FB /

CW00730889

Xmas !

Love :
Sid & Val -

Epsom Racecourse

DAVID HUNN

Epsom Racecourse

Its Story and its People

DAVIS-POYNTER
LONDON

First published in 1973 by
Davis-Poynter Limited
20 Garrick Street, London WC2E 9BJ

ISBN 0 7067 0099 6

Printed in Great Britain by
Bristol Typesetting Company Limited
Barton Manor St Philips Bristol

Contents

Acknowledgements

This book could not have been written, nor even contemplated, without the absolute co-operation of the Epsom Grand Stand Association and its Managing Director, Mr. Frank Coven, who for many months tolerated and accommodated the author as he plodded through their storeroom. More recent history was illuminated by the kindness of Lord George Wigg, then Chairman of the Horserace Betting Levy Board, ultimately the owners of Epsom Racecourse.

I am also greatly indebted for the help provided by the Metropolitan Police; by the libraries of the British Museum, the Borough of Epsom and Ewell, and *The Times* newspaper; and by Mrs Gwendolen Burns, who allowed access to the unique pictorial record of Epsom collected by her family.

The delights of almost every history of the area and of racing have been digested, and the flavour of many may touch these pages. Those old works from which quotations have been taken are the diaries of Samuel Pepys, Daniel Defoe and John Evelyn; *Letter to Eudoxa* by James Toland; *Eclipse and O'Kelly* by Thomas Cook; *Blue Riband of the Turf* by Louis Curzon; and *Atlas and Review of British Race-Courses* by F H Bayles.

From more recent years, I have used material from Edward Dorling's *Epsom and the Dorlings* (published by Stanley Paul), *Bred to the Purple* by Michael Seth-Smith (Leslie Frewin), and *The Jockey Club* by Roger Mortimer (Cassell). Though I have not quoted from it, Mr Mortimer's *History of the Derby Stakes* was constantly at hand. My thanks to all whose paths I crossed and whose wisdom helped me on my own way.

DH

The Downs are very famous for horse-matches as there
is not a properer place in the world for this sport.

James Toland, 1711

Prologue

'Think, when we talk of horses, that you see them, printing their proud hoofs i' the receiving earth'; but don't think this is a book about racehorses. Think, when we talk of Epsom racecourse, that you see this crown upon the Downs, this noble 'U', and realize this is not merely a track for the running of animals you are looking at, but a social phenomenon. Coming on the sight by chance, preferably from the direction of Epsom Downs station, the vantage point from which the grandstand is least offensive, a stranger might be tempted to regard it as a mirage.

There are no walls, no gates, no bars. There is a breathtaking span of open land, dipping, rolling, surging, green, and there, astride all this is, unmistakably, a racecourse. A course at which attendance is free and from which no one can be turned away. It's ridiculous, but it's true, and it's a fact that, for nearly 150 years, has angered those who make a profit from the racing there; but, just as bitterly and for just as long, those whose pleasure is taken in the enjoyment of those Downs have resented the intrusion of the racecourse.

This is the stuff of which drama is made, and time has seen an unbelievable parade of villains and heroes, of plots and counter-plots, of cunning, deceit, desperation and defiance, of comedy and mystery and even death. It is with these scenes, most of them played without an audience, that this book is concerned, rather than with the struggles for supremacy on the track so regularly witnessed by so many millions. When the field rounds the last bend of Tattenham Corner and thrums towards you, debanna-debanna, as you cling to your portion of the railing; when the mud stops flying and the agony of your anticipation subsides, then you may turn to your mate, lips tight, eyes bright, and give one of those odd little jerks of the jaw that mean 'That's what it's all about, buster, that is what it's all about!'

You would be wrong. Or, to be fair, you would not have been right until recently, when Epsom racecourse and Epsom Downs were bought for the nation – the racing nation – by the Horserace

Betting Levy Board. For 136 years, what that moment of bliss was about was bricks and mortar, and profit and loss, and dividends and rent and rates; it was about a lord of the manor who asked a fortune to allow horses across a whisper of his land, and another one who was conned by a Yorkshireman into starting the whole thing. Only incidentally was it about horses that won or lost and jockeys who cheated; more often it was about horses that were dyed, or died, and men who shot themselves because they had lost.

That final gallop up that cock-eyed 'straight' would not be happening but for you in the stands, you who pay good money to park your car and stroll to the paddock; it has never been much concerned with you on The Hill, for whom two railway lines were laid, two stations built, two million hot dogs steamed – you whose grandfathers used to walk ten, fifteen miles to the Derby, and back again that night. The race was not for your sake, but, oddly enough, the drama is. Ever since the first rails lined the course, the Downs have been a battlefield for human rights, personal rights; the fight of those who want to enjoy themselves against those who would like to charge them for the privilege. Before they recreate their performance on that Surrey arena, let some of the leading characters pass before you.

Those characters in the pageant to whom, perhaps, the greatest homage is due, are the monarchs of Nonsuch who moved like shadows behind the scenes, dimly perceived from a distance and seemingly incidental to the drama: but without them, the curtain might never have risen. Henry VIII, who built Nonsuch Palace; Elizabeth I, who 'stood at her standing in the further park, and there she saw a course'; James I, who positively encouraged horse-racing, and doubtless did so while the court rested on the edge of the Downs; Charles II, a great racing man, whose supreme importance here is the mighty part he played in the social development of Epsom town, where he took the waters, Barbara Villiers, Nell Gwynn and his pleasure.

While we're in the town, and before we reach the cast list of greater substance, a big hand, please, for Henry Wicker, the cowman who found those nasty waters in 1618; Samuel Pepys, who came to drink them and committed his enthusiasm to his diary; and Sally Mapp, the crazy bonesetter who set straight much that had been dislocated on the Downs.

And so up the hill, where the stage, as James Toland wrote, is 'covered with grass finer than Persian carpets'. Enter there, in 1769, a horse named Eclipse closely followed by an Irishman named O'Kelly. The former was so much faster than any horse ever seen that, within a year, it was carrying a starting price of 70–1 on; O'Kelly was no slouch either, and between them they drew the eyes of the racing world to Epsom Downs.

Close at hand are the young twelfth Earl of Derby, who lived on the Downs just one race-length from the winning post, and his Jockey Club buddy Sir Charles Bunbury. Between them they dreamed up the Oaks and the Derby, and Epsom has never looked back. At which point we must doff our caps to the Prince Regent, as he was to become, for whom the little Prince's Stand was built and who won the 1788 Derby with his horse Sir Thomas.

During his closing years as George IV, a villain appears on the scene. He lurks in the bushes for a while, and then appears with a magnificent flourish: Charles Bluck, gentleman, of Doncaster, leaseholder of one acre of the Downs for ninety years. On it he was to erect a stand for the accommodation of the visitors at the races. A roll of drums and hissing in the wings. The man from whom he acquired the acre was to stay in the centre of the racecourse stage for more than forty years: John Ivatt Briscoe, MP, Lord of the Manor of Epsom and freeholder of Epsom Downs.

The villain – for so, as you will see, he was inexorably cast – had a fairly short run, but it is a star part. Into his shoes stepped Ralph Lindsay, the first chairman of the Epsom Grand Stand Association (EGSA), a solicitor and also the steward of the manor of Epsom. Hanging on to the tails of his frock coat you will find William Chadwick, who built the stand and, by dint of the number of shares he accepted in lieu of payment, became, in due course, chairman himself, only to be overthrown in his turn.

Brushing aside a bevy of minor characters, who fight well for their places as the narrative unfolds, we make way for the mighty Dorlings. One must go back nearly two hundred years to take in old father William, who arrived in Epsom on horseback from Bexhill, bringing his printing press with him; then his son, the great, bearded Henry, in his time Epsom's Clerk of the Course, chairman, managing director and grandstand lessee, the man who reorganized, ruled and directed racing at Epsom; and his son, Henry Mayson Dorling, ruthless, unpopular, grand dictator of the Downs; and Henry's stepdaughter, the romantic and fascinating Mrs Beeton, who grew up in the grandstand and enters this cast list so unexpectedly.

Between them, the Dorlings span a century of racecourse history, crushing or conflicting with a host of other leading characters: from the Jockey Club, Lord George Bentinck, king of British racing; from the land-owning gentry that surrounded the course, James Stuart Strange, lord of the manor of Epsom who eventually sold out to the EGSA; Edward Studd, his opposite number at Walton-on-the-Hill, who would not; Archibald, fifth Earl of Rosebery, owner of Durdans and, thus, of the land the Association wanted for its paddock but couldn't get; John Barnard, whose own stand was always in the way – and still is.

Then on to the legendary Stanley Wootton, half a century of history on the Downs, former jockey, former trainer, farmer, massive landowner, the man with whom the EGSA could never establish an easy relationship; to Sir Brian Mountain, an emperor of insurance who, as Epsom's chairman, fortified his castle with dividends but let a bit of rot creep in at the foundations; and then Lord George Wigg, the remarkable man who, as chairman of the Horserace Betting Levy Board, came, in practice, to own Epsom Downs – the man whom Mr Wootton, like so many others, found he could trust: to whom he gave (if you use the word loosely) Walton Downs into safekeeping for ever.

It's quite a cast and quite a script!

CHAPTER TWO

Enter the villain

Christmas was coming, George IV was getting fat, and up on Epsom Downs someone nasty was roaming round the racecourse. His name was Charles Bluck.

For a while nobody noticed. There was much else to occupy the mind at the time: Britain was suffering her fourth Prime Minister in two years, and he looked like getting the boot before long; Peel was about to form the Metropolitan Police, agricultural labourers were stirring unhappily in the south, and the Royal menagerie had moved to Regent's Park. Who, in 1828, should worry about Charles Bluck?

Horses had been racing on the Downs for 200 years, to the growing disgust of Epsom residents: 'Great care is taken by the Urban District Council,' a local historian was to record some years later, 'to prevent infectious diseases from being imported into the town during the incursion of the unholy mob, and the streets are frequently watered with disinfectants.' The raging popularity of the Derby was – and still is – the deepest thorn in the fleshy side of Epsom's gentility, and in 1828 the Derby was already nearly 50 years old. Whatever the interest of Charles Bluck ('gentleman, of Doncaster') in the racecourse might be, it was unlikely to concern many of the gentlemen of Epsom.

The depth of Bluck's villainy is now impossible to assess accurately. It became confused, extended, perhaps exaggerated by the plot and counter-plot that it engendered. Skullduggery developed in dark corners wherever two or three were gathered together to make a guinea out of the Epsom Races, and noble though the precepts may have been of those gentlemen who eventually stopped Bluck, neither their methods nor their aims were clearly recorded in the notes they left behind. A century and a half later, one can be guided only by the historians nearest to the time, and their collective opinions on Bluck would lift the wig off a libel judge. Not untypically, he was said to be 'a rogue and a rascal, an unscrupulous knave, the biggest villain to go

unhanged'. His interest in the racecourse was 'an artful specula-
tion devised by a small horde of questionable characters' – of
whom, we are left in no doubt, the most questionable was
Charles Bluck himself.

His thread, rotten though it may have been, remains the most
fascinating in the vast tapestry of Epsom racecourse, if only for
the desperate efforts made to remove it. All he wanted to do (he
said) was to build on the Downs the sort of grandstand that
Doncaster already had. Accordingly, he attended the manorial
court of Epsom 'and represented that he was desirous of erecting
a stand for the accommodation of the visitors at the races'. He
petitioned the Lord of the Manor for the grant of one acre of
ground for 61 years, the land 'being parcel of the waste of the
Manor of Ebbisham'. If he had left it at that, perhaps all would
have been well; but, afraid that the plea of a stranger from the
north would not be acceptable in Epsom, Bluck then produced
his invisible backers: he was, he said, supported and sanctioned
in his plans by the Jockey Club (who even then controlled racing
over the country) and by 'the most distinguished members of the
Turf'.

John Briscoe, MP, the Lord of the Manor, was impressed, and
apparently did not take up the references – or perhaps Bluck
supplied forged ones. At all events, the lease was signed on 28th
November, 1828. Bluck had his acre for 90 years from 25th
March, 1829, at £30 a year. He undertook to complete, by the
following November, 'and finish in a good, substantial and work-
manlike manner, and to the entire satisfaction of the said John
Watt Briscoe and Anna Maria, his wife' a brick or stone stand
on which he would spend at least £5,000.

At that time, the only permanent buildings on that part of the
course were the small Prince's Stand (still the only one that
addresses itself happily to the eye), which was then a flat-topped
and battlemented affair; and the wooden rubbing house, in which
the horses were rubbed down after a race. A pub of the same
name now stands on the site. For race meetings, lines of wooden
and canvas stands, tents and marquees were put up to accommodate the gentry. The masses thronged, as they still do, on The
Hill on the other side of the finishing straight.

The signing of the lease to build what was to become the most
famous stand in the history of racing crystallized the opposition
to the Doncaster impostor. Ten days later he attended a meeting
of several gentlemen 'for the purpose of taking into consideration
the eligibility of establishing an association for building a grandstand . . .' They were prepared to spend four times as much as

Bluck to build a stand to accommodate 5,000 spectators 'with suitable refreshment rooms, offices and other apartments'.

Bluck was offered £1,000 to sub-let the ground to such an association at a peppercorn rent. The money, it was recorded in honeyed words that hardly concealed the vinegar in which they were soaked, was 'a compensation for the great trouble and expense which he had incurred in obtaining the said lease'. As a further inducement, Bluck was to be given the underlease of four rooms planned for the ground floor. To this he apparently agreed, on the further condition that he was paid £200 of his £1,000 on the spot (which he was), £500 by 20th January, 1829, and the remaining £300 by 20th April.

The hastily convened and, as yet, unofficial committee, having formed the Epsom Grand Stand Association, and thinking that it had disposed of the threat of Bluck, must have approached Christmas in a state of unusual excitement and trepidation. The site for the stand was apparently secure, though the actual transfer of the lease was some way off, and now, rapidly, £20,000 had to be raised. This the committee proposed to do by issuing 1,000 shares at £20 each and on 29th December (only a month after Bluck had obtained the lease himself) it was able to hold a meeting of subscribers to the Association.

It was held at the King's Head, Poultry, in the City of London. From the very start, the EGSA was not something in which residents of Epsom were primarily, or even partly, concerned – though in due course one local family acquired what amounted in practice to a controlling interest in it, one that they held for almost a century. By the time of that first general meeting, the Association's secretary, Edmund Sandford, had already received and replied to the first of an almost ceaseless flow of letters from local residents. They disputed the rights of the Lord of the Manor to grant such a lease, and of the Association to obtain sole rights to build a stand on the Downs; and complained, as some do to this day, that in putting a permanent building on the Downs, the Association was infringing on the rights of the tenants and commoners of Epsom.

Such records of that first shareholder's meeting as have survived – a few formal phrases almost lost in the legal paraphernalia of a later lease – are enough to suggest the warmth of self-congratulation that must have filled the upper room of the city pub that night. These men knew that they were on to a very good thing: they blessed the efforts already made by the committee, entrusted further negotiations to two of them, John Goodered and Philip Isaac, and asked only that the door should be firmly shut in Bluck's face. Goodered and Isaac were instructed to obtain an assignment of the whole term granted to Bluck by the Lord of the Manor, not merely the underlease, which left Bluck with at least one hand on the reins.

Within a fortnight the committee had much pleasure in informing the proprietors (shareholders) 'that they have engaged with an eminent Builder, who has erected several Public Works in the Metropolis, to build the Grand Stand and that he has undertaken to complete the same previous to the races in June next at a sum less than was anticipated. The works were commenced last week and the committee propose fixing an early date for laying the first stone'. That builder was William Chadwick, who was to play a long and powerful role in the Epsom drama: the committee didn't at the time inform the proprietors (perhaps it didn't know) that Chadwick already held some form of contract signed by Bluck, Sandford (who was not long to remain secretary of the Association) and a Mr Goodwin.

A month later the architect was appointed. Edward William Trendall, like most of the characters so far on the scene, was also to become more deeply involved than he expected. For the time being, however, his part was peaceful and professional. For a commission of 5 per cent of the builder's estimate of £14,000 (£6,000 less than the Association was prepared to spend), Trendall agreed to make all the necessary working drawings (five weeks after the work had begun) 'and to attend three times a week there during the progress of the works, and to report every Monday during the progress to the Secretary of the Committee'. For an additional fee of £10 10s, he was to make a drawing of the proposed Grand Stand 'for His Majesty'.

The secretary later reported to the shareholders: 'It appearing to the committee that His Majesty's patronage would be highly desirable, the design and plans of the building were in the month of January last prepared and sent to Lord Mountcharles, and several communications had with that nobleman on the subject of their being submitted to His Majesty, and his Lordship subsequently recommended that they should be sent to Mr Radcliffe, through whom they were more likely to reach His Majesty. The design and plans were therefore sent to that gentleman and communications had with him, but no answer has yet been had on the subject.' It was, in fact, another eleven years before a monarch visited the races.

While the bricks and mortar were being laid, Goodered and Isaacs set about further discomforting Bluck. It says a lot for his confidence and style that for at least six months of his historic year, despite the efforts being made to squeeze him out, Bluck not only kept a hand firmly in the Association's affairs, but, on at least one occasion, was actually asked by the committee to represent it; and because of his tenancy in law, Bluck's signature still appeared on legal documents.

On 17th February, Bluck attended a meeting of the committee at its request, ostensibly to arrange the agreement that had been made with him in early December – that he should sub-let the site for £1,000 and himself have a lease for four rooms. Now Goodered and Isaacs beat him down to £750, of which he had already been paid £200. For the rest, Bluck demanded 25 shares, valued at £500, and £50 cash. Glad not to have to find more cash, the committee agreed. As to the four rooms in the stand, which he wanted to use as refreshment rooms, Bluck offered a rent of £30 for the first seven years, £40 for the next seven, and £70 for a third period of seven years. The committee agreed, with the reservation that he was to use them during race weeks only, and informed the shareholders: 'The committee finding themselves unable to carry into effect the former agreement of the 8th December with Mr Bluck, a new arrangement of a more beneficial nature to the Association has been entered into with him. . . .'

But the vital question of who held the main lease had still not been resolved to the satisfaction of the Association. Bluck kept control, and in April the committee was forced to note that its underlease bound the Association to build to the amount of £14,000 by 1st January 1830 (six months beyond the estimated completion date promised), and that if the work were not completed by then, Bluck had the power of re-entry and occupation of the stand. It was a galling clause to have to record, but there was more to come.

With the financial situation decidedly unstable (the committee were trying to raise a £4,000 loan), attention was now turned to the race meeting, little more than a month away. Though the stand was far from finished, some accommodation had to be made for the public. What could Chadwick the builder do? Chadwick (whose power increased week by week, as the Association fell more and more into his debt), reckoned on 19th May 1829 that if he could obtain '£300 on Saturday next, and £300 the following Saturday, he could put the building in a fit state to receive company'. The money was found, and, for good measure a deputation from the committee which had gone to inspect the work, published these glowing remarks: 'The Deputation cannot conclude this Report without expressing their entire approbation of the manner in which the Builder continues to execute his contract. The Brickwork in particular deserves the warmest approbation, the bricks are sound, new, hard, and handsome, and the brick-mortar made of the best sand and lime that the neighbourhood affords. Nothing,' the report concluded reassuringly, 'can be apprehended from the weight of any concourse of spectators.'

However, things were not as good as they seemed. The deputation found 'Mr Trendall had caused to be erected a covered way to the door whereby a view of the most interesting part of the race – namely the last 150 yards – was entirely obstructed to a space which would be occupied by more than 150 persons'. So the first black mark went to Trendall. At least there were enough points of vantage, and some of shelter, for the committee to send invitations to some of the leading lights of society and the turf; to send Bluck, 'accompanied by any other gentlemen' to wait on the Duc d'Orleans and the Duc de Chartres and present them with free admission for the week; and to invite the Press for a preview of the unfinished building. This report appeared in *The Mirror of Literature, Amusement and Instruction* on Saturday, 30th May 1829, and deserves savouring in full:

> The building is 156 feet in width, including the Terrace, and 60 feet in depth, with a magnificent flight of steps in the centre. The columns of the portico are of Doric order, supporting a balcony, or gallery, which is to be covered by a verandah, erected on small ornamental iron pillars, placed over those below. There are four large and well-proportioned rooms for refreshments, etc., a spacious hall, leading through a screen of Doric columns to a large and elegant staircase of stone, and on each side of the staircase are retiring rooms of convenience for gentlemen.
>
> The first floor consists of a splendid room, 108 feet in length and 34 in width, divided into three compartments by ornamental columns and pilasters, supporting a richly panelled ceiling, and having a direct communication with the balcony, or gallery; on each side of the staircase there are retiring rooms for the ladies, with the same arrangements as those below for the gentlemen. The roof will contain about 2,000 persons standing; affording at the same time an opportunity for everyone to see the whole of the Derby Course, which at one time was considered doubtful.

Arrangements were made with 'Bishop the Officer' to secure his attendance during the race week, and a room in the basement 'appropriated to the use of the Magistrates' (free tickets for magistrates, too!) 'for the purpose of locking of Prisoners'. The insurance of the stand was increased from £3,000 to £6,000, and Charles Bluck was allowed ten of his 25 shares although the agreement had not yet been executed.

'Since the last meeting a grand stand has been constructed,' reported *The Times* racing man after the first day of the meeting. 'It is situated nearly opposite the Steward's stand, and at no great distance from the winning post, of exceedingly large dimensions; it promises, when completed, to be a very commodious building, well adapted to the purposes for which it has been erected. At present, however, it is in an unfinished state, and no doubt it is attributable to that circumstance, and to the scaffolding by which it is partially surrounded, that the grand stand is just now rather an unsightly object.

'Though not completed either within or without, the stand is opened for the use of spectators, and a certificate of its perfect security has been published. It is said that when finished the building will have cost the enterprising speculators £20,000. We trust the undertaking may adequately remunerate them: the rather, as a proper stand was decidedly a desideratum at Epsom.'

'Unsightly', indeed! Somebody must have put in some work on *The Times* man, because the next day he declared, somewhat ostentatiously, that 'nothing could be more splendid than the view of the Grand Stand', and after the third (Derby) day he gave them another boost: 'The effect of the new stand crowded from base to roof with spectators was extremely fine.' The *crème de la crème* – which on Derby day included the young Queen of Portugal – did not at this stage visit the grandstand, but remained with the elite of the Stewards' Stand (where the company in 1829 included also the Duc de Chartres, despite the EGSA's efforts to offer him free accommodation in the new stand).

As ever, the first day was the least impressive: 'The Cocknies who determined upon having as much as possible for their money, reserve themselves for the Oaks and Derby, and did not muster in very large numbers'. Came the great day, and even the rabble on The Hill moved the reporter: 'It was a perfect sylvan theatre, occupied from base to summit by more of lovely and brilliant than we almost ever before saw collected within an equal space'. How much of the week's success was due to that 'unsightly object' nobody knows, but it certainly seems to have been quite a meeting. *The Times* man concluded that there had not been one like it, 'in point of extent and brilliancy, these many years, and we understand there is nothing to be found elsewhere comparable to it'.

The next week Chadwick suggested that the committee might like to give him 200 shares (value £4,000) on account of the money owing to him. This was agreed. Four days later, he felt he might possibly be disappointed in disposing of the 200 shares allotted to him, and that it might be expedient for the committee to raise his £4,000 on mortgage. (Nobody would advance the cash on mortgage, and it was eventually raised on a 7 per cent annuity.) Not before time, the committee then began cutting the coat of the Grand Stand according to the cloth that it hoped to be able to lay its hands on. The omission of all unnecessary ornaments, it decided, would greatly decrease the extra charges that might arise. Trendall and Chadwick were instructed to forget the architraves and columns on the saloon floor, and to turn their attention 'chiefly to the convenience and strength of the building'. The insurance was, at the same time, raised to give a cover of £10,000.

With completion in sight, Chadwick then produced his original contract with Bluck and offered to surrender it to the committee, as soon as it executed a proper contract as security for him to finish the building. Perhaps it was this that shifted the balance of power; perhaps it was the disclosure of some other dark secret, but something certainly occurred between April and the end of June that weakened Bluck's hold on the Grand Stand affairs. His fight became increasingly petulant, the committee's actions more confident.

Its members were, however, considerably put out by what they called 'an offensive article' that appeared in the City column of the *Morning Herald* on 16th July. It was not signed and the editor declined to reveal the author's identity, but it smacked strongly of Charles Bluck. It opened with the sort of statement that today would have the editor swiftly in the law courts: 'Our attention has been called to as pretty a piece of joint-stock humbugging, in a small way, as ever we recollect to have heard of. It appears that, some time ago, an Association was concocted by a select number of jobbers, gamblers, and folk of that *ilk*, for the purpose of erecting a Grand Stand upon Epsom Race-ground. These gentry, in their prospectus, assure the public that they have purchased for 90 years the *exclusive* right of building a stand – well knowing that their exclusive right expires on the deaths of the Lord of the Manor and his wife, Mr and Mrs Briscoe, who are both over 60.' (The last statement was extremely unlikely, since neither died for another 41 years.)

The piece then turns 'to a trick of these gentry of a much more recent date. A few days ago these gentry advertised a first half-yearly dividend of five per cent, although, as we shall show, they have not derived a shilling profit from the concern, but the contrary. The dividend scheme, therefore, is an ingenious *decoy* to induce *flat* fish to enter the net of the associated worthies . . . The real cause why they pay this dividend is, of course, to induce the public to believe that the Stand is already a profitable concern . . .'

It goes on in considerable detail, and no doubt with some truth, since this dubious interim dividend was later much criticized by members of the EGSA themselves. The *Morning Herald* offered to insert any article in contradiction of the original, but none seems to have been offered.

During the race meeting the Jockey Club had evidently made it clear, though no record of it remains, that it was not in favour of the two front rooms on the ground floor being let to Bluck. One of the rooms, indeed, was already known as the Jockey Club Room, and those worthy gentlemen no doubt intended that it should remain so. The committee accordingly offered Bluck a reduction in rent of £10 a year for giving up his underlease of the Jockey Club Room, and another £10 a year plus five shares (worth £100) to give up the other front room.

Bluck's reply bore traces of desperation: 'Mr Bluck seeing as he does and being borne out by the opinion of the committee the great necessity of the two rooms mentioned being in the possession of the Association, has resolved to make a very great sacrifice and will therefore consent to the following terms . . .' He then, in a most extraordinarily misplaced arrangement of words, appeared to agree to give up the front two rooms (for ten shares, not five) and to retain the rear two at £10 a year, with exclusive rights to supply refreshments within the stand. He also required an undertaking from the committee that it would not let to any person or persons either of the two front rooms during the term of his lease, or there would be no deal.

'The committee will take into consideration,' he concluded, 'that Mr Bluck has already relinquished £250 (and) is now sacrificing the most valuable part of the property in parting with the two front rooms.'

The committee, which had already determined to use the space under the terrace for refreshment rooms, noted the communication and rejected its terms. Bluck continued to rent all four rooms. At the same meeting it resolved that the lease from the Lord of the Manor to Bluck should be assigned to the

Association, which would grant an underlease to Bluck on the terms agreed 'or hereafter to be settled'. It was obviously a matter that had already been arranged: four days later Bluck assigned his lease to the EGSA, the next day the Deed of Settlement of the Association was sealed.

That should have been the end of Bluck's involvement, save as sub-tenant and shareholder. But a quorum of dissatisfied members arranged for a special general meeting of the Association to be called in November, and a few days before it was due, all who were eligible to attend received an anonymous letter which ended: 'I have the honour to remain, Your most obedient Servant, A SHAREHOLDER.'

It was a long and detailed attack on the conduct of the Association, and particularly on the conduct of the Association's solicitor, Mr Lindsay, who had also been elected chairman of the committee: 'In order that you may perceive the absolute necessity of your attendance, either in person or by proxy, this circular is submitted to your consideration; and you are hereby respectfully reminded, that you ought not hereafter to complain, if the building should not be completed or answer the expectation of the Shareholders, unless you take this opportunity of supporting the tottering fabric.'

The writer pointed out that an overwhelming majority of the acting members of the committee were 'either partizans or intimate friends of Mr Lindsay, our solicitor, and Mr Chadwick, our builder, who sway every part of the management . . . therefore it is not to be wondered at that the affairs of the Association are in a lamentable state of derangement, complexity, and impending ruin . . .' Lindsay, the circular alleged, was not even a shareholder at the time he was elected to the chair, and was therefore ineligible. All the business of the Association since 21st May had been 'transacted by a usurped authority'. In seventeen subsequent detailed clauses, Bluck (who later admitted authorship) suggested matters that would repay examination by a select committee, including an investigation into the issuing of shares to Lindsay and Chadwick, and the size of their bills.

Unfortunately, not a word of that general meeting survives. (The first minute book of the Association covering the years up to 1844, disappeared some ten years later and was never recovered.) Bluck did get his select committee appointed to enquire into the affairs of the Association, and there seems no doubt that the enquiry was needed. Its findings were not fully revealed, but at the half-yearly meeting of the shareholders in January 1830, the Association's committee admitted: 'There appears to have been much which they regret should have taken place, yet they feel it would now tend to the injury of the Association, and to the sacrifice of the property embarked in it, if any enquiry into some of those matters were prosecuted with effect; and they therefore, in justice to themselves, and to the body of shareholders whom they represent, consider it expedient to allow matters, in some respects, to remain as they are at present, rather than frustrate the views of the subscribers at large, by further investigation.'

It was a shameless whitewashing job, and the best that can be said of it is that, whatever the official pronouncements, some of the findings of the select committee were taken to heart, though perhaps those that mattered most were heeded least. The investigators reported that the EGSA was 'an undertaking that cannot fail to be both useful and profitable', but they much regretted chairman Lindsay's decision to pay a dividend to shareholders before the stand was finished, and therefore before there was any profit; and they were 'obliged to disapprove of the amount of the expenses incurred (by the committee) at the spring races'.

As to Chadwick, he had received, they reported, £10,492 in cash and £2,200 in shares. The balance due would be £1,198 which he had agreed to take out in shares. 'Some parts of his contract the select committee are constrained to say they do not approve, but they have well-grounded hopes that no evil consequences will arise.'

The main committee answered one of Bluck's attacks on the chairman. His bill as solicitor was £477 12s 5d, in payment of which he had taken fifteen shares and £120, 'by which it will appear that he has presented you with upwards of Fifty Pounds'. Trendall, the architect, had been engaged 'upon terms highly advantageous to the Association'. The balance to him was £400, and he had very handsomely agreed to take £200 cash and the rest in shares.

The builder's work received its usual paeans of praise: 'the committee are much gratified to be able to state that the stand is now rapidly drawing towards completion, the unfinished parts, at present, being the staircase, verandah and balustrade in front of the terrace. They can confidently state, by an assurance received from the builder, that the building will be entirely finished many weeks before the Spring Races; when, to judge from its present appearance, they entertain not a doubt, it will be considered, in point of stability and neatness of structure, far superior to any similar accommodation in the kingdom.'

These are the heroes, then, nicely settled for the second act, but what of the villain, who had persisted, so obstinately, to the last page? The committee reserved its most pious speech for him: 'They beg to state, as their decided opinion, that the EGSA never was in such a flourishing state as at the present moment, and trust that in case future attempts should be made to destroy the harmony which it is so desirable should prevail among subscribers, by anonymous communication, or any other means, and throw the concern into anarchy, confusion, and unnecessary expense, it will meet with the silent contempt it so justly merits.'

CHAPTER THREE

A dose of salts

That was the beginning of the grandstand; the imprint of big business on a merry pursuit. It was not the beginning of racing on Epsom Downs, nor, by some 8,000 years, the beginning of Epsom. Cantering lightly past the Mesoliths and Neoliths, the Romans (who built Stane Street within a flint flick of the grandstand site), and Normans, it is worthwhile slowing down in sight of the Tudors. What was there to Epsom before the horses came, and why did they come? They came for a king and stayed because of a woman. An unlikely tale, but if strength can be gained by repetition, this charming fable is now as firm as rock.

As the 16th century ended, the area comprised three villages – Epsom, Ewell and Cuddington, of which the last had been bought by Henry VIII in 1537 and almost completely obliterated to make way for the great palace of Nonsuch – for its brief life as magnificent a royal residence as Hampton Court. Designed by a Florentine, Anthonio Toto dell Nunciata, it was said at the time to have been built 'with so much splendour and elegance that it stands a monument of art, and you would think the skill and science of architecture was exhausted on this one building.' It was an elaborately decorated two-storey palace, with five-storey towers at each end. Henry brought artists and craftsmen from all over Europe to work on it: 'who applied to the ornament of this mansion the finest and most curious skill they possesed in their several arts, embellishing it within and without with magnificent statues'.

In his last gross and faltering years Henry probably hunted deer in Nonsuch Park, as from his other pet palace in Bushey Park. Elizabeth did not inherit Nonsuch, but following a visit there, she bought it from the Earl of Arundel, who exchanged it for lands worth £534. In 1603 it passed to James I, attracting all the while the glamorous glitter of courtier and courtesan, the splendour of regal entertainment.

Little of this affected the village life of Epsom (only a couple of miles away) or the nearer and senior settlement of Ewell, both of which pottered on from smallholding to smithy, from manor house to mud patch. By now some of the horse-riding noblemen had roamed further afield, out of the gates of Nonsuch and on to the firm green slopes to the south-west, already a favourite spot for foot runners. Elizabeth may well have sat side-saddle, watching some of the young bloods of her court gallop against each other, over the hill and back again. ('On Monday was a great supper made for her, but before night she stood at her standing in the further park, and there she saw a course.') James almost certainly rode out, and probably saw to it that, for the entertainment of his guests, some organized form of horse racing was arranged while the court was in residence: the prize, customarily, would have been a silver bell. More glorious days were to come, with Charles II, but first – the cowman.

It was in 1618, so it is said, that Henry Wicker drove a few cattle to find water on the common, half a mile to the west of the old village of Epsom. Coming across a damp patch of mud, he pushed his stick into it and a large puddle appeared. Happy to have to look no further, Wicker settled down and waited for the cows to drink their fill. But they didn't drink. They sniffed and stamped, snorted, dipped a nose in here and there. Water it might be, but drinkable it was not.

Touching his tongue to a wet finger, Wicker agreed. If this was ordinary water, he was the Lord of the Manor. They moved on elsewhere for their drink, but not before the cowman had carefully marked the spot. He came back later and, dabbling his hands in the water, noticed that it stung the raw scratch that crossed his knuckles. Before long the villagers were collecting water in buckets from the pool that never dried, taking it back home and bathing septic places on their families, their dogs, their cattle. The water was, a local historian recorded, particularly effective when used 'as an external application to ulcerated sores and scorbutic eruptions'.

For 15 or 20 years, that seemed to be the limit of its use: 'vulnerary and abstersive' – handy stuff for cleaning wounds. Then some labourers, less sensitive to the taste than the cows had been, drank a few handfuls while they were working nearby, and shortly found the water had other, equally positive, effects: it could purge as well as purify. According to Manning's *History and Antiquities of the County of Surrey*, the water contained eight parts nitre and one part earth. It was 'diluent, absorbent, diuretic, gently purging the innocent in operation'. The first pharmaceutical analysis of the content of the water does not seem to have been made for another 50 years.

In 1695 Dr Nehemiah Grew published, in Latin, an account of the Epsom springs, their constituents and properties: *Tractatus de Salis*, 'a treatise of the Nature and Use of the Bitter Purging Salt, Easily Known from all Counterfeits by its Bitter taste'. On evaporating a gallon of Epsom water, Dr Grew found two drams of impure magnesium sulphate. The secret was out, and soon pharmacists were preparing Epsom salts artificially in unlimited quantities, though it was another century before they were accepted in general medical practice.

By then the fame of the waters had spread far and wide. Realizing that they had a useful find on their hands, the elders of the village piped the stuff up to a tap and built a wooden shed round it. Had they suspected that Wicker had unearthed the equivalent of a liquid gold mine for Epsom, they might have done the thing in more style. It was not until near the end of the century, the peak of Epsom's medicinal popularity, that the Lord of the Manor built an assembly room at the wells.

None of this was irrelevant to the town's horse-racing future. By the time the Roundheads and Royalists were active, visitors were arriving to take the waters. The more visitors, the more horses; the more horses, the more races. In 1648, racing on the Downs was a frequent enough event to be used as cover for a meeting of Charles' supporters. On 16th May, according to Clarendon's *History of the Rebellion*, 'after the king had addressed the two Houses of Parliament at Guildford, a meeting of Royalists was held on Banstead Downs under the pretence of a horse race, and 600 horses were collected and marched to Reigate'. (The Downs then still took their name from the busy village to the north-east, rather than the nearer but sleepier one to the north-west.)

With the end of the civil war and the restoration of the monarchy came the golden age of Epsom and the real establishment of racing. As one pries through histories of the day in the hope of finding a sensible account, disappointment is illuminated only by an occasional sentence: 'Commonly upon market days here all the country gentlemen appoint a friendly meeting . . . to match their horses' (Haywood, 1653). In a line squeezed between paragraphs of his diary, Pepys, on 27th May 1663, makes his first reference to the popularity of racing at Epsom: 'This day there was great thronging to Bansted Downes, upon a great horse race and foot race; I am sorry I could not go thither.' However, Charles II frequently did. Aged thirty when he returned from France to the throne, he came to Epsom at his amorous peak. He had Barbara Villiers tucked up in Nonsuch

Palace (he later gave it to her and named her Duchess of Cleveland) and sometimes stayed himself at the King's Head in Epsom (the nearest inn to the Downs) with Nell Gwynn apparently stowed away in the next house and readily available through a secret door.

By now the place was the rage of fashionable society, quite outstripping Tunbridge Wells. Everybody went to what used to be an insignificant rural village to drink the waters. A new town was springing up near the wells to accommodate the incessant flow of visitors. As Pepys makes clear by his entry for 25th July, 1663, this the town was sometimes quite unable to do:

> Then having intended this day to go to Bansted Downs to see a famous race, I sent Will to get himself ready to go with me, and I also by and by home and put on my riding suit; and so by boate to Whitehall, where I hear that the Race is put off because the Lords do sit in parliament today. . . .
> [With his servant Will, and a friend, Mr Creed, Pepys instead passed the afternoon with acquaintances at Clapham.]
> Towards evening we bade them Adieu and took horses, being resolved that instead of the race which fails us, we would go to Epsum; so we set out; and being gone a little way, I sent home Will to look to the house, and Creed and I rid forward – the road being full of citizens going and coming toward Epsum – where, when we came, we could hear of no lodging, the town so full. But what was better, I went towards Ashted, my old place of pleasure . . .

The next day, Sunday, Pepys and his companion took the waters, which are as near Ashtead as they are Epsom. Immediately, and with relish, he makes clear what most historians have been delicately reluctant to mention: that in view of the efficiently purgative nature of the waters, it was fortunate that the wells were hard by the common, among the shielding shrubs of which there were areas agreed to be left for the convenience of women, and others for the relief of men. So firm was the agreement that a contemporary map marks them.

> Lord's day. Up and to the Wells, where great store of Citizens; which was the greatest part of the company, though there were some others of better Quality. I met many that I knew; and we drunk each of us two pots and so walked away – it being very pleasant to see how everybody turns up his tail, here one and there another, in a bush, and the women in their Quarters and the like. Thence I walked Creed to Mr

Minnes's house [George Mynnes or Mynne, Lord of the Manor of Horton, lived at Woodcote Park] which hath now a good way made to it, and finely walked round; and thence to Durdans and walked round it and within the Court yard and to the bowling green, where I have seen so much mirth in my time; but now no family in it (my Lord Barkeley, whose it is, being with his family at London).

Later that day, tired of their stay at Ashstead:

> . . . and so mounted either to go toward London home or to find out a new lodging. And so rode through Epsum the whole town over, seeing the various companies that were there walking; which was very pleasant to see how they are there without knowing almost what to do, but only in the morning to drink waters. But Lord, to see how many I met there of Citizens that I could not have thought to have seen there, or that they had ever had it in their heads or purses to go down thither.

They rode on to Ewell ('Yowell, beyond Nonesuch-house a mile'), stayed Sunday night there, and returned for another dose of the waters on Monday:

> It being a much warmer day than Yesterday, there was a great store of gallant company, more then to my greater pleasure . . . We drank each of us three cups; and so after riding up to the horsemen upon the Hill where they were making of matches to run, we went away and to Yowell, where we find our Breakfast, the remains of supper last night hasht.

The 'making of matches to run' was a less formal affair than 'a great horse race'. With the waters taken, and a limit to the numbers of hours that could be passed in inns and coffee-houses, there was no more enjoyable pursuit in the area (in daylight, possibly no other pursuit) than to ride up the lane to the Downs. There they could race against each other, or encourage others to do so, and make a wager on it either way; even indulge in the wild goose chase, or steeple hunting, later described by Pownall: 'Two horsemen, drunk or sober, in or out of their wits, fix upon a steeple, or some other conspicuous distant object, to which they make a straight cut, over hedge, ditch and gate.'

Robert Black records, in *Horse-Racing in England*, the sort of wager that was typical of the thoughtless indolence of the young gallants of the day: 'A stupid and cruel match was run at Epsom between Mr Girdwood's Crop and Mr Harris's roan horse for 100 guineas. Crop was to go 100 miles before the roan went eighty. By the time the roan had gone eighty, Crop had done only 94, and both horses had long been so dead beat they could hardly crawl, and people walked in front of them enticing them on with sieves full of oats. Crop was so bad that he was expected to die, and was sold for £5.'

Of equal stupidity and greater eccentricity was the wager played out some years later, when a form of continuous race track had been established on the Downs. For twenty guineas, a local farmer is said to have bet he could drive a hundred ducks five times round the course in fourteen hours. He was within a hundred yards of winning the money when one of the ducks dropped dead.

By 1675 there was such frequent activity on the Downs that the owner of Woodcote Park had to apply for, and was granted, a deed of partition that recognized his right to a sheepwalk on the Downs for 400 sheep. The repercussions of this arrangement were to jolt the EGSA more than 150 years later, when it was discovered that the sheepwalk, then the right of Baron de Teissier, covered the ground on which lay the new stand, the winning post and the judges' stand. As the Association committee put it in a report in 1829: 'It became necessary that steps should be taken to conciliate that gentleman and effect an arrangement of his claim, such a measure appearing best calculated to promote the interests of this Association, and after various interviews having been had it was at length determined that the Baron should receive the sum of £1 as a consideration for the ground . . .' That massive compensation (accepted by the Baron) was considerably extended by his solicitor's costs of £44 5s 2d.

There was point in Pownall's reference to horsemen 'drunk or sober, in or out of their wits'. It was long to be the habit at Epsom to interrupt racing with a heavy lunch in the town, and in the 17th century – before owners began engaging jockeys to do the riding for them – afternoon racing, without rails and sometimes without a course, must have been a hazardous business. The very first reference to a horse race in the area is in the parish register of Banstead, among the list of burials for 1625: 'William Stanley who in running the race fell from his horse and brake his neck.'

The hurly-burly is well reflected in a report by a Colonel Cooke in 1679, describing a meeting that would almost certainly have been held on the straight course of four miles, from a point

somewhere north of Banstead village to the finish above Epsom:
'At Banstead twelve horses ran for three plates, a plate a heat,
when Roger Pope's horse threw and bruised him and Tom
Wharton's threw him and he was taken up for dead, yet is alive
again, but much battered, and this they call sport! The Duke of
Monmouth escaped narrowly. There was so vast a crowd no
other could be expected.'

That particular meeting took place at the same time as a Bill
was being introduced in the House of Commons to exclude the
Duke of York from succession to the throne. 'Some struggled to
have delayed the second reading,' wrote Colonel Cooke, 'urging
the thinness of the House occasioned by a dog match at Hampton
Court and a horse match at Banstead Downs; but no argument
could stem the tide, and read it was.'

In the same year that Charles II granted that sheepwalk right,
his mistress, the Duchess of Cleveland, who had borne him three
sons, began to demolish Nonsuch Palace. The materials were
sold and used in many of the fine houses that were then being
built in the area between the wells and the Downs. The greatest
of these was Durdans. This was itself not far short of a palace,
and was built almost entirely of Nonsuch remains for the first
Earl of Berkeley (Keeper of the House of Nonsuch) on that
gentle and sumptuous slope that now leads down from the Paddock to the south-west corner of the town.

Once part of the Manor of Horton, the original house of
Durdans was in 1650 the home of Sir Robert Coke, the Lord
Chief Justice, whose wife Theophila was a Berkeley. She left it
to her nephew, George, the ninth Lord Berkeley, in 1652, and
it was in his time that the place became a mecca for high society.
Long before he became the first Earl, he had entertained royalty
there. Both Pepys and the other great diarist of the day, John
Evelyn, were fellow-guests on one notable occasion, and it was
Evelyn (whose brother Richard lived nearby, at Woodcote Park)
who recorded the details: 'September 1, 1662: Being by my L:
Geo: Berkeley invited, I went to Durdens, where dined his
Majestie, the Queene, Duke, Dutchesse, Prince Rupert, Pr:
Edward, and aboundance of Noble men . . .'

' His Majestie' was still Charles II; his poor queen, Catherine
of Portugal. The Duke was his brother James, of York, who
succeeded him to the throne – for, though Charles had several
children, none was by his wife. Rupert, an interesting character,
was the son of Frederick V of Bohemia and Elizabeth, daughter
of James I. He came to England in 1642 to fight for the royalist
cause, and became the commander of the king's fleet.

The house was later the country home of the Earl of Guild-ford, and (on loan) of Frederick, Prince of Wales, son of George II and father of George III. In mid-18th century it was de-molished, rebuilt, destroyed by fire, and eventually built again on a smaller scale. It was bought in 1874 by the fifth Earl of Rosebery, whose influence on racing at Epsom was tremendous. In his time, and afterwards, the Epsom racecourse authorities were to be involved in long and anguished negotiations over land belonging to Durdans (of which today's Paddock was a part), and over the even bigger estates of neighbouring Woodcote Park, and the manor of Walton-on-the-Hill, to the south of the course.

The wealthy aristocrats who settled in these mansions, attrac-ted by the waters and held by the turf, were themselves magnets for their fellows. There was nowhere, London society decided, quite like Epsom. The numbers flocking there were so great that in 1684 the first daily post outside London covered, with some difficulty, the 16 miles to Epsom Wells, but only in May, June, and July, the drinking season: at other times the road was often impassable, and it might take a carriage eight or ten hours to get through.

Charles II ran his span, James II came and went, and so did William and Mary. They all contributed greatly to the develop-ment of horse-racing in general, though there is no firm evidence of their activities on the Downs. William was the first to employ a trainer – the legendary Tregonwell Frampton, who for a handsome reputed salary of £1,000 a year was 'Keeper of the Running Horses to His Sacred Majesty King William III,' a post he also held with Queen Anne and the first two Georges. Frampton, the first professional trainer and 'the father of the Turf', was resident at Newmarket, but was no doubt influential in Queen Anne's founding of the Royal Ascot meeting. The statement has also been published that he induced the Queen to inaugurate racing at Epsom, but without much substantiation. The Queen's consort, Prince George of Denmark, did often come over from Windsor to take the waters, which was enough to ensure the wells were not forgotten. Some of those who were elegant, rich enough, and fancied themselves a touch poorly, took off west to the new health fad – Cheltenham Spa. But at least three died regretting the change:

> *Here I lies with my two daughters*
> *All through drinking of Cheltenham waters;*
> *If only we'd stuck to Epsom salts*
> *We shouldn't be lying in these here vaults.*

John Evelyn had recorded a different tale of the Epsom waters in 1670. His brother Richard had died in agony, leaving a widow and one daughter and 'a most noble seat at Woodcote, neere Epsom'. A post-mortem was ordered. 'It was not a spectacle,' he said, 'that I desired to be present at.' But he records the details, on 10th March, in gruesome detail:

> My brother being opened, a stone was taken out of his bladder, not bigger than a nutmeg, somewhat flatt, and oval, not sharp, one part excepted, which was a little rugged: but his livar so faulty that in likelyhood (it could not) have lasted much longer, and his kidnis almost quite consumed: all of this doubtlesse the effects of his intollerable pains proceeding from the stone; and that perhaps by his drinking too excessively of Epsom Waters, when in full health, and that he had no neede of them, being all his lifetime of a sound and healthy constitution.

As the waters began to lose their popularity a cunning pharmacist and quack doctor decided the time had come to discover new wells. Having just established himself as a public benefactor by building almshouses for twelve poor widows, he built the New Wells of Epsom. He opened them in 1706 in a nicely convenient position, promoted them with the enthusiasm of a 20th century bingo hall proprietor, and managed to disguise from many patrons the fact that if there were any health-giving qualities in the new waters they came not from any miraculous gift of nature, but out of the bottles in his back room.

Thomas Allen's splendid *History of Surrey* seizes this villain firmly by the scruff of his neck: 'The waters gradually lost their reputation through the knavery of one Levingston, an apothecary, who having purchased a piece of land here, built a large house, with an assembly room, and sunk a well. By means of concerts, balls, and other diversions, he contrived to allure the company from the old well; and at length, getting the lease of the latter into his hands, he locked up the place. The new water, however, was found not to possess the virtues of the old, and Epsom began to be deserted.' (The old well was in fact reopened in 1727 and continued with some success, but the invention of sea-bathing in 1753 ended Epsom's run. The Old Well House was demolished in 1804, but the well itself is still preserved in the garden of a private house.)

With the waters failing, and Nonsuch no more, it would have been no surprise to find that Epsom had lost that appeal to the nobility without which horse racing could scarcely prosper.

But the quality of the turf itself was the guarantee of success. There was by then sufficient racing on Banstead Downs to warrant the appointment of a Clerk of the Course to control the frequent but irregular meetings.

The *London Gazette* announced, in January 1695, that two plates would be run for annually for three years. The stake money demanded of entrants was three guineas seven days before the race, or five guineas later. Such meetings certainly captured the imagination of James Toland, a gentleman of leisure who was quite overwhelmed by the combination of the horses, the Downs, the village, and the waters – even the new waters. He wrote a long letter about the Epsom scene to his lady love, and was so pleased with his efforts that in 1711 he caused it to be published. It is a hymn of praise to Epsom in which he perhaps allows its virtues to run away with reality in the cause of persuading the lady to abandon the well-known delights of London and sample, with him, those of rural Surrey. The letter must be the most elegant and complete compliment Epsom has ever received: and does make clear some of the qualities that turned the place from obscurity to a shrine for all who followed fashion.

The village, says Toland, 'much frequented for its most healthy Air and excellent mineral Waters, is distant about fourteen Italian miles from London bridge and twelve from Fox-hall. It is deliciously situated in a warm, even bottom, anciently called Flower-dale, between the finest Downs in the world on one side . . . and certain clay hills on the other side, which are variously chequered with woods and groves of oak, ash, elm, and beech, with both the poplars, the intoxicating yew, and the florid white-beam.'

In the village, he assured his lady (whose name was Eudoxa), 'you would think yourself in some enchanted camp, to see the peasants ride to every house with the choicest fruits, herbs, roots, and flowers, with all sorts of tame and wild fowl, with the rarest fish and venison, and with every kind of butcher's meat, among which Banstead-down mutton is the most relishing dainty.

'When you are on top of the Downs, 'tis one of the loveliest prospects imaginable, to view in the vale below such an agreeable mixture of trees and buildings that a stranger is at a loss to know whether it be a town in a wood, or a wood in a town.'

As to those Downs, he went on, they are 'covered with grass finer than Persian carpets, and perfumed with wild thyme and juniper . . . and for sheep-walks, riding, hunting, racing, shooting, or games of most sorts for exercise of the body or recreation of the mind . . . they are nowhere else to be paralleled.'

And, getting closer to our point: 'You can never miss of it on the fine grounds of the new orbicular Race, which may well be termed a rural Cirque.' This clearly establishes the existence by 1711 of a racecourse of the kind of which we are familiar today, though Toland also refers to 'the four-mile course over the Warren-house to Carshalton'. Banstead-downs, he writes, 'are very famous for horse-matches, as there is not a properer place in the world for this sport'.

In a breathless build-up to the climax of his appeal, he concludes: '. . . whether you go to some cricket match . . . or chuse to breath your horse at a Race . . . whether, I say, you delight in any or every one of these, Epsom is the place you must like before all others.'

There is no record of whether the gentleman's eloquence persuaded Eudoxa to abandon her more sophisticated haunts and join him on the Downs. He certainly deserved some satisfaction.

Toland, incidentally, repeats the claim that John Aubrey had made 30 years earlier, that from the Downs it is possible to see 'nine or ten counties in whole or in part'. This seems impossibly extravagant until a clear day and a pair of binoculars come to one's aid. You may then spy parts of Surrey, Hampshire, Berkshire, Buckinghamshire, Oxfordshire, Middlesex, Hertfordshire, the Tower of London and Kent: not far short of their estimates. Aubrey, that wily old raconteur, did actually say that he could encompass the range from the chapel of the manor house at Banstead. Those who wish to emulate him will find success rather surer from the top of the grandstand.

CHAPTER FOUR

Many atrocities

Blessed with the Downs and purged by the salts, Epsom, you might think, had had its share of luck. But in the 18th century two more natural phenomena arose to hoist the flag over the town and draw first the carriage trade and then what would later be called the coach trade. Both were living freaks: the most remarkable woman of her day, and the most remarkable horse of any day. The Downs had Eclipse, which never ran second. The town had Crazy Sally.

Her name may have been Sally Wallis or even Wallin, but just as likely it may not. It may have been Sally Fenton, or not. Her notoriety survives as Mrs Mapp the bonesetter, a wondrous and no doubt welcome figure in a day when a bad fracture was likely to lead either to deformity or a swift chop with the surgeon's cleaver.

'In 1736 a woman came to Epsom in the character of a bone-setter,' relates Manning, 'and made no inconsiderable figure for some time . . . The concourse of people who attended her was incredible, and it was supposed she got twenty guineas a day. She had strength enough to put in any man's shoulder without assistance.' An issue of *The Gentleman's Magazine* that year declares: 'Her Bandages are extraordinary neat, and her dexterity in reducing dislocations and setting of fractured Bones wonderful.'

She was said to inherit her skill from her father, who operated as a bonesetter in Hindon, a Wiltshire village near Warminster. Her sister, says Manning, was 'that Polly Peachum who was married to the Duke of Bolton.' This would be the actress known as Miss Fenton, the first to play the heroine in Gay's exciting success 'The Beggar's Opera', first staged in 1727. The performance made her for a time the most celebrated actress in London, before she became the Duchess of Bolton.

If Epsom's bonesetter was her sister, neither made much of it. The girl left home after a family quarrel and wandered about the country calling herself Crazy Sally, before finding Epsom ideally receptive to her talents. Her success was so stupendous that any Londoner who could afford to get to Epsom and pay her fees did so rather than risk a visit to the doctor. The medical profession was none too pleased, and, to expose the charlatan, hired an impostor to take to her his supposedly dislocated wrist, which the surgeons hoped she would pretend to mend and charge him for it. Sally spotted the deception immediately. She took the man's wrist in her hands, wrenched it out of joint, and sent him back to the fools who had paid him.

At the height of her triumphs she fell for the wrong man, a Mr Mapp 'from which no persuasions could prevent her'. They married, but within a fortnight he was away, and much of her savings with him. She was not one of nature's beauties, and hurried off – unsuccessfully – to find him. A tragedy for metropolitan fractures, and indeed for Epsom, which was prospering from her presence almost as richly as it had done when the waters were all the rage.

It all helped to keep the Downs lively, and there was no doubt that the popularity of the gallops and the frequency of the falls alone brought the bonesetter a few customers, though there was one potential client who did escape the lady's remarkable services: 'A curious accident befell the jockey who rode the winner of the Sweepstakes. Just before he came in at the Winning Post, being crossed by a gentleman on horseback, the rider was thrown, but his leg hanging in the stirrup, the horse of course carried his weight in, and won miraculously without hurting the rider.'

By the time Crazy Sally settled in the village, race meetings were held every spring (and often in the autumn) and had been since 1730. Even before that, Daniel Defoe, on his gentle journey through England, had found the Downs full enough: 'When on the Publick Race Days they are covered with Coaches and Ladies, and an innumerable Company of Horsemen, as well Gentlemen as Citizens, attending the Sport; and then adding to the beauty of the Sight, the Racers flying over the Course, as if they either touched not or felt the Ground they run upon; I think no Sight, except that of a Victorious Army, under the Command of a Protestant King of Great Britain, could exceed it.'

The town in the season, he reported, 'is full of Company, and all disposed to Mirth and Pleasantry.' Even the businessmen, straight from the City, 'look as if they had left their London thoughts behind them . . . as if they came hither to unbend the Bow of the Mind, and to give themselves a loose to their Innocent Pleasures.' Some even commuted by horse to and from the City: 'I know one Citizen that practised it for several Years together, and scarce ever lay a night in London during the whole Season.'

Defoe's admiration of the beauty of Epsom's countryside is almost as ecstatic as Toland's: 'It is like a great Park filled with little Groves, Lodges, and Retreats for coolness of Air, and shade from the Sun; and I believe, I may say, it is not matched in the World, on that account; at least, not in so little a space of Ground.' He uncompromisingly underlines the difference between Epsom in season and Epsom out of season, when it returned to the natural desolation of a country village: 'In the winter, no place for pleasure. Homes shut up, windows fastened, curtains taken down, furniture removed, walls out of repair, leaves off the trees, and people out of town. Roads deep, stiff, full of sloughs, and in a word, impassable.'

About six weeks before the spring race meeting, the hunter's stakes were occasionally run for: 'At one of which the celebrated horse, Madcap, won the prize and proved the best plate horse in England' (Allen). Prize money at the main meetings was raised by charging a fee to all the stall-holders who wanted to sell their wares at the course, and to those who put up marquees and temporary stands at the winning post. As Defoe indicated, it was clearly a money-making occasion. Less literate hands were at it in 1735:

> On Epsom Downs when racing does begin,
> Large companies from every part come in,
> Tag-rag and Bob-tail, Lords and Ladies meet,
> And Squires without Estates, each other greet . . .

Should there be any doubt, the Rev Thomas Cox, in the *History of Surrey*, begun in 1715 and finished in 1731, notes that the racecourse was then much frequented.

The races were still held in heats, a practice that persisted at Epsom until The Oaks were run in 1779. Events began at the Banstead end of the four mile straight course, usually at about 11.0 a.m. Heats were held through the morning, after which the company would retire to the town for a long tavern lunch, returning some hours later for the final stages of the day. It was thus not uncommon for a horse in the final run-off to be then engaged for the fourth time that day, racing over an undulating course considerably longer than the distance from Hyde Park Corner to St Paul's – not forgetting that each time it had to get back to Hyde Park on its own legs.

Such stamina seems unbelievable. That there were enough horses able to withstand such a day's racing is largely due to the ruthless measures taken by Henry VIII to raise both the quantity and the quality of horses in England. Every brood mare, he had decreed, must be fourteen hands high. Magistrates were empowered and directed to scour the commons and memorial wastes at Michaelmas and put to death all stallions and mares under the specified height. He laid down a minimum scale of horse ownership that ensured nobody shirked their equine duty. It ranged from archbishops and dukes, who were 'obliged to keep seven trotting horses for the saddle, each to be fourteen hands high and of the age of three years' to the one-horse obligation of any layman 'whose wife wore a French hood or velvet bonnet'.

It may have been the result of such dogmas that a large and rather ugly colt was foaled in 1764 at the Duke of Cumberland's stud in Windsor Great Park. It was sold the next year to William Wildman, 'a butcher of much prosperity', for a good price despite its looks – 70 or 80 guineas. Finding it bad-tempered to the extent of being unmanageable, he sent it to a rough-rider at Epsom: the yearling was ridden all day and occasionally all night as well, but nothing broke its spirit. The horse seemed prepared to go on running for ever.

Eclipse, as it was called, gained some local fame for its pace and determination, and Wildman was encouraged to give it a trial against a good runner. They were taken up to the Epsom course very early one morning – a time of discreet inconvenience still adhered to for trials of the greatest interest – and set them off. Those who make it their business to be in the know on such matters arrived too late to see anything, but they found an old woman who had been up on the Downs since dawn.

Yes, she said, she had seen something: a horse with one white leg running away at a monstrous rate, and another a great way behind. She was sure the other would never catch up, 'not if he ran to the world's end'. So, at least, the conversation was reported around the taverns of the town later in the day; and so the myth of Eclipse was launched – perhaps the only myth among a million since, springing from racing stables, that proved true – totally true – however ludicrous the exaggerations appeared.

Eclipse was still no beauty. Higher behind than before, the body was mounted on long legs (the off hind one partly white), and stood over fifteen hands high. At the end of a long neck, a small, odd head. In a trial of equine elegance, Eclipse would have been laughed out of the ring. But when it came to travelling, the others could stay at home – and often did.

The horse was five before it ran its first race. Carrying eight stone, it entered a 50 guinea plate at Epsom on 3rd May, 1769.

Local excitement over the trial run had shortened the starting odds to 4–1 on. An Irishman at the rails went further, and made a bet so bold and so dramatic that it has echoed through history: 'Eclipse first, the rest nowhere.' And that was the official result, a runner being declared 'distanced' (or 'nowhere') if it was not within 240 yards of the winner as it passed the finishing post. Such horses were automatically disqualified from running in subsequent heats of the same plate. Though the field were more or less together at three miles (opposite the Law Courts at the end of the Strand, you might say), Eclipse's jockey sat still and the horse ran away with it, as if passing St Paul's by the time its rivals reached Ludgate Circus.

From that moment there could have been no doubt that Epsom was nursing the most extraordinary race horse ever born. After two more easy wins, the Irishman (whose name was O'Kelly) offered Wildman 650 guineas for a half-share in Eclipse at Ascot on 29th May. Oddly enough, the owner accepted. Even more puzzling, at the end of the season (five more races, five more wins) he sold O'Kelly the other half-share for 1,100 guineas. Undoubtedly, as Theodore Cook wrote in *Eclipse and O'Kelly*, 'no better bargain in horseflesh was ever made'.

By the end of that first year's racing, Eclipse had won 680 guineas. In 1770 O'Kelly entered him for nine races: Eclipse won three and walked-over six, winning 1,469 guineas. By then the horse was starting at odds down to 70–1 on, and no other horse alive was able (or willing) to race against him. O'Kelly, who in prize money had barely covered the purchase price, then withdrew Eclipse from the track. This god among all quadrupeds was, said Cook, 'never beaten, never whipped, never felt the tickling of a spur, or was ever for a moment distressed . . . outfooting, outstriding and outlasting every horse which started against him.'

Retirement to stud was the beginning rather than the end of Eclipse's mightiest achievements and earning power. At Clay Hill, on the Downs, the stallion earned O'Kelly £25,000, at fees which began at 50 guineas and did not drop below thirty for the rest of its life. Breeders say loosely that the mark of Eclipse is on nine out of every ten classic winners even today. Certainly by 1906, when Cook wrote his book, 82 of the 127 Derby winners were Eclipse descendants, as were 30 of the 34 runners in that year's race. Eclipse sired three Derby winners in its first four years at stud; in its one failure, the first Derby in 1780, only the second and third were Eclipse foals.

One will perhaps never look upon its like again. But on

making enquiries of a commissionaire at the Museum of Natural History in South Kensington, one may be escorted to a sub-basement and look upon its skeleton – preserved for posterity in a plastic cocoon, though not on exhibition to the public. A pity; Eclipse deserved honouring.

It is a wonder that the right skeleton arrived at the museum, to which it was presented by the Royal College of Veterinary Surgeons. When Cook was preparing to write his book, he was shown six 'undoubted' skeletons, nine 'authentic' feet, enough hair from the tail of Eclipse to have stuffed the largest arm-chair in the Jockey Club, and sufficient hide from the great beast to carpet the yard at Tattersall's.

The sadly brief racing life of Eclipse, glittering though it was, scarcely reflects the value of the horse to Epsom. Before its time, racing there still carried the air of a passing pursuit: the serious dedication that had long been applied on the Heath at Newmarket was rarely in evidence on the Downs. But within a decade of Eclipse switching its endeavours from turf to stud, Epsom had given birth to two of the most famous races in the world – the Oaks and the Derby. The moment of conception of the Oaks, in 1779, changed the face of racing on the Downs; the birth of the Derby decided the destiny of the town.

The precise pattern of a race meeting at Epsom at that time is preserved in a remarkable document still in the possession of the Epsom Grand Stand Association. It appears to be a contemporary copy of the original articles of agreement for the spring meeting of 1778, 'made concluded and agreed upon . . . by and between the several inhabitants of the Parish of Epsom in the County of Surrey for and towards the raising of the under-mentioned 4 several plates.' It is signed by the two stewards of the meeting, Robert Hudson and Edward Knipe, Junior.

It was a four-day meeting: On Wednesday the race was open to 'any horse mare or gelding to carry nine stone the best of three heats four miles each heat'; on Thursday, '5 and 6 years old and aged horses etc. that never won thirty pounds (matches excepted).' The five-year-olds were to carry 8 stone 4 lb., the six-year-olds 8 stone 11 lb., and the 'aged horses etc.' 9 stone 4 lb. Again, there were three heats of four miles each. Friday must have been welcome: heats of only 2 miles, for four-year-olds with 8 stone 7 lb. up. Back to 4 mile heats on Saturday, for five-year-olds (8 stone 7 lbs.), six-year-olds, and aged horses (9 stone). For all races, mares and fillies were allowed 3 pounds.

Fewer than three 'reputed running horses etc.' would not be accepted as constituting a proper start, and all horses had to be at Epsom 'ten clear days before the first day of starting and there continue until the day of running at such of the subscribers stables in Epsom as shall subscribe four guineas or upwards towards these plates.' Entry fees were fairly steep: 3 guineas a horse, 5 shillings 'towards the repairs of ye rails' and 5 shillings 'to ye Clerk of ye Course'; or, at the post, 6 guineas a horse, 5 shillings for the rails, and half a guinea for the Clerk. Further financial penalties awaited any owner whose horse was not plated by the subscribing smiths in Epsom: 2s. 6d. a horse.

The cost of putting up booths by the course was on a sliding scale that increased the further from Epsom the owner lived: 'to wit every person who shall erect a booth or shed who lives in Epsom to contribute 1 guinea. If within twelve miles of Epsom 2 guineas and if further than twelve miles 3 guineas for each booth or shed.' The rate was to be paid to the Clerk 'before the breaking up of the ground otherwise such booth etc. shall be destroyed.' They were to be built only 'on a strait line the same side of ye hill the rubbing house stands leading towards Ashstead.'

Half an hour was allowed for rubbing down between heats. The plate in each case went to the horse that won two of the three heats. If the three heats were shared between three horses, those three were to run a fourth heat. Finally, it was agreed that any rider who 'shall or do wip or lay hold of any rider, his horse saddle or bridle' should be deemed a distant horse, which would disqualify the mount from running for that plate.

One line in this ancient document makes it clear that this particular meeting in 1778 was an unusual one: 'All horses etc. that shall run for any of these plates shall start exactly at 5 o'clock in the afternoon.' The traditional pattern of morning heats, midday carousal, and afternoon heats was passed over on that occasion in favour of a hectic evening's racing. If any of the plates went to a fourth heat – and they frequently did – it could hardly have started before eight o'clock, remembering the mounts had 4 miles to canter back to the start after rubbing down.

It may have been this very meeting that sired the Oaks and the Derby. Among the owners almost certainly involved in those plates were Sir Charles Bunbury and the young twelfth Earl of Derby, and neither of them can have watched their horses covering perhaps 32 miles in one evening for a prize of a few sovereigns with much pleasure. Bunbury, who had owned racehorses for 15 years, was a steward of the Jockey Club, which is about as senior position as one can hold in the racing world. He had watched with interest the experiment of Lieutenant-General

Anthony St Leger at Doncaster in 1776, when he initiated the first major race to be decided on one running only.

Derby's interest was just as vital. He had a 180 acre country home at Woodmansterne, probably within sight of the start of the four-mile course, and was the most influential landowner in the district. Early in 1779 Bunbury was one of a roystering house-party there and after a great deal of choice claret, and over what the Earl of Rosebery called 'Lord Derby's curious port', these youngish bloods (Derby was 27) decided that the strain of all those heats was too much, and they were going to show Epsom the sort of race that should be held on the Downs.

A month or two later, at the spring meeting, Epsom racegoers saw a 1½ mile race for three-year-old fillies, no heats, no re-runs. It was called the Oaks – the name of Lord Derby's house – and was won, not unhappily, by the Earl's own horse Bridget. It may have been that night, back at The Oaks, that the same men took another alcoholically-induced step, the sound of which still cracks annually over the racing world. Focusing as it did all the excitement (and all the betting) into one short and shining race, the Oaks had been a splendid success. Next year they would sponsor an even shorter one for three-year-old colts as well – just one straight mile.

'Your turn for the name, Charles,' said Derby happily. 'We'll call this one the Bunbury.' 'Not a bit, old man,' said Bunbury, 'your house, your idea, you have it.' They tossed a sovereign for the privilege, and called the race the Derby. Bunbury kept his name in the history books by winning it with Diomed.

'Thursday May 4th 1780. The Derby Stakes of 50 guineas each, half forfeit for 3-year-old colts 8 stone and fillies 7 stone 11lb. One mile (36 subs).' That was how it began. Of the 36 entries, 9 ran. Bunbury's chestnut colt started favourite at 6–4 and secured his noble owner the whole of the prize money of 1,075 guineas. It was a fine young horse, unbeaten in its first three years' racing, but subsequently declined and was retired as a six-year-old with a stud fee of only 5 guineas (compare that with Eclipse's 50 guineas 13 years earlier). According to Roger Mortimer's *History of the Derby Stakes,* Bunbury sold Diomed at the age of 20 for 50 guineas. It was shipped to the United States and promptly sold to a Virginian breeder for 1,000 guineas. The new owner's intuitive gamble came off: Diomed responded to the new climate so successfully that it sired a line of excellent winners and became America's equine hero.

Bunbury remained a powerful racing man, and in 1801 brought off an astonishing double when Eleanor won both the

Derby and the Oaks. His trainer died during that meeting, but lives in his last words, which a priest was hastily summoned to hear: 'Depend on it,' said the unfortunate man, as the priest made ready with the final blessing, 'Eleanor is a damned fine mare.'

The card for that first Derby meeting was still mostly concerned with plates run for in heats. The first day offered a Noblemen's and Gentlemen's Plate of £50 (two 4-mile heats), and as an appetizer for the Derby eight horses contested three 4-mile heats for £50: also, 'to add to the interest of the meeting a Main of Cocks will be fought, the property of the Gentlemen of Surrey.' On the third day, the Oaks was followed by the 2 mile Ladies' Plate, and business was concluded on Saturday with heats of the 4-mile Town Plate.

The settling of bets between gentlemen (the rabble did their business at the betting post, half-way up the Hill) usually took place several days later at Tattersall's, in London. Winnings were not always guaranteed: 'It was plain that many accounts were deranged by the non-appearance of two parties, who lost heavily on both races. One is a Mr R-p-y, whose losses are variously stated – the average about £7,000. His case is quite hopeless, as he had apprized his victims that "from the unexpected termination of the Derby and the Oaks, he cannot meet his differences." Nothing could be done more coolly.

'The only great winner was Mr Forth, who had nothing to do but sit still and receive tribute: it was a glorious sight to see the rolls of banknotes forced upon him every minute, and the perfect non-chalance with which he pocketted them. He wins nearly £30,000.'

The Earl of Derby's private life was a matter of great interest in the locality, and indeed to society at large. At the age of 21 he had bought The Oaks, on the edge of the Downs, from Captain John Burgoyne, who later achieved notoriety as the general who lost the American War of Independence. Burgoyne had bought the Elizabethan building (previously 'Lambert's Oaks' and subsequently often confused with a nearby alehouse also called 'The Oaks') as a home for his distinguished bride – Lady Charlotte Stanley, daughter of the 11th Earl of Derby. The 12th Earl was his grandson, and Lady Charlotte's nephew.

He moved into The Oaks with his bride, Lady Elizabeth Hamilton, sister and heiress to the Duke of Hamilton. They had a son and three daughters before the Countess left him in favour of the Duke of Dorset. Derby was expected to sue for divorce, but refrained from doing so when he learned how much that would please his wife, whose great hope then was to become Duchess of Dorset. The marriage remained undissolved until her death in 1792, after which the Earl, then 40, married an actress ten years his junior – one whose face was familiar at The Oaks house parties.

The Earl's race, meanwhile, gained in popularity year by year, drawing greater crowds than had ever been seen before on any racecourse. After four years on the original 1 mile course, it was lengthened in 1784 to $1\frac{1}{2}$ miles – approximately the distance over which it has been run ever since. In 1788 the Derby had its first royal winner: the horse was Sir Thomas, and the owner was the Prince of Wales (later George IV), who had so often attended the race and was more than any man responsible for race-going being at last considered a thoroughly fashionable pursuit. Three years later the profligate 'Prinny' was involved in a racing scandal at Newmarket, when one of his horses finished last one day (after drinking a bucket of water, some said) and first the next.

His brother, the Duke of York, won with Prince Leopold in 1816, and with Moses in 1822, and year by year the royal party in the original Prince's Stand became less comfortable and more cramped, including as it did the giants of high society – the Dukes of Bedford and Somerset, Lord Jersey, and the notorious Beau Brummell.

As we have seen, Prince's at this time was the only permanent stand on the Downs. Maps of the period, in fact, mark it as 'The Stand'. No evidence of its date of construction seems to have survived though an engraving does exist showing the Derby winner of 1793, Waxy, standing on the course with the little stand in the background; and since in 1780 'Their Majestys were on the Downes to see the day's sport,' the stand might well have been up even then.

It was a rather odd and charming edifice, looking less like a race stand than a tower from some Ruritanian castle: small, square, and battlemented, and faced with three Gothic arches, the centre one nearly twice the height of the others. It seems too small to warrant so many entrances, and the smaller doors may have been to storage chambers under the stairs. The main door probably opened on to a dining hall from which a staircase ran round both sides of the tower to the flat roof – a vantage point from which the privileged could enjoy an unrivalled view in comparative comfort.

When the racing bored them, or perhaps in the long intervals between races, they found much else on which to wager their money: whether this old peer would last the year out, or that young damsel remain unwed another twelve months. Marriage frequently interested them, and one of their faithfully recorded wagers, signed by Beau Brummell, Lord Charles Maines, Lord Lorne, and E. H. Delme, promises that each will give 100 guineas to the last of them to be married.

Elsewhere on the course, the company was rather less elegant. Pownall wrote in 1825: 'If the weather be fine, there are seldom less than 60,000 assembled here when the Derby stakes are contested. Of these the vicious and unprincipled form a tolerable proportion . . . It therefore generally follows that many atrocities are committed; and those who fortunately escape the numerous accidents which occur, have to lament the loss of some portion of their property.'

The atrocities were not all committed on the course, for the country lanes, muddy and potholed, leading from the Downs, were a natural hunting ground for thieves and vandals as the gentry made their way back to London after the meeting. Gangs of villains hid in the hedges and ditches, rushing solitary carriages, and thinking nothing of overturning them if there was any opposition to their demands. After the meeting in May 1795, it was reported that several carriages were broken to pieces on the way home, more than thirty robbed, and one lady left with a broken arm.

At these times, there can have been little doubt of the truth of Francis Grose's celebrated maxim:

> *Sutton for mutton, Cashalton for beeves,*
> *Epsom for whores, Ewell for thieves.*

CHAPTER FIVE

Intermission I

This chapter will be short, but it might be painful: a small slice of less than engrossing history of some of the families and estates that surrounded the Downs. Skip it if you insist, but don't blame me if later you find some threads broken in the tapestry of your knowledge. If only we knew all about them, the stories would be fascinating; scratching at the surface, we find a spot of colour here and there, and must make do with it. The presence of these people, and the massive amount of land they held, was later to prove the greatest obstacle to the development of the racecourse.

We know about The Oaks and Lord Derby, but he was the other side of Banstead and not relevant here. The Earl of Rosebery (who later bought The Oaks) was relevant enough, but at this stage in the story he had not arrived at Durdans. At this time, the beginning of the 19th century, the great house, twice demolished, had lately suffered destruction by fire during rebuilding, and was to be rebuilt on a smaller scale and pass into the hands of the Heathcote family.

Next to Durdans was Woodcote Park (350 acres, 1 mile south of Epsom, and contiguous to the racecourse, as it says in the books: it is now the Royal Automobile Club country seat). In AD 940, long before there was a house there, it became part of the lands of Chertsey Abbey, granted in a charter drawn up at 'the royal town, called in English, Kingston' and signed 'Athelstan, rex totius Britanniae'. By the time Pepys' friend George Mynnes lived there it was the seat of the Lord of the Manor of Horton. Mynnes left the manor to his daughter, Mrs Elizabeth Evelyn, whose unfortunate husband died with that stone in his bladder. (John Evelyn wrote that his brother Richard married the 'daughter of Esquire Minn lately deceased: by which he had a great Estate, both in Land and monie'.)

Her disposal of Woodcote Park, where she had built a new house in 1648, led to a spicy scandal: she left it to a distant relative, the fourth Lord Baltimore, a Roman Catholic who had opposed James II in Ireland and was outlawed as a traitor. The family enjoyed at Woodcote a debauched reputation, which by 1768 had gone rather too far, when the sixth Baltimore was then tried at Kingston Assizes for the rape of a young milliner. He narrowly escaped conviction (claiming the maid was ready and willing), sold the estate, and went to Naples to die. It is said that he travelled across Europe with eight women, a physician and two black eunuchs. His exotic will is remarkable for its extraordinarily generous bequests to Italian servants. The manor was subsequently bought by a rich merchant of French extraction, Lewis Teissier, whose son became Baron de Teissier. Woodcote House seems to have stayed out of racecourse history, though it was once home of the Lords of the Manors of Cheam, Ewell and Cuddington.

You can't step far into the history of land-owning around Epsom without falling over a Carew, who seem, at their peak, to have been Lords of the Manors of Banstead, Walton-on-the-Hill, and Epsom. Sir Nicholas Carew was a Gentleman of the Privy Chamber, Master of the King's Horse, and Knight of the Garter during the reign of Henry VIII. The King presented him with the manor of Walton in 1533 – at one time the residence of Anne of Cleves – and of Epsom in 1538: after which he discovered that Carew was plotting to overthrow him. A Catholic, Carew made 'a godly confession, both of his fault and his superstitious faith', but was beheaded on Tower Hill just the same. All his estates reverted to the Crown – including the manor of Banstead, which Carew had leased from Queen Catherine (of Aragon), who had continued to hold the manor after her divorce from Henry.

The Carew family appear never to have regained possession of Epsom, though Walton, at least, was later restored to and held by the family until the death of Sir Nicholas Hacket Carew in 1762. Defoe records in 1724 that one of the Carews, a notorious gambler, lost all his lands and houses in one night's gaming – 'some say at one cast of the dice'. But before the necessary legal formalities of the transfer could be completed, the winner was frustrated by the death of the loser, whose estate was thus preserved for his heirs. It eventually came into the hands of Richard Gee, who, by an Act of Parliament in 1780, took the name and arms of Carew. Remember the manor of Walton-on-the-Hill, more than a square mile of highly-prized land on the south side of the racecourse: racing teeth were never more grievously gnashed than over this turf.

The *Victoria History of the County of Surrey* states that the manor of Epsom too was returned to the Carews, in 1576. Others are firm that it remained Crown land until 1589, when Queen Elizabeth gave it to Edward d'Arcy, a groom of the Privy Chamber. Its past is charming: still legally known as Ebbisham, it was Ebba's Ham (Ebba's aunt, Eanher, was Queen of the Isle of Wight in the 6th century AD). Its future was of vital concern to the racing world, since much of the racecourse, and later the grandstand buildings, lay on the manorial wastes of Epsom. There is no record, until the 19th century, of what charge, if any, the Lords of the Manor made for racing there, and of what control, if any, they exercised over it – points that were later to be matters of life or death to racing on the Downs. (The later Carews worked up their income from racing over Walton land from £50 to £300 a year.)

To return to the late 17th century: the widow of George Mynnes (of Woodcote Park) bought the manor of Epsom, and on her death it passed to her daughter, Mrs Evelyn – already, from her father, Lord of the Manor of Horton. From her it went to Christopher Buckle, Lord of the Manor of Banstead. He built at Banstead an extravagant house in Nork Park, later bought (in 1812) by the Earl of Egmont and coveted in part by those who wanted a 5 furlong straight. The Epsom manor went up for auction, and was bought in 1770 by Sir Joseph Mawbey; his son, with the same name, was Lord of the Manor from 1798 to 1817, when he was succeeded by his eldest daughter, Emily. She died a year later, the manor passing to her sister, Anna Maria Mawbey, than whom no woman can have had a greater influence on a classic racecourse until Mrs Topham took over Aintree. In 1819 Anna Maria married John Ivatt Briscoe, MP for East Surrey. It was his legal right to administer her estates, and he did so for 50 years. For 40 of them he guided and re-strained the efforts of the Epsom Grand Stand Association in a way that it occasionally found frustrating, but his encouragement of the sport was unfailing and his generosity almost incredible; not only did he allow racing over the manorial lands without charge, but he actually made an annual donation to the race fund.

Without the co-operation of this Lord of the Manor, no race could ever be held, no rails erected, no bets laid, no sod cut, no stone cemented to stone nor girder raised; it was in his power to banish from the Downs not the people of Epsom, whose rights he had to guard, but their garish toys – the carriages and coaches, the swings and the stalls, the knaves, the knives, the naked ladies.

CHAPTER SIX

The reception of company

Even 50 years after the first Derby, gazeteer writers could still refer to Epsom as 'a large and remarkably pleasant village on the road from London to Dorking and Guildford.' At the last census, in 1821, it had only 452 houses and 2,890 inhabitants. The historian J. C. Whyte reckoned that 20 years later, the population had only increased to 4,000 and noted then: 'In the centre of the town is a large sheet of water' – now, of course, a car park. The medicinal waters were well forgotten by the time the grandstand was up: 'The principal cause of the celebrity which this place now enjoys is the races, which are held twice a year on the Downs in the vicinity.'

The placing in the calendar of the two meetings was somewhat irregular, and several 20th century racing historians have been considerably confused. When the EGSA was formed there was one in the week before Whitsun and one in October. The first, the long-established spring meeting, included the Derby and the Oaks and was the high spot of the racing calendar: 'Several of the royal family, and most of the nobility, attend these races.'

Ten years later a meeting was established in April, and it has survived ever since as the spring meeting. In 1840, Whyte noted it was 'very thinly attended, and the sport is very indifferent'. By then the Derby week was known as the summer meeting – though snow fell while the race was being run in 1839 – and the October meeting had been dropped.

An anonymous historian, doubtless a resident, was one of many who did not appreciate the honour that was being done to their sleepy little town: 'Its perennial slumber was broken twice a year by race meetings, when the followers and camp followers of the Turf stormed the neighbourhood during a few agitated days, then struck their tents and left the town, sodden and exhausted. Thereafter the calm recommenced, and the inhabitants could saunter over miles of open turf to breathe the purest air in England.'

The situation had not greatly changed a century later, and probably never will. What happens on the Downs is still of little concern to the residents of Epsom, except that when it is happening front gates are closed and children counted frequently. There are some who still maintain their rights were sold down the river when Charles Bluck laid his first brick, and that it is a diabolical liberty to stop a man of Epsom galloping his own horse on his own Downs. There will always be some to fight for usurped rights, and though the Epsom Grand Stand Association has taken infinite pains to tie up its own extremely expensive rights in a fair and lawful manner, the spirited opposition it has met for nearly 150 years has kept both its members and the zealous residents on their toes.

Whatever the local feelings about the Derby crowds in 1828, Bluck knew that there was money to be made out of funnelling a few thousand individuals into a grandstand. The determined and eventually victorious anti-Bluck faction was not opposed to that idea, but could probably see that, with better organization than Bluck could command, there was a brighter rainbow and a fatter crock of gold at the end of it. But some of them at least cared enough for racing to want to set up conditions for a meeting that would allow maximum participation in the event, with minimum prevarication. Up till then, placing bets had been more difficult than trying to catch a cockroach in a coal cellar. As the *Illustrated London News* racing expert summed it up a few years later: 'Up to the first quarter of this century, you went to Newmarket, where the existence of the animal you staked your money on could no more be known to you till he came to the starting post (and not then, unless you had a good telescope) than the state of the Emperor of Morocco's bile. You went to Epsom, and found the jockeys starting themselves; or to Doncaster, and saw them deciding how they came in . . .'

Starts, even when accompanied by an official, remained a chaotic business and seldom took place precisely at the time advertised. The pleasure of watching a race at all was severely curtailed by the fact that, on Derby days at least, it was not safe for a lady or gentleman to leave the carriage and be exposed to the rampaging, pick-pocketing mob that surged outside.

It was not a scene, by contemporary accounts, that differed greatly from the one that engulfs the Downs today: 'All sorts of persons and things were mingled together in inextricable confusion – giants, dwarfs, peers, blacklegs, etc., etc . . . There was an entire street of canvas "hells", particularly cool looking and inviting, for all who pleased to avail themselves of the opportunity of entering a suburban St James's. Add to this Jews, jockies, persons equally intent upon cheating and being cheated – gipsies capable of telling everybodies future but their own – horses at full speed – a beautiful expanse of wooded country – St Paul's seen dim and indistinct as a shadow in the extreme distance, and the reader, who has never been at Epsom during race week, if such there be, will have aggregate of the physical and moral *materiel* which constitutes the scene.' (*The Times*, 3rd June, 1829.)

At least getting there is now a slightly more regular procedure, if an infinitely less colourful one: 'Some, more adventurous than others, made their appearance at a very early hour on the road leading from London to Epsom in every possible (and we had almost said impossible) species of vehicles. The glittering barouche – the humble tax-cart which, "contrived a double debt to pay", carries about legs of beef six days in the week and the butcher's rib (seldom a spare rib) on the seventh – these and all intermediate and anomalous conveyances were put in requisition, and drawn by animals as various in character and appearance as the vehicles themselves.

'Few casualties occurred in their progress of a more serious nature than the occasional crash of an axletree, or tumbling of a spavined donkey. With the exception of such accidents, and now and then a temporary ebullition of anger or ginger-beer, matters went off as smoothly as could be expected till their arrival at the Downs.'

The second chapter of this story was concerned with the drama of Charles Bluck and the establishment of the EGSA. It left us suspended in 1830, after that embarrassing business of the investigation by the select committee into the early running of the Association ('There appears to have been much that they regret should have taken place . . .'). Before we carry on from that point, there are a few stitches to pick up from 1829 – nothing vital, but worth a few minutes.

You'll remember that the grandstand was not completed in time for the spring meeting of that year. In fact, builder Chadwick had quite a job to squeeze £600 out of the committee so that he could make the place fit for some sort of occupation, (there was, incidentally, a fatal accident to one of the workmen: the committee and Chadwick agreed to go fifty-fifty on his funeral expenses 'so that he may be decently interred'). The accounts for 1829 showed that £192 was taken in the stand at the spring meeting, indicating an attendance of some 750 people a day, in addition to shareholders. Before the October race meeting, 50 bills were printed 'and stuck up in the most public situation leading from London to Epsom'. Despite this, it seems to have been a financial disaster: they took only £4 1s 6d at the grandstand door. The building was then said to be 'in a state of great forwardness', but Chadwick declined to proceed without more money: he had received only £6,750 and was owed another £6,050.

Money-raising continued to be the most urgent matter on the committee's agenda. By the time Chadwick and Trendall (the architect) had been paid up to date, Bluck paid off, and the old committee compensated, there was a balance in the bank of £29 9s 8d. By the end of the year there was cash in hand of £130, to meet debts that had risen to £516. At the half-yearly meeting of shareholders at the British Coffee House, Cockspur Street, in January 1830, the committee phrased the situation delicately:

'As your funds have not been lately in so flourishing a state as could be wished, your committee have considered, as a subject of the greatest importance, the reduction of the heavy expenses which have hitherto attended the management of your affairs . . . They are most happy to state that they have engaged as a secretary, Mr Weatherby, of Oxendon Street, a gentleman well-known to many proprietors as the publisher of the *Racing Calendar*, and have made arrangements with him to undertake the management of the concern, in future, at less than one-third of the expenses attending the late establishment in Wellington Street.'

The details, not all of which were reported to the meeting, were that Weatherby (whose family still publish the *Racing Calendar* and are secretaries to the Jockey Club) had offered to take over the job, to provide an office, accommodation for the committee, stationery, firing, and candles for 110 guineas a year. Sandford, the original secretary, was paid his due salary and a bonus of £32 10s, 'on account of his attention to your affairs and his sudden dismissal' (he had a fortnight's notice). He was also presented with the furniture in the Wellington Street office. His clerk, Leon, received no such consideration. On 9th December he was paid the past year's salary of £75 that was that day due to him, and fired. By the time of the January meeting he had asked for a quarter's salary as redundancy money, 'which your committee submit for your consideration, but at the same time beg to express it as their opinion that he has no claim.'

(The meeting in fact voted him the money, to the discomfiture of their committee.)

The select committee weighed in at this meeting with their report on the grandstand that was quoted earlier ('. . . rapidly drawing towards completion . . . it will be considered . . . far superior to any similar accommodation in the kingdom'); but despite its unfinished state, it had already been rated 'to the relief of the poor of the Parish of Epsom' at an annual rent of £500. This was the first of many battles the committee had with the town over rates: 'unwarrantable and illegal', it claimed. This time they came off best, and later in the year they were reduced to £350.

By April the buildings were 'advanced nearly to completion', and the front page of the *Morning Chronicle* carried this historic notice on the 12th of that month:

EPSOM GRAND STAND

The Committee beg to inform the Nobility and Gentry frequenting Epsom Races, that this elegant building will be ready for the reception of company at the ensuing Meeting, which commences on the 25th May. The Committee have provided a room for the Members of the Jockey Club and the New Rooms at Newmarket, and for the Stewards of the Races. The remainder of the building, comprising a convenient betting-room, saloon, balcony, roof, refreshment, and separate retiring room for Ladies, with attendance and other accommodations, WILL be OPEN to the PUBLIC. Refreshments of every description will be provided by Mr Charles Wright at the most reasonable prices, a list of which will be seen at the Stand. The whole arrangement will be under the direction of the Committee, who are resolved that the strictest order shall be preserved. Ladies and Gentlemen will find their pleasure and comfort greatly increased by repairing to the Stand, as they will enjoy a full view of the whole Course. They will have the Grand Saloon, which is 110 feet by 40, as a promenade, and they will have every accommodation around them. The advantages of which, when compared to the confinement of a carriage, are obvious. Prices of admission, Tuesday and Wednesday, 3s each; Thursday and Friday, 5s each. Tickets for the week, 12s.

The magistrates for the County of Surrey are respectfully informed that they will be admitted free.

It was not the only good news in April: Mr Briscoe, the Lord of the Manor of Epsom, had signified his willingness to return the first year's ground rent (£30). And the month saw both the end of the villain who began it all, and the first mention in the records of the family that came to mean so much to Epsom racecourse. The chairman of the committee (Mr Weston, who had succeeded the solicitor, Lindsay) had bought Bluck's lease of the four basement rooms for £350, and handed it to the Association – who paid him 5% per annum for the loan.

No more, it seems, was ever heard of Charles Bluck. The entrance? It could only be a Dorling, the whole family of whom will take up a lot of space in any history of the racecourse. For the moment, let us turn to William Dorling, a printer, who was already renowned for publishing, on every race day, the 'Only Genuine Race Card Approved by Authority'.

Shortly before the opening of the grandstand, the committee noted: 'that Mr Dorling's offer be accepted to mention the prices of admission to the stand at the bottom of his lists, and that the horses will saddle before the stand; that there is no printing now required for which they can give him an order, but they will bear his application in mind'. Who would have thought that within 15 years the Dorlings would be running the racecourse?

Though the Association had done their best to interest the king in the new grandstand, there was no hope that he would visit it. George IV was now 68, and on his deathbed. The day before the meeting opened, the report on his condition in the *Windsor Express* left little hope of recovery. 'It must not be disguised,' they said, 'that at His Majesty's period of life the absence of actual improvement, even though there was no marked deterioration, was in itself an unfavourable symptom. Towards the latter part of last week, at the most fearful part of the disorder, so extreme were the royal sufferings, and so violent the symptoms, that the medical attendants declared that any other frame must have succumbed to the disease.'

As the Londoners began to arrive for the four-day meeting, so the cost of living in Epsom mysteriously took a turn for the worse. It did not escape the notice of *The Times* racing correspondent: 'The charges made by townspeople and others was as usual outrageously high. Even the bakers raise the price of bread during race week, and the inhabitants of Epsom are not exempted from the increased charges.' Derby day was its customary success, despite a heavy shower 'mixed with hail nearly the size of French beans' an hour before the race – which was more than an hour late in starting. But, notwithstanding the attraction of the completed grandstand, the meeting as a whole was not taken to the heart of society as warmly as the Association hoped it would be.

The Times did not carry a report of the first day's racing at all, and after the second day had only this to say: 'The weather still continuing uncertain, these races have not come off as yet with their usual *éclat*. Today, the course was not more numerously attended than yesterday, and the company were compelled to seek shelter from the numerous showers. In the saloon of the Grand Stand, the visitors amused themselves previously to, and in the interval of the races, the ladies with novels and chat, the gentlemen with the racing calendar, and gourmands of either sex with lobster, salad, and champagne.

'About two o'clock, shortly before the commencement of the running, one of the heaviest and most intense showers came on. The rain was as penetrating as a flight of arrows, and descended as thickly and rapidly. In three seconds it cleared the course more effectually than the new police, active though they have been in discharging this and other duties here during the last two days. Neither their vigilance, however, nor the inclemency of the weather, were sufficient to put a stop to the out-of-door, any more than the inn-door, gambling: the professors of the art of concealing the pea from the investigations of too curious inquirers plied their thimbles as busily as tailors.'

The sport, *The Times* man reported, was 'fair'. Business clearly was not. Even the lobster salad failed to show a good profit, and a Mr Topham reported to the committee that, having lost money by the supply of refreshments at the stand, he was therefore 'unable to make any payment to Mrs Wright, and was willing to submit his accounts to her solicitor'.

Trendall's star was still on the wane, and heading for extinction. Immediately after the meeting, he was asked 'to go into the accounts for the building of the stand'. A few weeks later he wrote 'requesting that the appointment of a surveyor of the building might be conferred on him'. The committee did not think any such appointment necessary. Trendall himself, like Chadwick the builder, was by now a member of the committee as well as being a considerable shareholder (in this year alone he took 200 shares in lieu of payment for his professional services), and by 1833 his signature was appearing on the Association's cheques. But at the annual meeting that year he was one of three committee members due to retire and was not re-elected.

Shortly afterwards, notes begin about Mr Vaile, who had obviously been called in to do a very considerable amount of work on the grandstand. The nature of the work remains a mystery, but he sent in a bill for £129. A sub-committee was appointed to investigate the charge, which they arbitarily reduced to £91 7s 10d, 'which sum they recommend should be tendered to him'. Mr Vaile, not surprisingly, refused to accept it: '. . . and the trustees having been threatened by Mr Vaile's solicitors with legal proceedings, the committee in order to keep the Association from litigation have agreed to pay, and Mr Vaile has agreed to accept, £105 in full discharge of his account.

'Resolved that the secretary do write to Mr Trendall and inform him that they expect him to pay such part of Mr Vaile's bill as has been incurred in consequence of his professional neglect, and beg the name of his solicitor in order that action may be served upon him.' Presumably Trendall paid up. There is no record of the action being pursued, nor is Mr Trendall's name ever mentioned again.

Financial problems were a long way from being settled – in fact they were to grow steadily worse – and though there was no doubt that every year more and more people were attending the Derby, not enough of them were using the grandstand, which was still the only major source of income for the Association. The October race meeting was not a roaring success, and the stand was of course only a liability for the other 359 days of the year. It still required a major effort to get to Epsom, and particularly to get up to the Downs (a road from the town was made in 1834). Surfaces remained atrocious for many years, and at times of heavy rain were likely to disappear altogether; the nearest railway was as yet 17 years away. The inns of the neighbourhood were only capable of accommodating a few dozen visitors, and unless the racegoer was fortunate enough to have friends in the area, he was faced with the prospect, at the end of each day, of either sleeping in his carriage, or under a hedge, or suffering the journey back home again – an event that was likely to include at least one attempted robbery with assault.

All such hazards and disturbances could probably have been overcome a century later by deft or deafening public relations. In 1831 almost the only effective method of passing on information was by word of mouth. There were 50 posters on the road from London, but newspaper advertising was so discreet as to be practically invisible.

Before Derby week this humble nudge appeared in the *Morning Post*, the *Morning Herald*, *John Bull* and the *Racing Calendar*:

EPSOM RACES

The public are respectfully informed that the Grand Stand

will be opened on the four race days, that good refreshments will be provided as last year, and every attention paid to their accommodation.

Tickets of admission to the front rooms on the Terrace floor may be obtained by application to Mr Weston.

After the meeting, *The Times* and *Morning Herald* were chosen for a new attempt to make the stand pay:

To tavern keepers, etc. The spacious building on Epsom Downs known as the Grand Stand may be hired for the purpose of an hotel, or for public entertainments etc., and the person hiring would be entitled to the receipts arising from the admission of company at the October races. He might also have the privilege of serving refreshments at the opening Meeting next year. The celebrity of the surroundings and the great internal accommodation of the house render it a very desirable situation for entertainments during the summer.

There do not seem to have been any takers. In October, prices of admission to the stand were reduced: to the Roof only, 6d; to the Saloon, Balcony and Retiring Room, 1s; to the Privilege Rooms and additional parts, 2s. The mid-summer annual accounts of 1830 showed a balance of £305. In 1831, there was a profit on the year of £553. Two years later, there was a running deficit of £12 10s 6d, and in 1834, despite race receipts of £900, the balance was down to £47 14s 7d. By 1837, the committee were glad enough to find a Mr Careless prepared to rent the stand, exclusive of the housekeeper's accommodation, for a year. But, after the October race meeting in 1832, the committee chairman 'having reported the misconduct of the housekeeper, the secretary was ordered to write and admonish him and to tell him that his salary will be £5 a year only from 1st November'.

At that price, it was hardly surprising that he misbehaved again and was fired. (The details were not disclosed.) A new housekeeper was appointed at £10 a year: 'the best terms your committee could obtain'.

Meanwhile, the roof began to leak, and the committee empowered Mr Chadwick to keep it watertight as long as he didn't spend more than 30s. The insurance on the stand was reduced to £5,000, and when the Association was pressed for payment of the poor rate in April 1835, the chairman 'undertook to call upon them to let the rate stand until after the Derby'. Times were indeed hard – though not so hard that the five members of the committee could not continue to receive their dues. They were ordered, as usual, to attend at the races and be paid one guinea for each day of attendance and their expenses, not exceeding 10s 6d a day. Each man was thus getting in Derby week nearly as much as the wretched housekeeper had been paid for the year.

Another loan of £550 was raised that year and it must have come as some relief when, the following summer, the efficient Mr Weatherby informed the committee that his other engagements were interfering too much with the business of the Association, and he would be forced to resign the office of secretary. The chairman, a merchant banker, persuaded one of his clerks to undertake the necessary duties for £10 a year. The business of the Association continued to be conducted in this stringent fashion for some time, with the committee handing out a Christmas bonus of 5 guineas to their chairman's clerks for favours received.

Two items contrived to lighten the gloom over the Downs as the Association's first decade of business faded: Amato and Queen Victoria. The first was a horse owned and bred by Sir Gilbert Heathcote at Durdans. It was entered for the 1838 Derby, and having neither won nor run a race in its life, started at 30–1. It proceeded to win by a length, returned to Durdans' gentle pastures and never ran again. Sir Gilbert buried the horse in his grounds, and built a considerable monument over the grave. (The nearest pub to the spot was later named The Amato. It nurtured one of Epsom's charming legends: that at dawn on every Derby day, the name of the winner would be found chalked on the well outside.)

This was the year that the railway brought racegoers closer than ever to Epsom, though it was far from close enough to have satisfied today's customers. The nearest station, Stoat's Nest, lay on the London to Brighton line about midway between what are now the stations of Purley and Coulsdon North. It was 7 miles from the racecourse, but a walk of that distance at both ends of the day was not regarded as an insuperable problem by our ancestors, and Stoat's Nest was well patronized during meetings.

Nevertheless, it must have been with some joy that racegoers received the news that a rival line, the London and South-Western, was to run special excursion trains on their Southampton line on Derby day, 1838. There was no station near Epsom at which they could dismount, but the company chairman, a notable racing man called Sir John Easthope, announced that eight trains would stop at the point where his railway line crossed the road from Kingston to Ewell (a point now marked by Surbiton Station). It left the travellers with a mere 5 miles to walk to the Downs. Sir John had no idea of the extent of the enthusiasm which his announcement would arouse.

The trains were to leave from the company's terminus at Nine Elms, between Battersea and Waterloo. Early in the morning a crowd of about 5,000 stormed the station, taking possession of all the carriages they could find and causing 'much damage and disorder'. The police were called to disperse them, and the railway company transported as many as they could – a small proportion of the total – to the alighting point. Despite the confusion, Sir John was so well pleased with his scheme that he repeated it further down the line for the Ascot meeting.

The first rail link to Epsom (from Croydon via Sutton) came just in time for the 1847 Derby, but, before that, Queen Victoria had made her celebrated visit to the course, her first since she had gone there as a small girl. Nothing so exciting had yet happened to the Association, whose committee had been greatly disappointed by the lack of royal interest in racing since the building of the grandstand. What was usually the paddock became the royal promenade, and the committee asked the owner of The Warren (a hunting lodge built for Charles II on the far side of the course) if they might use his paddock. Until then he had agreed, for J. C. Whyte had noted only a year earlier that, at a price of one shilling, the saddling and parading in the grounds of The Warren had attracted vast crowds, 'including nearly half the male portion of the peerage'. But the wind of religious scruple was blowing over the owner: his objection to betting, and therefore to racing, forbade it, and saddling was carried out at Langley Bottom, to which Prince Albert rode before the race.

Preparations for Her Majesty involved, regrettably, the expenditure of some £200 on the stand. But as the committee pointed out to shareholders, the regal fixtures and fittings were retained, and 'a few pounds outlay will in future be sufficient to prepare for Her reception, and from the admiration Her Majesty expressed the committee are of the opinion that Her visits will be annual.' Alas, admiration or not, she never returned. But the effect of the visit was to raise attendance at the stand by 25 per cent, and to allow the committee at the next annual meeting to distribute a four per cent dividend to shareholders.

Only one incident of that royal visit seems remarkable enough to record. The Derby was won by Little Wonder – at 14 hands $3\frac{1}{2}$ inches, hardly out of the pony class. When the Queen presented its very young and small jockey, McDonald, with a goldmounted whip and asked him how much he weighed, he obeyed stable instructions and declined to divulge such a secret. Prince Albert is reported to have been highly amused; Her Majesty, perhaps, was not.

The story has been told and retold a thousand times in books and bars, which does not necessarily lessen its accuracy. But it is a fact, conveniently overlooked, that at Ascot six years earlier the Queen had asked the same question of Bell, 'a mere child of four stone', whose mount had just won the Ascot Stakes. To Bell the Queen gave £10, but from him she is said to have received the same answer: 'Please, ma'am, my master says I'm never to tell.'

By the time of the Queen's visit, but not because of it, the committee had obtained the approval of the shareholders for the removal of a close-boarded fence from the front of the stand, and to enclose the open ground which lay before it with a 'handsome and substantial open iron railing'. Though this was going to cost £300, the committee persuaded a general meeting that 'such inclosure would be a very desirable object, and likely to promote the interest of the Association'. That done, it was able to assure the next annual meeting that receipts at the stand were increasing, and to anticipate 'a very considerable increase in their receipts in future from being enabled to make a different arrangement with regard to the booths erected at the races'. The committee had now convinced itself that: 'if certain alterations could be effected the Concern will be one of the most profitable speculations of the present day'. (Later, not happy with the choice of words, they changed 'speculations' to 'undertakings'.)

The truth is that in spite of the fact that a slowly increasing number of racegoers used the comforts of the grandstand, it still did not pay its way. The fault probably lay in the common problem of poorly-organized race meetings. Until order and clarity could be produced on the course, the full potential of the stand was not likely to be realized: until those who paid for admission were sure they were going to see the horses saddled, paraded, and started on time, they might as well take a chance elsewhere – in the adjacent Barnard's Stands, for instance, which, though temporary erections of wood and canvas, for whose seats there was great competition. Unfortunately for the shareholders of the Epsom Grand Stand Association, the organization of the races had nothing to do with their committee. The meetings were arranged by the stewards through the Clerk of the Course, whose appointment was in the hands of the Lord of the Manor. Those whose chief concern was for the wellbeing of the patrons of the stand were likely to be frustrated until both affairs could be directed by the same hand.

In 1841, the committee decided that the only way they could guarantee an income for the shareholders was by letting the stand. They offered it to Charles Langlands, a member of the EGSA and well-known local businessman who also, like John Barnard, had temporary stands on the course for meetings. He turned down their suggestion that he should take it at £1,000 a year, but the following July he and Barnard together offered to lease it at £900.

The committee still stuck out for their £1,000, and, in December 1843, had a letter from the Lord of the Manor to say that he had received an offer to rent the stand at that figure: 'I submit to you the propriety of immediately concerning a General Meeting of the proprietors on the subject.' No record remains of who made that offer, or why it was not accepted, but the 1844 meetings came and went and still the Association had not found a tenant.

There was a sensational Derby that year, the story of which has been told before and will be told again as long as horses run. The winner, Running Rein, was disqualified – but not until a splendid piece of detective work by Lord George Bentinck had unmasked the villain. The owner of the second horse, Orlando, called for an inquiry, alleging that Running Rein was more than three years old. The stewards withheld the stakes and agreed to the inquiry, the second in consecutive years of which Running Rein had been the subject.

The previous year, at Newmarket, the horse had beaten other two-year-olds with suspicious ease, but its owner had been cleared by a stable lad who swore that the horse was indeed Running Rein, at whose birth he had been present only two years previously. This time, Bentinck, who came between Sir Charles Bunbury and Admiral Henry Rous as the turf's autocrat of the day, was convinced there had been a deception and was determined to prove it.

Suspecting that the horse's legs had been dyed to cover its real identity, Bentinck called on all the chemists between the home of the owner, a Mr Goodman, and his club, which he visited every day. Bentinck hoped that one of them would tell him of a recent sale of a large quantity of dye: not one could recall such a sale. But at a Regent Street hairdresser's he found what he wanted: a man whose description fitted Goodman had bought a large bottle of hair dye. The female assistant who made the sale went with Lord George to Goodman's club and identified him. Goodman confessed that 'Running Rein' was in fact a four-year-old, Maccabeus.

Goodman was barred from the turf, Orlando declared the winner, a lot of punters were pleased to collect. None was more pleased than one young officer, who had backed Orlando so heavily to win that the loss ruined him. He was about to blow out his brains when word reached him that Running Rein was to be disqualified: he saved the bullet and won £30,000.

Less vitally, but to equal astonishment, it was discovered that Maccabeus was not the only four-year-old in the 1844 Derby. Leander broke a fetlock at Tattenham Corner and was destroyed, but its trainer was so livid at insinuations of deceit that he had the corpse exhumed, cut off the lower jaw, boiled it clean and sent it to a veterinary surgeon to prove it was only three years old. Alas, the vet did not agree. Aghast, the trainer dug up the body again and sent the upper jaw to another expert, with the same result.

Both stories are fully recounted by one of the family in *Epsom and the Dorlings*, the compelling tale of a horse-racing dynasty, which was about to lay its hands on the course; in November 1844 the EGSA committee offered the grandstand once more to Barnard and Langlands, at £1,000 a year. Again they refused, and in May, 1845 the Epsom stewards recommended Mr Briscoe, the Lord of the Manor, to reappoint as Clerk of the Course Henry Dorling, who had held the job since 1839. Within five weeks he was also the lessee of the grandstand. The Downs had their first dictator.

CHAPTER SEVEN

We Dorlings

'We Dorlings are, and always have been, an extremely ordinary family. It is only circumstance, allied to the pioneering spirit of William Dorling and the far-sightedness of his son Henry, that has made us of some consequence to the Epsom race course.' So wrote Edward Dorling, William's great-grandson, a century after Henry took over the grandstand.

William the pioneer had been a printer and stationer in Bexhill, and brought his family and the tools of his trade to Epsom at the beginning of the 19th century. He sold writing paper, 'portable pens', hymn books, lavender water, shaving cakes, and pianofortes, and established the first printing press ever seen in Epsom. When the Epsom Grand Stand Association was formed, William attended the inaugural meeting with his son Henry, and his eldest grandson, Henry Mayson Dorling. They all took shares.

By then, father William was already closely connected with Epsom racing circles. Owners, trainers, jockeys, and touts supplied him, on the morning of every race meeting, with information on runners and riders. Dorling gathered it, checked it, sifted it, and rode back into town to print it. He had been doing this since May 1827, when he produced 'Dorling's Genuine Card List from Mr Farrall's only Copy'. (Farrall was the Clerk of the Course.) Henry's eye must have been on the business of racing from the start. The family biographer leaves no clue as to how Henry landed the job of Clerk of the Course in 1839 – not at that time an exacting one, but one that certainly required some expert knowledge as well as firm authority and organizing ability.

There is no doubt that when he was appointed Henry knew exactly what his next move would be, and one presumes he had done a good deal of diplomatic lobbying around the manorial court and among the racecourse stewards. He was a man of naturally persuasive manner, and personal charm. To be quite fair he was a gentle dictator – unlike his son, who succeeded him, and became the terror of the Downs.

Shortly after his appointment as Clerk of the Course, Henry Dorling proposed to the EGSA committee that if they would give £100 of Plate to the Race Fund, he would arrange that all races except the Derby and the Oaks would be saddled in front of the stand, as they were at Ascot and Goodwood. In this, he said, he had the support of the Jockey Club and the Epsom stewards. It was only the beginning; by the time the committee met again a fortnight later, they had before them a letter from the Clerk: 'I find on consulting with several influential parties that it will be useless to proceed further with my plan for the improvement of the stand unless some more liberal donation be made to the Race Fund than was at first contemplated . . .'

The 'influential parties' were undoubtedly the Stewards of the Jockey Club, and particularly Lord George Bentinck. To them, and later to the Epsom stewards, he made immensely precise proposals for the improvement of racing, the course, and the stand. Bentinck acknowledged them thus: 'I have submitted your proposal to Lords Exeter and Stradbroke, and also to Colonel Aston, and have found them all warm in approbation of it – provided always that you guarantee the £500 additional and all the improvements detailed in your letter to the Stewards. To enable yourself to do this the first step appears to be that you should obtain a lease of the Grand Stand for a term of years with power to renew; and no time should be lost in doing this.'

Henry Dorling was already ahead of them. That letter to the committee contained an almost contemptuously brief summary of the proposals he had made to the Jockey Club – insofar as they concerned the Association – which boiled down to his asking them to alter the stand and the lawn before it, and to award the Race Fund £300, in return for which *all* races would be saddled in front of the stand – and continued: 'In consideration of the trouble and expense I have been and may be put to for the purpose of advancing your interests, you shall agree to pay me during my life an annuity of 5% upon the increased revenue of the stand. And in case you do not feel disposed to agree to the foregoing proposition, I beg to inform you that I am willing to take the Stand on lease for 21 years at a rental of £1,000.'

The committee did not hesitate. A week later, on 30th June, 1845, Henry Dorling commenced his tenancy of the grandstand. That very day, as Clerk of the Course, he presented his detailed proposals to the stewards of Epsom races. The letter in which they lie is an historic document, and an astonishing one; in it, with one magnificent sweep, the new broom seems to have cleared away most of the confusion and decay into which racing

67

at Epsom had fallen, and to assemble a pattern for racing so admirable that, once adopted, it has persisted largely to the present day. Gradually and inexplicably, as his great-grandson was later to write, Epsom racecourse had begun to be looked upon as a place of the past. Its hard-won prestige had faded. Henry Dorling did not immediately turn the meetings into gold-plated successes – that took time – but he immediately reversed the trend and began to build an exemplary reputation on the Downs. This, at last, was the sort of horse-racing that people wanted to see.

My Lords and Gentlemen, [he wrote]. It is the opinion of many of the most respectable Inhabitants of Epsom, and its neighbourhood, that if the Stewards approved, measures might be taken, that would materially improve Epsom Races, very much benefit the Town, and add greatly to the comfort and convenience of those Noblemen and Gentlemen, who patronize the Turf.

I have consulted with Mr Lindsay, the Steward of the Manor of Epsom, who fully concurs with me in this application; and who states that Mr Briscoe will gladly avail himself of any opportunity to improve the Races, on any plan that may be recommended to him by the Stewards.

The following proposals are therefore most respectfully submitted:

That as a sure means of preventing the tumult and confusion, and the frequent accidents which have lately occurred at the Start for the Derby, and the Oaks, that the Stewards will be pleased to direct in future, that all Horses running at Epsom shall be saddled on the Course, in front of the Grand Stand, in the following manner.

The Course to be thoroughly and effectually cleared, at least a quarter of an hour before the Bell rings for Saddling. The Horses in the Race to be brought on the Course from the Pull-up, or from any other convenient or quiet place, which may be enclosed and kept clear by the Police. No Horseman to be admitted on the Course under any pretence; nor any other Person except Members of the Jockey Club; owners of Horses running at Epsom; Trainers and Jockies engaged in the Race; and, as it has been suggested, Persons holding half-a-guinea Tickets, the product of which might be added to a Race. As the Horses were saddled, and mounted, they might draw off quietly up the Course, taking their preliminary canters on their way round to the Starting Place; on arriving at which, as but very few persons would be likely to be there assembled, and the course quite clear, there is a great probability of an equal and favourable start taking place.

This Plan, if acted on, would considerably increase the number of spectators in the Grand Stand, and other temporary Stands, as there is no doubt that many persons who are obliged now, to ride about Epsom Downs, on hired Hacks, would gladly avail themselves of the comfort and security afforded by the Grand Stand, which needs but little alteration and improvement, to render it the most commodious, as it is now, much the largest in the Kingdom.

The Lessee of the Grand Stand in consideration of the benefit that he expects to derive from the adoption of the proposed plan, offers, in case the Stewards shall order that the Horses be saddled as before stated: –

1. To give the sum of £300 annually, to any Race, or Races, at Epsom, as the Stewards may think proper to direct.

2. To enlarge the Lawn in front of the Stand, making an acre in all, to make the enclosure continuous to the Rail of the Course, and to slope it gradually as at Goodwood and Ascot.

3. To place the conditions of admission under the control of the Stewards, so that all defaulters, or other disreputable persons, might be forthwith expelled on their being recognized; and he also engages to make such other similar regulations from time to time, as the Stewards may require.

4. To devote a spacious and convenient *private* Room for the reception of the Stewards, and of the Members of the Jockey Club, as well as an office for their secretary, adjoining.

5. To appropriate several suitable Rooms in the Basement of the Building as a Weighing Room, a retiring or dressing Room for Jockies, an office for the Clerk of the Course, and the Judge, etc. etc., all continuous, and well adapted for the purpose, as well as close under the eye of the Stewards; also to give up a space at the back of the Stand for the reception of the Hacks belonging to Trainers and Jockies without any charge.

It is also most respectfully suggested, that the Judge's chair should be removed from its present position to the upper side of the course, as at Ascot, so as to bring the whole of the business of the meeting on one side of the course, and so to obviate the necessity of crossing and re-crossing, which has been found to be production of much inconvenience. Trainers, Jockies and others, when wanted, could be found by their masters, which is not the case at present on Epsom Downs.

As the Temporary Stands, and Booths, would benefit by the proposed arrangement, in the same ratio as the Grand Stand, it is proposed that they should contribute an increased sum to the Races by having the Ground they stand upon, let to them by *Public* competition as at Ascot, and Goodwood. At present, the space on which the temporary stands and Booths are erected, together with the whole of the Standing for Carriages on Epsom Downs, is let by *Private Contract* to an individual for the sum of £600 a year, of which Mr Briscoe retains £150, leaving £450 for Racing purposes. There is no doubt that the ground would fetch considerably more, if it were put up to fair and open competition: indeed, there are parties in Epsom ready to give £800 for it immediately, and I am authorized to state that Mr Briscoe is willing to raise an increased sum in the manner beforementioned provided that the Stewards recommend him to do so.

The forgoing propositions, if acted upon, would produce Public Money for the Epsom Meeting of 1846, and future years, amounting to the sum of One thousand pounds: – namely –

From the Lord of the Manor	–	650
”　　the Lessee of the Grand Stand	–	300
”　　the County Members	–	50
		£1000.

being exactly double the sum given in the year 1845. The £200 from the Derby and Oaks, just about covers the expense of the Police, etc.

The State of the Course and Exercise ground is at present extremely bad, owing to the practice that prevails of ripping up the surface in search of Flints, and carrying away great quantities of Turf and Mould for Sale. The Right, or Deputation of the Lord of the Manor to do so, is at present vested in an individual, who pays about ten pounds a year for the privilege, and whom it is supposed makes a considerable profit, to the great detriment of the Course and training ground. I am empowered to state, that Mr Briscoe (on his receiving a communication from the Stewards to that effect) is willing to place his authority into the hands of the Clerk of the Course, or of any other person, they may think proper to nominate.

In case your Lordships should honour me with your approval of any of the foregoing propositions, I shall be proud to attend at any time or place for the purpose of personal explanation, and I have taken the liberty of bringing the matter forward thus early, to give time for advertising the Additional stakes, as well as to make the necessary alterations in the Stand.

> I have the Honour to be
> My Lords and Gentlemen
> Your Obedient Humble Servant,
> Henry Dorling
> Clerk of the Course.

Though the grandstand was now Dorling's castle, he was only the sub-tenant, and the responsibility still lay with the EGSA (whose chairman by now was William Chadwick, the builder). In May 1846, the committee visited the stand and 'found the alterations etc. being performed satisfactorily by Mr Dorling and approved of everything that was being done by him'. In July, after the Derby meeting, the committee reported to the share-holders that 'the tenant is reaping a rich harvest for the money he has expended'; but the rent was secure and the property consequently improved in value.

A press cutting shows that while Dorling's moves were having some effect, there was still a good deal of room for improvement. The reporter of *The Pictorial Times* first turned his attention to the course: 'The racing commenced, or should have commenced, at two o'clock, but from a want of punctuality not at all credit-able to a management which in other respects gave so much scope for commendation, was not brought to a close until nearly half-past six. Much dissatisfaction was expressed on this head.' All the grandstand seemed to suffer from was over-popularity: 'The Stand was the centre of attraction to all who proposed to them-selves a cool and comfortable enjoyment of the racing. The character of its visitors was perhaps less aristocratic than of old; But a more fashionable display we have never met in this spacious and, as now ordered, most convenient edifice . . . The crush was so great as to lead to a slight suspicion that many found their way in whose features would not be recognized at Tattersalls, whereat the bona fide subscribers grumbled exceed-ingly.'

Though Dorling must have been covering his rent very hand-somely, the Association's accounts showed that their expenses were still a good deal higher than their income: by £91 in 1846, and by twice that sum the following year. At this time Mr Briscoe was contributing about £500 a year to the race fund; Captain Charles Carew, Lord of the Manor of Walton, £21; and Lord George Bentinck, £200. Among their regular incidental expenses, the Association listed payments at the minor meeting of £10 to the judge, £5 to the starter, £34 17s 6d to the police, 18s 0d to three telegraph men, and 15s 6d 'to hire of course keeper's hack'. The judge did no better at the Derby meeting, but the starter's fee went up to £20 and police expenses rose to £125 8s 6d. Their efforts also resulted in the Association having to pay £10 for a room in which the magistrates could deal with offenders, and £4 12s 6d for the presence of the magistrates' clerk. Two labourers working four days in the Paddock cost £1 between them. With little to offer in the way of dividends to shareholders, the committee were at least able to report consider- able reductions in management expenses: their five members now met only twice a year, at a total cost to the Association of £25, including the secretary's remuneration – and in 1847 this was reduced by the appointment of a new secretary for only £5 a year.

With such gruesome financial pressures on them, the com- mittee were no doubt sometimes inclined to apportion Mr Briscoe's donation to plug deficits rather than to increase the stake money for the races, for which purpose it was intended. In September 1846 a somewhat acrimonious correspondence began between the Lord of the Manor's steward and the Association, following the circulation of the annual accounts: 'You were paid £498 15s. I am at a loss to discover anything like this sum appropriated to stakes. If it has been otherwise applied I think the particulars should be shown, which are doubtless comprised in the account between the Clerk of the Course and the Stewards.'

The following reply came from the Association: 'If it is the pleasure of the Stewards of Epsom Races that you should be furnished with a copy of our account with them, we shall be happy to send it, and we have no doubt that Mr Dorling will be ready to do the same.'

The following May, the steward of the Manor wrote: 'We believe it is unnecessary to remind you that the amount is pre- sented by Mr and Mrs Briscoe, and that that gentleman expects that a sum not exceeding £100 shall be appropriated to any other than racing purposes, or in other words that the amount to be expended on the Downs or otherwise (except as stakes) shall not exceed that sum.

'I am also to state that it is not now the wish of Mr and Mrs

Briscoe that the addition to the stakes should be advertised as presented by them . . . It is not wished that their *names* should appear . . .

'We abstain from reiterating the surprise of Mr Briscoe on finding that a sum of only £220 out of the £498 15s. contributed by him was applied to racing purposes last year, his direction to apply £100 this year to other purposes will prevent a recurrence of the irregularity.'

This was followed, three days later, just in case any doubt should remain, by: 'We have paid into the Bank of England to your credit £502 1s 6d, relying that £402 1s 6d. is applied to racing purposes such as additions to the stakes etc.'

At the same time, the Lord of the Manor was more than a little put out by the way in which Dorling was not only carrying out those major alterations and improvements that he had detailed, but also a few minor matters that seemed to him, as Clerk and grandstand lessee, necessary if he was going to get racing at Epsom into shape. For at least five years, flights of protest, some of them barbed, winged their way from the manor house to the offices of the Association in May 1847:

> We understand that Sir Gilbert Heathcote, who is accommodated by the express direction of the Lord of the Manor in the old Judges' Stand, was by no means pleased last year at the Clerk of the Course having thrown ropes across the course confining the horses before starting to the short space in front of the Grand Stand. There can be no doubt of the motive of this, but it is rather beyond the mark to prevent one of the Stewards having the opportunity of seeing the horses before his own box. It is therefore expected that the rope will be placed next to the old Judges' Stand and not as before.

> We have no hesitation in saying that the Law Charges this year are considerably augmented by Dorling's unwarrantable incroachments and unaccountable conduct in relation to the Downs and the old Judges' Stand etc.

> We are glad to hear that Mr Dorling is satisfied with the explanation regarding the supposed charge of commission and we hope in future he will ascertain the facts before he ventures on such unfounded statements. We expect he will retract them as publicly as he made them, at the Eagle and elsewhere.

Throughout this prolonged and somewhat unfriendly correspondence, the committee seem to have stood by its tenant, and continued to report to the shareholders its approval of Dorling's activities: 'There is reason to believe the tenant is deriving a large beneficial interest in the undertaking, and it will no doubt prove ultimately a most profitable investment to the share-holders.' In January 1850 the chairman reported to the committee that in view of 'the encroachments made by the tenant', the Lord of the Manor would not be satisfied unless a fresh lease for the stand was negotiated, at an increased rent. The committee closely examined Dorling's activities, and informed Briscoe that it saw no reasonable grounds for applying for a new lease, since the new fence that the lessee had put up (on the east side of the stand) only enclosed the acre of ground to which the Association was entitled.

The Lord of the Manor was shortly to list his complaints against Dorling in a long letter to the Jockey Club Stewards, but while we wait for that, there are other matters with which we must catch up. Prime among them is the alteration to the Derby course, which Dorling did not mention in his original proposals, but which he organized in time for his second classic meeting in 1847. Since 1784, when the Derby had been extended to $1\frac{1}{2}$ miles, the start had been high on The Hill, behind Sir Gilbert Heathcote's cottage, Downs House, (known as Sherwood's) and thus out of sight of the grandstand patrons. This in no way suited Dorling's plans to bring the best of all possible worlds to his stand. He moved the start much nearer, low on The Hill in full view of the stands: the field was then faced with a severe uphill pull of three or four furlongs, before joining the old course on the far side of Tattenham Corner. This occasioned, to put it mildly, a certain amount of criticism.

As the *Illustrated London News* had it: 'It is a singular anomaly that the greatest race in the world should be run over perhaps the worst and most dangerous course we have. The elder trainers and jockeys may well sigh for the days of the old Derby course, with its nice gentle rise of three-quarters of a mile, which nearly settled the thing before Tattenham Corner. All that is changed now. However, the Grand Stand folk like to see the race from end to end, and they must have their way.'

Dorling clearly rated this innovation as one of his greatest, and the opposition wounded him. He pointed out that the 905 yards of the new course rose in fact one foot less than the first 905 yards of the old course, so what could all the fuss be about? He chose to ignore the more pertinent fact that over the first 500 yards the new course rose 84 feet – a gradient of 1 in 18, compared to 1 in 23 in the old course. It was this that caused the slow pace at the start so that the goats and the sheep tended to reach Tattenham Corner almost together and in considerable chaos. As one jockey put it: 'We are like a great floating body. It's a mercy the coroner isn't called in once a year at Epsom; no horse can be said to be fairly on his legs when we come crashing round that turn. How we get round it, I don't know.'

One correspondent, at least, found something to write about at that spring meeting other than Dorling's new Derby course. On 22nd May, 1847, *The Pictorial Times* (the paper that the previous year had criticized Dorling for unpunctuality) presented this chill picture of the day's events: 'By Epsom Races, the millions understand the Derby day; the general public make the meeting consist of but two – the anniversaries of the Derby and the Oaks. Thus, Tuesday last did not draw a dozen equipages to the Surrey Downs.

'The wind is at East – the rain falls coldly – and at six p.m. once more the hill is deserted – all sorts of rumours rife among the gossips who wend their ways home. Foremost among these was the fact that a felonious attempt to "nobble" one of the leading favourites, in a great training, had been discovered; that the perpetrators were in actual custody; that the promoters, or instigators, were well known; and that the matter would be presently in a criminal court. It is a consummation devoutly to be wished! They hung a poor wretch, called Dawson, for poisoning some racehorses at Newmarket.'

It was in 1847, too, on 18th May, that Lord George Bentinck moved in the House of Commons 'that this House at its rising do adjourn till Thursday' (by which day the Derby would be over). The acceptance of the motion was the first public nod by the establishment that Derby day was a holiday – acknowledged though not enforced, in which all business in the London area seemed as surely suspended as it now is on Christmas Eve. By 1860 there was considerable parliamentary opposition to the practice, and the Prime Minister, Lord Palmerston, firmly stated: 'To adjourn for that day is part of the unwritten law of Parliament.' By the last decade of the century the adjournment motion was no longer carried – a fact much regretted in 1894, when the Members were not present at Epsom in any great strength to see Lord Rosebery, then Prime Minister, lead in Ladas, his Derby winner. (Much power to the elbow of Lord Mersey, who in 1971 proposed an adjournment of the Upper House for similarly hedonistic reasons.)

It was ironic that Bentinck should have proposed that motion in 1847. By then he had given up his racing interests for politics, and sold his stud for £10,000. One of the horses, Surplice, passed to Lord Clifden: in 1848, to Bentinck's mortification, he saw it win the Derby. Disraeli, in his *Life of Lord George Bentinck*, recalled how the day following the race he came across Lord George in the library of the House. He gave 'a sort of superb groan'.

' "All my life I have been trying for this, and for what have I sacrificed it?" he murmured. It was in vain to offer solace.

"You do not know what the Derby is," he moaned out.

"Yes, I do. It is the blue ribbon of the Turf."

"It is the blue ribbon of the Turf," he slowly repeated to himself; and sitting down at the table, he buried himself in a folio of statistics.' Within eighteen months, Lord George was dead; his heart failed seven days after Surplice won the Leger.

A less controversial innovation than Dorling's new Derby course had been his founding, in 1846, of the Great Metropolitan Handicap, still the big attraction of the early-season meeting. It is still run over a magnificently eccentric, probably unique, course, starting at the winning post and moving down the finishing straight the wrong way. Just short of Tattenham Corner, the course veers right on a vast reverse-S bend, joining the main course near the mile post, and in good time to enjoy the full Tattenham Corner bend before returning up the finishing straight and home.

It was not only the course that made the Great Met remarkable, but the manner of its inception. Trying to raise prize money for the new race, Dorling called on a friend and former neighbour of his in the City of London, Samuel Beeton, a publican with a deep interest in the sport. Beeton opened a subscription list for it in his own pub, and persuaded many other publicans to do the same (those that served as betting shops as well were happy to oblige). They raised £300 the first year and £500 the second, and the race became nationally known as the Publicans' Derby. Five years after the Great Met began, subscription lists were opened in pubs all over the London area for the City and Suburban Handicap, another great April success. The publicans unfortunately closed the subscription lists when the Gaming Act of 1854 made it illegal for them to handle bets, but the races went on.

Before we lose sight of Mr Beeton, a word, a long word, about a more intimate link that he had with Epsom racecourse. He had inherited the pub, the Dolphin Tavern in Milk Street, from his father in 1836; by which time his eldest son (also Samuel) was five years old. In that same year a first child was born to a family just down the road from the pub, the Maysons. The young wife's mother, a widow known as Granny Jerram, kept a boarding house in Milk Street at which one of the guests in earlier years was Henry Dorling.

That link would be enough to establish Dorling's acquaintance with Beeton, but the tie was to be much stronger. Dorling had, by all accounts, fallen deeply in love with his landlady's daughter at the same time as did his close friend Benjamin Mayson. Elizabeth Jerram married Mayson, and Dorling married another almost immediately (calling his first son, you may have noticed, Henry Mayson Dorling).

When Mrs Mayson was expecting her fourth child, her husband died. When Mrs Dorling had had her fourth child, she died. In 1843 Henry and Elizabeth re-met and were married first over the anvil at Gretna Green, and then in church at Islington. The new family, with Granny Jerram and the eight children, settled at Epsom in the house close by the site of the new railway station and proceeded immediately to set about raising a new crop of children. Their fertility was phenomenal: the first was born in the first year of marriage, and after seven years they had added six to the original eight.

They went on producing for a further twelve years, by which time Elizabeth was 47 and her eldest daughter, Isabella, was 26. The total number of children then was 21 – four each and thirteen belonging to both. When Henry Dorling took over the grandstand in 1845 they already had Granny and ten offspring to house (and Mrs Dorling was, of course, pregnant with a son later to be christened William George Bentinck Dorling). Though Henry had a house in London, a home with the printing business at Epsom, and was shortly to build a large country house in Croydon (where the public library now stands), it occurred to his practical wife that it would be an awful waste of a large building and huge grounds if the family failed to occupy the stand.

This they did, triumphantly and noisily, living in committee rooms, saloons, kitchens, and grand balconies, with the Downs as their playground. In race weeks, they were banished to their other residences. Of course, by the time the last Dorling child was born (in 1862), the platoon was not at its maximum strength. Though all the babies were strong and healthy, a rarity in those days, two died as children, and others had married and left home long before their parents had finished providing them with infant brothers and sisters. One such was Isabella Mayson.

Her mother had always kept in touch with the old friends of Milk Street, who included the Beetons of Dolphin Tavern. In due course it was natural that Isabella and young Samuel should meet (she had gone to finishing school in Heidelberg with two of the Beeton daughters). He was known, after his mother's maiden name, as Samuel Orchart Beeton. At 21 he was apprenticed to a printer and book-binder, and soon this bright and beautiful lad was himself publishing reprints of *Uncle Tom's Cabin*.

The inevitable romance rivals that of Browning and Barrett, and was chronicled in absorbing detail by the late Nancy Spain (a great-grand-daughter of Henry Dorling) in *The Beeton Story*. Those who enjoy long and literary Victorian romances, spiced with tragedy, should read it. Here it has no place but to lead us to its climax: Beeton went into periodical publication, with *The Englishwomen's Domestic Magazine* and *The Boy's Own Journal*; Isabella married him at Epsom in July, 1856, and together – for this was, as you will by now suspect, *the* Mrs Beeton – they produced the incomparable *Book of Household Management*, its 556,000 words (six times the length of this book) compiled and edited by a girl who was only 23 when she began the job.

Isabella was, at same time, producing children, but with nothing like the success of her mother at Epsom. At 21 she had a boy, Samuel Orchart, who died at three months; at 23, another Samuel Orchart, who died before he was three. The year he died a third son, Orchart, was born, and two years later, Mayson Beeton: they both died in 1947. Isabella herself, in her 29th year, died eight days after Mayson's birth.

Have we strayed a long way from Epsom? Not really. Henry Dorling's wife had her last baby only three years before the death of Mrs Beeton, so through the tragedies of grandchildren dying, there was still the sound of children crying. Too often, perhaps, for the Clerk of the Course to get much peace in his office. On one occasion, relates his grandson Edward, the great papa shouted down the grandstand corridor: 'For heaven's sake, Elizabeth, what is all that noise about?' His wife is said to have replied: 'That, Henry, is your children and my children fighting our children.'

CHAPTER EIGHT

Numerous complaints

Domestic disturbances apart, Henry Dorling's position at Epsom
was awkward enough to have worried a lesser man. The tenant
of the Association, and obliged to fulfil the conditions of his lease
from them, he was under constant criticism from the Lord of the
Manor for his excesses both as Clerk and grandstand manager;
at the same time he was encouraged by the Jockey Club Stewards
who recognized in him a man with both the determination and
the power to run the best-organized meetings in the country. In
1846 his most important ally on high, Lord George Bentinck,
began to drop out of racing and concentrate on politics: 'I wrote
to Lord George nearly two months ago,' the steward of the Lord
of the Manor wrote to Dorling in March. 'His reply was that he
was so much engaged with his parliamentary duties that he would
not attend to racing matters. Some ten days ago Mr Briscoe
called on him, but he seemed indifferent about the matter at the
moment.'

Bentinck's power in the Jockey Club passed to Admiral the
Hon. Henry John Rous (who, 30 years later, died after
having a fit at the Epsom spring meeting), who wrote to
Dorling:

> You will observe a very great increase of members since the
> enlargement of the Stand, and I have terrible complaints of
> the crowded state, especially on a Derby or Oaks day – for as
> you know we are obliged to receive distinguished Foreigners,
> who attend in greater numbers every year, as well as Members
> of the Royal Family and their suites. It is therefore an absolute
> necessity that you should enlarge the Stand and extend it
> nearly to the Rails of the Course. I have to add about ten
> candidates – young noblemen who keep horses – to your
> present list and I have nothing to expect but reproaches from
> men I have no power to admit, and from members of the
> Stand who with good reason complain they can't see the races
> with any comfort. As you must well know that all the sup-
> porters of Epsom Races are members of the Stand, why not

enlarge it? Nothing pays so well or can be more remunerative to your own interests.

As Clerk of the Course, Dorling could not afford to offend the Jockey Club; as lessee of the grandstand, the more tickets he could sell the more money he made; but extending the stand 'nearly to the Rails of the Course' would have been in direct contravention of his lease from the EGSA, and theirs from Briscoe. Already the terracing of the lawn and its extension to the course had got him into trouble, as we shall soon see.

When trouble hit Henry Dorling, it usually came in the name of Ralph Lindsay, a two-headed lawyer who was the EGSA's solicitor and who, you may remember, became its chairman without first (according to Charles Bluck) owning any shares. After the investigations by a select committee into the affairs of the Association in 1830, Lindsay did not escape without censure, and subsequently left the chair and the committee, though continuing to act as the Association's solicitor. But Lindsay, a partner in a firm of solicitors in the City, was also the steward of the Manor of Epsom, and the signatory of all the letters quoted in the last chapter that were critical of Dorling's activities. In April 1850, Lindsay (as steward) wrote to C. and J. Weatherby, secretaries to the Jockey Club.

After discussing the legal and other charges which Mr Briscoe had to deduct from his Downs income before making his usual donation to the Race Fund, Lindsay wrote:

> Much may be done that would lessen those expenses if all parties (and in this we cannot exclude the Clerk of the Course) would take care to avoid doing anything in relation to the Downs which requires the intervention of the Lord of the Manor or ourselves.
>
> We refer to the subjoined unauthorized acts which have been committed since the appointment of the present Clerk of the Course, merely to show the necessity and propriety of our constant attention and not by way of complaint against any individual, although it is hoped that any alterations which may be deemed expedient and useful in the future, may receive the previous written sanction of the Lord of the Manor or ourselves: –
>
> > The stoppage of the 16 feet roadway in front of the Grand Stand between the site of the Stand and Race course and adding it to the lawn.
> >
> > The enclosure by post and rail at the east side of about a fourth of an acre of ground the waste of the Manor.

The demolition of the walls of Mrs Briscoe's freehold tenement near the one mile post formerly let to Farrall and the laying of the site into a new course, for the benefit of the lessee of the land.

The erection of a Building on the Grand Stand Ground projecting out of a straight line from the front of the Grand Stand thereby intercepting the view from Barnard's stands.

The lowering the ground on each side of the stand to some depth and carrying the soil to and raising the front lawn – contrary to an express Covenant in his lease, also intercepting the view, and which it is stated although not the proximate, was the *remanet*, cause of the accident, the Visitors to Barnard's platform rushing to a point not intercepted by the lawn to witness the race.

The formation of the Metropolitan course (for purposes which are too obvious) depriving the copyholders of the Herbage.

The removal of from 80 to 100 yards of the post and chains placed by Barnard near Tattenham's Corner for the standing of Carriages and replacing them in another position, thus preventing the view, to Barnard's injury some £30 a year usually received for standing of Carriages there.

We beg also to express our surprise at hearing from Mr Briscoe that Mr Dorling, without the least foundation, asserted that we had deducted on a former occasion £35 as a Commission or poundage on the rent paid for the Downs which although we might have been justified in making, we have, under the circumstances abstained from doing . . .

We may add that it has become a matter of great doubt whether the office of Clerk of the Course, is not incompatible with that of Lessee of the Grand Stand, especially as one result has been the recent alteration of the Derby Course which we hear is so much complained of.

Lindsay's connection with the EGSA was severed long before Henry Dorling's, but now it is time to return once more to William Chadwick, the builder, under whose chairmanship Lindsay had returned to the committee. Like Lindsay, and through him, Chadwick's early operations with the EGSA were not entirely above suspicion. He had amassed so many shares in lieu of payment for building the grandstand that it was only a matter of time before he worked himself onto the committee and into the chair. In that position, as far as the scanty evidence goes, he seems to have had the interests of the Association firmly enough in mind, and was clearly a determined supporter of Henry Dorling.

Appearances, however, were deceptive (they so often are in the minutes). At the general meeting in July 1850, attention was called to the absence of Mr Chadwick: 'it was suggested whether under existing circumstances that gentleman should not be called upon to retire from the committee'. (The circumstances themselves were not explained.) The meeting agreed to leave the matter in the hands of the committee, whose secretary was subsequently instructed to write to Chadwick 'suggesting the propriety of that gentleman's solicitor'. Two years later, Chadwick appeared again in the chair at the annual shareholders' meeting, to which he was unanimously re-elected, although he never attended another committee meeting. It was as though, having won the election, he determined never again to sit at a table with the men who had asked for his resignation.

Lindsay had kept up his attacks against Dorling. In November 1850 he demanded on behalf of Briscoe an extra £5 a year rent because Dorling had planted an ornamental shrub behind the stand. 'I begged Mr Briscoe to let it stay,' Dorling wrote to the committee, 'as being purely ornamental and of no real use.' The committee praised the very honourable manner in which Dorling had fulfilled his engagements to the Association. (Later they complained to Briscoe that 'a public house or beer shop has been erected close to the rear of the Grand Stand, greatly injurious to our tenant'.)

The committee began to use the services of another solicitor, though Lindsay was still a committee member. He protested, but to no avail, and, in April 1857, sold his shares in the EGSA, rendering himself once again ineligible to sit on the committee.

John Barnard, who had nearly become the grandstand tenant himself, continued to play a central part. His family had for many years put up temporary race stands – since 1829 it had been immediately to the west of the grandstand – and it was to him that Dorling referred in his original letter of proposals to the Epsom stewards. The space on which the temporary stands and booths were erected was let by private contract, together with the parking space for coaches and carriages, for the sum of £600 a year; on the open market Dorling thought it would raise much more, and he believed there were people in Epsom ready to pay £800 for it. By 1847 Barnard was paying £700 a year, but in 1850 he asked the Lord of the Manor to reduce the rent to £600 again. His profit in the previous year, he said, had been only £110. He considered this altogether inadequate for the risk, since two-thirds of the income was from the standing of carriages on Derby day only: 'It is manifest that in the event of unfavourable weather the profits would be considerably diminished.'

Following up another of Dorling's suggestions, Briscoe had appointed Barnard to superintend the Downs and the digging of flints, 'with a view to prevent their being got in improper places, whereby the turf may be injured'. Barnard volunteered to co-operate with the stewards to keep the Downs in good order – vital for him, since it affected the hard standing that he rented for carriage parking; and without that, Dorling pointed out weightily to Briscoe, Barnard would not be able to pay the very heavy rent required of him for the privilege of letting booths.

Ten years later Barnard further consolidated his position on the Downs by building on his patch next to the grandstand 'a brick erection', which, as the horrified EGSA complained to Briscoe, was forbidden by the terms of their lease from the Lord of the Manor, which allowed no other permanent building on the Downs. A year later Briscoe had still taken no action against Barnard, but he did refuse the Association's application for more ground for building to the west of the stand. He promised he would take an early opportunity to inspect Barnard's building and see if it was, as the Association claimed, in continuous breach of contract. It had probably been removed by 1865, when a Mr Grant Heatley Tod Heatly put up what Dorling called 'a most objectionable erection' on the south side of the course, next to the Stewards' stand. It was three storeys high and completely blocked the view of the Derby start from the Jockey Club section of the grandstand.

Heatly agreed to remove it if it could be accommodated elsewhere, and eventually the EGSA and Briscoe agreed to let him build a booth on top of the judges' stand. When it was finished, this prominent vantage point was occupied by Briscoe himself and Timothy Barnard, John's father.

After 1850, there was unquestionably a turn for the better in the affairs of the EGSA. Not only did the accounts show a small profit for the first time since it had let the grandstand, but there was a sense of fuller interest, greater prestige, and real permanence about the business. It was due more to Dorling's determined policy of improvement and organization rather than to any particular event, but no doubt the return of royalty in 1856 gave a considerable boost.

Victoria brought her Albert in 1840, but since then had shown little interest. Now Albert came to the Derby with Prince Frederick of Prussia, 27-year-old son of the German Emperor, who was about to marry the Queen's daughter, Victoria. (He later became Emperor, but reigned for only a few weeks before his death in 1888.) The visit was an event to which Dorling would no doubt like to have given a good deal of preparation, but he was informed of it only on the previous afternoon.

The *Illustrated London News* recorded that an apartment was prepared for royal visitors next to the private saloon, 'which was filled with the leading female members of the aristocracy'. The room itself was 'tastefully fitted up with crimson hangings and handsome lace curtains. On the table was a beautiful bust in parian (a porcelain resembling marble) of the late Lord George Bentinck, and over the looking-glass hung the Royal arms in needlework, executed by the Misses Dorling.' According to the reporter, there was no cheering when the princes appeared, 'but no lack of curiosity to obtain a glimpse of the future husband of the eldest daughter of our beloved Queen'.

The Association now began an incessant campaign to acquire more land, both for building and for racing. Since the grandstand had been built, the only addition to the original acre had been a patch of land near the mile post that Briscoe let to Dorling for £5 a year. The agreement between Briscoe and Dorling makes it clear that the plot, 40 yards by 56, 'was formerly with the Stable Shed and Buildings thereon (but which have been blown down) in the tenure of occupation of His Royal Highness the Duke of York deceased'. Dorling used the land to soften the bend at the entrance to Tattenham Corner.

'In consequence of numerous complaints arising from the more respectable organs of the Public Press, as likewise from other influential quarters, of the great want of space in the Grand Stand and the enclosure', the EGSA committee went to Briscoe with the idea that it should extend the stand to provide a weighing room, offices for the Stewards, Clerk of the Course, and Clerk of the Scales, 'and more accommodation for noblemen and gentlemen, members of the Jockey Club, and other influential persons'. He appeared to be favourably disposed towards the idea, and at his request, plans and drawings were prepared. But the EGSA was not the only body to appreciate the desirability of building on the Downs now that racing was making money.

The London and Epsom Downs Railway Company wanted to build a station only 220 yards from the grandstand, but were frustrated by spirited opposition both from the Association and in Parliament. Briscoe agreed to sell another company, the Banstead and Epsom Downs Railway Company, a plot about five furlongs from the stand, a much more acceptable proposition and one that gave birth to Epsom Downs station, and vastly increased public attendance at the races.

An even more urgent and aggravating matter was the proposal for the future of the Rubbing House site. There had been a public house of that name for many years on the site of the old rubbing house, where horses were rubbed down between heats in the days of the straight four-mile course from Banstead. In 1841 Briscoe had leased the pub to Edmund Clives for 21 years. The lease had been taken over by a firm of brewers, Pagdens, but on 3rd June, 1857, a fire broke out 'and consumed the said Rubbing House and the stablings and outbuildings thereto belonging'. Briscoe's fire insurance policy proved altogether inadequate for the cost of rebuilding. He agreed with Pagdens that if they would spend £1,000 on a new inn, he would pay £500 of it and grant them a 40 year lease at £30 a year.

Though the agreement was signed, and building plans drawn up, they may not have been immediately executed: for in 1863 a prospectus proposing a new hotel, the Downs Hotel, for the site was circulated. It was to be a massive affair costing £80,000 – five times as much as the Grand Stand had cost 35 years earlier – and appeared to the EGSA to be less an hotel than another grandstand.

It protested vigorously to Briscoe that such a building would be in direct competition with the Grand Stand, and a contravention of the terms of their lease; eliciting the reply from Ralph Lindsay that the land on which the Rubbing House stood was Briscoe's freehold and not subject to the prohibitions of the EGSA lease. The committee's anxiety was understandable: the present pub, on the same site, stands in an ideal position, a hundred yards past the winning post and facing down the finishing straight. It is said to be the only pub on a racecourse in England, and for those whose interest in horses is not too detailed, provides a most charming retreat: food and drink to hand, and bookies within hailing distance. The present private first-floor balcony is no threat to the monopoly of the stands, but the Downs Hotel, as proposed, certainly would have been.

In the event, the protests registered with Briscoe, and the original grandiose plans of the Downs Hotel Company were much modified. Meanwhile, the committee badgered him relentlessly to approve their plans for the extension of the grandstand. Briscoe was in no hurry, and in 1865, a year after the plans had been submitted to him, the committee had to report to the annual meeting of shareholders that all their efforts to obtain a concession had been unsuccessful. The same meeting instructed the committee to remonstrate strongly with Briscoe against the way in which he was allowing stands to be constructed along the course. It was, it said, fraught with danger to their interests and 'contrary to the arrangements under which they were induced to subscribe their money in constructing their present noble building'.

The situation had not improved six months later, when Dorling informed the committee that he did not want to renew his 21-year lease, due to expire in the summer, which had been offered him at £2,000 a year instead of the £1,000 he had been paying. He pointed out that the financial obligations of running the business were increasing rapidly. He had been compelled to pay the Lord of the Manor of Walton-on-the-Hill £300 a year for a licence to run over that part of the course which crossed his land, and this was due to be increased to £500. Dorling had himself added £1,000 a year to the stakes, and this, too, would have to be increased if Epsom were to keep pace with Ascot.

He offered instead to manage the stand for the Association, and the shareholders in June, 1866, approved the committee's proposal to appoint Dorling and its chairman, Francis Knowles, as joint managing directors of the EGSA at salaries of £500 a year each. The meeting heard glumly that Briscoe was still unmoved by the committee's continuing plea for additional ground adjacent to the stand; and that a large sum was now necessary both for the enlargement of the stand and for the construction of better accommodation, 'which contrasted unfavourably with the facilities offered by other race stands'.

In April 1867, more than three years after he had asked to see the plans, Briscoe signified that he would allow offices to be built between the grandstand and Barnard's stand, but with firm conditions. He refused to grant the land to the Association, and would only treat with Dorling as Clerk of the Course; the extension was not to be for a stand, only for offices; it was to be removed if he wished it; and after six years, it was to become his property.

Despite such stringent constraints, the committee wanted to move quickly in order to have the offices in use for the Derby meeting at the beginning of June, but the builders' tenders were so high that the permanent construction was deferred, and a temporary weighing room and jockey room erected instead. They also managed 'a sort of saddling enclosure in the Paddock', which was a great boon in bad weather.

The Derby that year was a notable one, and not just because it was won by a racing outsider – Hermit, which started at 66–1.

The horse was owned by Lord Henry Chaplin, who three years earlier (before succeeding to the peerage) had been engaged to Lady Florence Paget. She, however, was swept off her feet by a noble gentleman referred to in *The Times* as 'that mad plunger, Lord Hastings', whom she married.

Through the winter of 1866–7 Hermit was rated as a possible Derby winner, but a few weeks before the race it broke a blood vessel, and the consequent setback to training and fitness caused the bookmakers to dismiss it as a serious contender. The Duke of Hamilton regarded its chances as so remote that he laid a gigantic bet, £180,000 to £6,000, against its winning. At the request of the Prince of Wales, the bet was cancelled – fortunately for the Duke.

Others were not so lucky. Lord Hastings, not content with taking Lord Chaplin's fiancée, proposed to take his fortune with another huge bet on the race. Chaplin, however, maintained his faith in Hermit, and won £141,000. Hastings lost almost all he had, and eighteen months later, at the age of 26, killed himself.

Back at the grandstand, Charles Dickens had been on one of his assignments for *Household Words*. In the kitchens he found 1,200 wine glasses, twice as many tumblers, and 3,000 plates and dishes. The chef, he said, had put in his orders for the Derby day feast: 65 lambs for roasting, 350 pigeon pies, 500 spring chickens, and 800 eggs. The salad was to be put in a huge tub, and mixed with birch broom – a new one.

By the end of the year, with the racing over, a tender for the permanent extension on the west end of the grandstand was agreed at £987. The subsequent addition of a balcony for the use of jockeys, trainers, and the press – standing room only – brought the cost up to £1,200, but made those offices 'the most commodious and suitable for the purpose in the kingdom'.

In spite of its considerable debts and financial commitments, the Association could now pay such a bill without strain. It was the first year in which all the profits of the concern returned to them, instead of going largely to Dorling, and the EGSA made £6,806; the next year, the figure was £7,410 – and that was after putting more than £4,000 into the Race Fund. So encouraged was the Association that, as soon as the new race offices were finished, it invited tenders for extensive alterations and improvements to the stand: but the cost of living was rising, too. All the tenders received were between £10,000 and £13,000, and the plans were deferred.

In August 1867, the Association negotiated a new two-year agreement with Mr Carew, Lord of Walton Manor, to continue racing over his land (the south side of the course) at the same rent of £300 a year (Dorling had an increase to £500). At the same time it resolved privately to construct, if possible, a new course that would avoid Walton territory. However, a survey showed that this would be extremely difficult, and when Carew sold the manor, early in 1868, to Edward Studd, the Association took the first opportunity to point out that it held a lease until August, 1869, and would be glad to arrange a further lease on the same terms.

It was the start of a long war. Studd (whose great-grandson Peter was Lord Mayor of London in 1968) had no intention of being charitable to Epsom races. He exchanged letters for 18 months with the EGSA during which the fate of the racecourse was in the balance. The Association protested that it could not possibly meet his terms; Studd knew he had the upper hand, and in the end he got exactly what he had asked for. The battles were formal, and bitter: their flavour is best conveyed by extracts from some of these letters that survive. The first came from Dorling and Knowles after their initial meeting with Studd's legal adviser:

> When we saw you hereon the other day you intimated that £300 would not be taken. We hope however that your client will reconsider such determination. We believe that your client is indisposed to do anything that would militate against the success of the races, and our clients would remind him that the Lord of the adjoining Manor of Epsom, over which the races are principally run (and who is not a racing man at all), returns to the races the greater part of the amount he receives, the amount he retains being considerably less than what has hitherto been paid for the use of Walton Manor, and in fact takes nothing for the course itself . . .

Following Studd's examination of the newly-signed lease, his solicitors wrote to the EGSA solicitors thus:

> He declines to grant your clients a lease at the rent they offer. It is far below the sum he considers should be paid. Mr Studd will not recognize the agreement with Mr Carew of which you have sent us a copy, as Mr Carew had no power to make such an agreement and Mr Studd did not buy subject to it.

Dorling and Knowles next had an interview with Studd's legal adviser to find out what kind of a deal he was after. The answer so shocked them that the committee immediately resolved 'that the proposed alterations in the race course avoiding Walton

Manor be carried out as quickly as possible'; and the joint managing directors tried another approach to Studd:

> We saw Dr Shorthouse yesterday and he stated to us that you would require £2,500 down in addition to £1,000 per annum for permission to run Epsom Races over that portion of Walton Manor for which we have hitherto paid Mr Carew £300 per annum. We respectfully submit that you should reconsider these terms, as the amount is much beyond what we think fair for so small a portion of Epsom Race Course . . . We are willing to pay you an equitable yearly rent, having no means at hand to pay money down.

It produced an angry reply direct from Studd:

> I am in receipt of yours of the 17th instant, and in reply can only say that after the manner in which you have treated me in the matter I must decline altering my determination.

To which Knowles and Dorling replied:

> We can only express regret that you should have been advised to require terms with which we really have not the means to comply – involving us also in the expense of varying the Race Course in order to prevent future uncertainty.
>
> We are sorry you would not grant us the interview we solicited in the first instance, as we considered that if the peculiar position of the Epsom Grand Stand Association with regard to Epsom races had been properly explained to you, you might have been induced, like Mr Briscoe and Mr Heathcote, to patronize the races and to take an interest in furthering our endeavours to minister to the amusement of the People.
>
> We are not cognisant of having wilfully done anything that might be construed as offensive to yourself during the progress of this protracted negotiation, which in the interest of all we are sorry has been brought to such an unsatisfactory termination.

Three days later Studd wrote:

> I have just returned from Worcester and have received your letter of the 27th instant. I cannot realize your remark 'We are not cognisant of having wilfully done anything that might be construed as offensive to yourself during the progress of this protracted negotiation.'
>
> In the first place you were advised by the solicitors for the

executors of the Carew Estate that your holding for that portion of the Derby course belonging to Walton Manor had expired, and that you had better come to terms with the new proprietor. Instead of doing so you paid no regard to his communication and had a notice served on Mr Dorling. You marked out a new course, and when that was found unsuitable you wrote me for an interview, and though you were referred to my solicitors, you not only failed to come to terms with them, terms that would have been favourable to yourselves, but you produced a document which if valid would have deprived me of my rights of rents.

The EGSA committee, somewhat deflated, paused only to tell Briscoe what was going on and to suggest that Barnard would have to chip in if they were forced to raise the price, then requested their solicitors to write to Studd's solicitors to apply formally for an interview. The following reply was received:

We received your letter of the 6th instant and have seen Mr Studd upon it. He thinks a meeting between him and your clients will be of no advantage, as he adheres to his terms for the proposed lease . . . It is right we should add it is Mr Studd's intention to give half the £2,500 to a certain race or races.

Nearly a month later the EGSA replied more succinctly than usual:

We are instructed to inform you that the terms asked are so high that they cannot be entertained. Our clients will however be willing to treat on the following basis: 99 years at £750 per annum.

The answer was another rebuff:

Mr Studd declines the offer made by your letter . . .

It was now the end of 1868, and ten months since Studd had moved into Walton. At the next committee meeting, chairman Knowles reported his belief that Studd would sell his rights over Walton Downs for £15,500, and such an offer was immediately made; he declined to sell. His solicitors advised the EGSA that it was wasting its time in offering anything other than what Studd demanded – £2,500 down and £1,000 a year for 21 years. Knowles offered £1,000 a year for a 21-year lease terminable by the Association after 7 or 14 years. Studd's solicitors declined to communicate the offer. Knowles repeated the offer plus the

£2,500 premium, stipulating that half was to be returned to the race fund.

With a weary sigh almost audible a century later. Studd agreed that the lease should be terminable at 7 or 14 years, but only with a year's notice; he refused the condition relating to the race fund and stated that the money must be for two *really good* stakes for the benefit of the racing public:

> Since I saw you I have consulted the highest authorities on this point, and they are all of the opinion that this is the proper course to be pursued under the circumstances. You will therefore please consider this is finally decided upon; and in fact I may as well mention, at once, that further discussion upon any of the points would be a mere waste of time, as the whole of them have already been ventilated, and none of the terms offered will be departed from.

He got his two races, one the day before the Derby, one the day after. The EGSA committee was stunned, its prosperity severely curtailed. It was by no means the last blow it received in its struggle for the domination of the Downs.

CHAPTER NINE

Intermission II

On 30th May, 1829, a member of the EGSA committee was asked 'to make such arrangements with Bishop the Officer to secure his attendance on the race week as he may think proper'. Thus modestly began the long involvement of the police with Epsom races. In that first year of the grandstand, and for long afterwards, the county magistrates were respectfully informed that they would be admitted free; and a room in the basement of the stand was appropriated to their use 'for the purpose of the locking of prisoners'. That practice persisted when the new stand was built and continued until the combination of better facilities for transporting the wrong-doers to the local police station and a slightly more civilized regard for those in custody occurred. 'They are human beings, after all,' one policeman said, 'and that room was a bit much.'

How many people Bishop took into custody in 1829 is not recorded, but he presumably found the job more than he could cope with. After Derby week the following year, the Association had to foot a bill for £7 for constables. Twenty years later, policing the summer meeting had become so big and efficient an operation that it cost the racecourse authorities £125 and resulted in their having to pay £10 to hire a room for the magistrates and £4 2s 6d for the expenses of their clerk in dealing with the offenders. A few years ago, in 1963, the EGSA's police bill reached £12,000 for the year.

The complications of the job are immense, and without the co-operation of the public, would be overwhelming, for the police on Derby day are faced not only with the sudden invasion of enough people to fill Southampton or Aberdeen, but also with the fact that this mob swarms over land which, though a public common for the rest of the year, is, during a race meeting, private property – the back garden of the grandstand. So far as is known, the situation is unique, and often uniquely baffling. Murder, rape and robbery will be as firmly dealt with by the law in your garden as in the High Street; but while, for instance, the parking of cars within the racecourse would be a public offence for the rest of the year, during the meeting it is strictly not the police's concern. They will be in attendance while officers of the EGSA, or of the Downs Conservators, attempt to persuade the drivers to go elsewhere.

It is no secret that these two bodies are very keen that the police should take a more active part in enforcing the by-laws made by the Downs Conservators under the 1936 Epsom and Walton Downs Regulation Act. (The Epilogue to this book contains the recommendations on this point made by the Working Party on the Act.) They are unlikely to succeed; the attitude of the police is to avoid involvement in private disputes as far as is consistent with keeping the peace. In November 1971, the Commissioner of Metropolitan Police indicated that he would oppose any greater police involvement in what, strictly speaking, was an amenity problem encountered on only a few days each year. The limits to the existing powers of the police for keeping order during Epsom races are limits that they clearly do not wish to extend.

Their attitude is quite understandable when conditions on the racecourse are taken into account: it is absolutely open, unguarded, unguardable. Suppose, for instance, that legislation were eventually approved to instruct the police to stand shoulder to shoulder with the Conservators in one of their periodic bids to keep caravans off the Downs. Suppose 'the travelling people' did not co-operate – and they never have done in this matter – how could the law possibly be enforced? The Conservators, the EGSA and a private security corps have distinctly failed in the past to impose their will on the caravanners, and there is little chance that the addition of the police would bring success. As one seasoned campaigner has said, you could only keep the caravans off the Downs by surrounding the course night and day with a wall of men – or a wall of brick. Apart from almost certainly being unsuccessful, for the police to take part in such a campaign would also inevitably be an unfortunate public relations exercise.

So the police turn out only in such numbers as are requested by the Association, or are found necessary by experience, but are careful of the legal area in which they operate. Just after the war, for instance, the Association got steamed up about spivs who hired orange boxes to give people in the free strips a better view. They wanted police action, but there was none, for no indictable offence had been committed. Nor, for the same reason, did they stop the gipsies making a slick buck by charging high prices for 'private' car parks on the Downs; as long as the motorists were not being defrauded, there was no reason for police action. If the Conservators, acting under the authority given them by the 1936 Act, were to attempt to remove these unofficial car park attendants, the police would go along too – but only to see it all went off peaceably.

Because it is their duty to prevent and detect crime, the police would always be adequately represented in any public gathering of this size; and because it is their duty to control traffic on the highway, they will always have a massive problem on the approach roads to Epsom on Derby day. But beyond those obvious tasks, which are in the public interest, the racecourse executive has to pay for the help of the police at the course, and wherever else it may be needed.

Anybody may apply for the services of the police at a private function, or on private premises to protect property or preserve order, and providing the Chief Constable – or in the Metropolitan area, the Commissioner – approves the purpose and can spare the men, all the applicant needs is the money. Probably to deter frivolous copper-hirers, the rate charged per man is substantially more than the rate earned per man. Thus a constable costs nearly £2 an hour (minimum charge for three hours), or £15.72 a day. Sergeants work out at more than £18 a day and inspectors at £21.44. Chief superintendents come for £3.65 an hour, close on £30 a day.

You pay extra for uniform branch officers in plain clothes, and much more if you want them disguised in morning or evening dress – to watch for sleight of hand in the Club Stand, for instance. Horses are available at £1.15 a day (the racecourse use five) and dogs at 95p, conveyance extra. Travelling expenses to and from the job, a refreshment allowance, and reasonable accommodation must also be provided.

Although the Epsom Downs arrangements are so splendidly streamlined that the EGSA has to hire fewer policemen now than it did in 1850, and the bill is less than half what it was in the mid-1960s, these little extras do add up. For the four days of the Derby meeting in 1972, the 59 men cost the Association nearly £5,000, and the extras topped £600: £23 for horses, £122 for meals, £136 for marquees and £151 for transport. A few years earlier, there were twice as many men on the bill, and twice as many deployed by the police for their own purposes. Some of these purposes were more habitual than necessary, and when the pruning operation began it was not difficult to cut back; one man, for instance, was posted at a road junction that had been sealed off; four were discovered by a senior officer, so the story goes, enjoying a hand of whist behind the bushes on the Walton side of the course. Year after year they had been detailed for duty there, but had never found out what they were supposed to be doing.

The basis of the 'private' police work on the Downs is the manning of those points at which roads or footpaths cross the course, and to provide a token show of law and order in the most densely populated areas. It is only a token: the number of policemen, for instance, who line the finishing straight for the royal arrival could not hope to prevent a determined individual from assaulting the Queen's person, or at least her car. Nor is there any way in which they could stop the public jumping over the fence in front of the horses, as one woman did with such tragic result in 1913.

The 'welshing' of bookmakers who could not, or did not propose to, meet their commitments used to be a major problem, but the fraternity have put their own house in order on that matter. In Derby week 1972, the police made only twenty arrests on the Downs, the majority for unlawful gaming. It has always been so: it's not that you can't sit round a blanket and empty your pockets in a pontoon school, but conducting an exhibition of the three-card trick with intent to defraud is another matter, and something of that kind has been popular as long as two or three suckers were gathered together. It was as long ago as 1830 that *The Times* man at Epsom noted: 'The professors of the art of concealing the pea from the investigations of too curious inquirers plied their thimbles as busily as tailors.'

Apart from that, there is a fair sprinkling of thieving from motor vehicles, a pickpocket or two, a bit of cheating over tickets and inevitably, in a crowd like that, an indecent assault once in a while. Later in the day sterner matters may arise: there was an alleged rape on the Downs a few years ago, during an investigation of which the lady concerned complained that it was all right with him, and she didn't mind that one, but when *he* started as well it was too much. Derby day drunks are a nuisance in the town in the evening, but unless one is being objectionable the attitude on the Downs is a tolerant one. Once there was a lady who, after an afternoon on the gin and tonic, insisted on being arrested as a drunk because she had lost her husband. She was accommodated in the local police station and, in due course, it was discovered that her husband had returned to Doncaster without her.

It is almost unbelievable that 50 or 60 men can now achieve, on Derby day, what, sixty years ago, needed 705 police on the

course, another 90 put there by police order, and 800 more looking after things elsewhere. Today fewer than 400 police are
involved in special Derby duty of any kind, and they include
nearly 40 traffic wardens. A helicopter is used to help traffic
control now, and before that police shared the Automobile
Association's spotter plane, but this method is scarcely novel:
in 1932 they were using an autogiro, the helicopter of its
day, and traffic control from the air actually began in Britain
with the use of an airship to spot the Derby day traffic jams in
1921.

These were more likely to be caused by horses and carts than
by cars, and going a little further back we can see that the
pedestrians gave the police as sore a traffic problem as they have
now. In 1887, 1,460 police were deployed on Derby duty: 607
were on the racecourse and in the vicinity of the grandstand
(paid for by the EGSA); 65 attended the private stands, Barnards
and Langlands; the South Western Railway Company ordered
9 policemen for stations on the line from Waterloo; the London,
Brighton and South Coast Railway needed 48 men, some to be
posted at stations as far away as New Cross, Norwood and
London Bridge, and 26 to keep order at Epsom Downs station
(to which the police added another 11).

As well as 193 police on duty at fixed points on the roads of
Epsom, and another 60 ready for traffic control, there were 34
on the roads of Wandsworth, 30 in Sutton, 21 in Tooting, and
175 spread over Brixton, Clapham and Croydon. On the police
orders for the meeting this directive appears: 'At the close of
the races each day the Police on duty are to prevent missiles
being thrown by persons in carriages or on foot, particularly at
the following points: the Hill, the crossings on the course, Epsom
Town, Epsom Downs to Rose Hill Gate, and Clapham Common.' By 1911 Clapham Common had been dropped from the
list, but the custom of 'throw out your mouldies' – believed
originally to refer to stale pieces of bread left behind in the picnic
bag, though the cry later rang out from the urchins at the road-
side in the expectation of receiving unwanted coins – persisted
down the generations. A news photograph, taken in 1908, shows
Edward VII throwing coins to the gipsies as he arrived on the
course. Injuries to the children scrabbling for coins between the
coach wheels were frequent, and more recently, though the police
have done their best to discourage the habit, one child was killed.
But the tradition persists, although the bounty is scarcer.

By 1911 there were just as many police controlling traffic
between London and Epsom, and even more on the course

(nearly 800), but the need for a show of authority at the intermediate railway stations had passed with the breaking up of the
racecourse gangs. Tattenham Corner station was open and the
South Eastern and Chatham Railway Company thought 7 policemen there would be adequate. The only sign of the law at Epsom
Downs were the 11 men used to control the crowds leaving the
station and pouring over Longdown Lane.

The owner of Durdans still booked a couple of constables for
his personal protection – the estate lies on one of the roads from
the stand to the town – just as in 1850 the owner of Woodcote
Park, Baron de Teissier, paid £2 10s for extra police, and the
Sutton Vestry Book records the resolution at about the same time
'that the sum of four pounds be allowed out of the Highway
Rate for the protection of the village during Epsom Race week.'
That sum would probably have paid for 3 constables a day
throughout the meeting, and a fourth on Derby day.

The following schedule shows the complete police requirement
at Epsom racecourse for Derby week, 1850:

1 superintendent	6 days @ 13s 6d	–	£4 1s od
1 inspector	" @ 9s od	–	£2 14s od
1 "	4 days @ 6s 6d	–	£1 6s od
8 sergeants	" @ 3s 6d	–	£5 12s od
63 constables	" @ 3s od	–	£37 16s od

Extra for Derby and Oaks:

1 inspector mounted	2 days @ 6s 6d	–	13s od
1 sergeant "	3 days @ 3s 6d	–	10s od
1 constable "	2 days @ 3s od	–	6s od

The total amounts to £52 18s 6d. No mention is made of
travelling expenses or meal allowances, but lodgings had to be
paid for at the rate of 15s a head for the superintendent and
inspectors, 10s for the sergeants and 4s for the men (for the entire
meeting), which would have been about enough to provide a dry
ditch and a handful of hay. The EGSA's financial commitment
for maintaining law and order is completed by the hire of two
flies for 7s od to convey gambling implements to Epsom.

A true martinet

Studd's licence to the EGSA allowed them 'to run races over those parts of the course that extend over Six Mile Hill' at the hard price of £1,000 a year. As well as the premium of £1,250 to the Lord of the Manor of Walton, they had to pay a further £1,250 'to be appropriated as Gifts by the Lord to the two following races: The Walton Manor Stakes (750 sovereigns) and The Six Mile Hill Handicap (500 sovereigns)'. The Association wanted to enclose its expensive piece of racecourse with posts and chains so that it would not be damaged either by trainers or the public throughout the year; but Studd would only allow them to have it fenced off for three days each side of a race meeting.

A marginal note by his solicitors (Farrer Ouvry & Co.) on the draft licence explains: 'The Lord would prefer that no posts and chains were set up except at race times as the trainers and the public complain very much on that head and we understand that some public expression of feeling on the subject may be expected shortly. If the only object of the Lessees is to keep the course in order the Lord would probably covenant to do that at his own expense if the keeping up of the posts and chains were waived altogether.'

Public feeling on the question of access to the Downs has been expressed intermittently and with varying intensity for 150 years, and in 1888 it was to be demonstrated in the High Court, but for the time being the local people were not too awkward. The EGSA, in fact, was making one of its regular attempts to appeal against a rate assessment – which, you may recall, it had done even before the grandstand was completed. The rating story at this time (1869) was as follows: in 1845 (when Henry Dorling first took the lease), the rateable value was £450; in 1852 it was increased to £3,840, and reduced on appeal to £1,400; in 1866, it was increased to £3,800, and reduced again, on objection, to £2,500. With the fortunes of the Association booming in 1867, a dividend of £5,000 was paid to shareholders, and the following year the rateable value was reassessed at £4,500, one-seventh of the rate of the entire parish of Epsom. The stands at Ascot and Goodwood were then rated at £1,600 and £1,450. This time the appeal only brought the figure down to £4,102, but even this helped at a time when the Association needed all the money it could find for its programme of expansion.

Even before the result of the appeal was known, its next negotiation was completed. It was one for which the jockeys at least were grateful: the committee persuaded the owner of Durdans to let them use his paddock during race meetings. At that time, the Durdans paddock extended right over what are now the EGSA offices and the stable block, over the run-out beyond the winning post, up to and including the present parade ring. Horses finishing at top speed had very little space to slow down in before they were faced with the Durdans boundary, and some had been known to wheel right and gallop down Chalk Lane towards the town before they could be brought under control.

Arthur Heathcote agreed to open the paddock to the racecourse for the six days of racing in 1869 for £1,000. 'The welfare of the Association has been seriously imperilled by the exorbitant terms demanded,' the committee reported to the shareholders three months later, referring to their two latest negotiations. Heathcote almost immediately died, and the following year his heirs, the Reverend Thomas and Mr Francis Heathcote, arranged a somewhat less demanding lease: they granted the EGSA use of the paddock and the Rubbing House Field (nine acres together) for 21 years at £1,050 a year, plus 15 free passes to the paddock and 2 to the grandstand. There were to be no buildings there except for the sale of refreshments and tickets.

The death of Arthur Heathcote was the first of several that closely affected the EGSA. In August 1870, the Lord of the Manor of Epsom, John Ivatt Briscoe, was buried at Wimbledon. A better friend to racing never lived at Epsom. His wife, the actual owner of the Manor, had followed him by the end of the year, and her successor, Henry Blackburn, survived only eighteen months. In the same summer, the EGSA secretary wrote to say he 'felt so very ill he would have to resign his appointment'. George Judd, a member of the committee, took over the job and was dead in eight months; and on 20th March 1873 the death occurred of Henry Dorling, who had controlled racing at Epsom for nearly 30 years.

In his last years, Dorling had taken two more steps of huge importance to the Association. A month after the death of Mrs Briscoe, he obtained from her successor a three-year lease on the land on Epsom Downs previously let directly by Briscoe for the temporary stands, the booths, and the parking of carriages. It cost the Association £1,500 a year, but it immediately sub-let it to Messrs John Barnard and Charles Langlands for the same sum – plus a donation to the race fund of £300 in 1871 and £500 in each of the next two years. The gain to the Association in terms of authority was obvious; unfortunately the gain to racing was temporarily nullified by Blackburn's decision to discontinue Briscoe's £500 annual donation, but his successor restored it.

Dorling also persuaded the committee that it was time the Association exercised greater control over the free use that racehorse trainers made of the Downs. It was a move that led to a considerable rebellion, but an important one in the EGSA's march towards domination. This was the notice that was published in October 1869:

> Notice is hereby given that towards defraying the expense of the Exercise Ground on Epsom Downs, and of so much of the Course as lies within the Manor of Epsom, and until further notice, a fee of ten shillings and sixpence will be charged yearly for every horse which, with permission of the Lord of the Manor, goes there for any race meeting, or runs any private trial or public race thereon; and a fee of one guinea will be charged annually for every horse which, with such permission as above mentioned, shall be trained on such Downs.

We have seen enough of Dorling's achievements since 1845. Almost everything to do with racing at Epsom that was worthwhile had its source in his wisdom and enthusiasm, (he had relented at last about the 'new' Derby course, with its severe climb, and gave it a new start high on the south side, where it has remained ever since). It was he who introduced what is now known as the spring (April) meeting, with its two great attractions of the Great Metropolitan and the City and Suburban; and re-shaped the mechanics of racing in a way that was accepted as a model on all courses. He had also built a row of private boxes under the grandstand roof veranda 'for the better accommodation of nobility'. This was no doubt to answer such requests as he once had from the Duchess of Richmond, who 'would prefer a portion of the Grand Stand railed off, if she could have it to Herself, but should Mr Dorling not be able to do this, the Duchess would then like to have the stand that Lord George used to have'.

Henry was succeeded as Clerk of the Course, and as a committee member, by his eldest son Henry Mayson Dorling, who was soon instructed by Admiral Rous that 'on no consideration was he to interfere with the Derby track'. Three years later another Dorling, Henry Mayson's brother Edward Jonathan, joined him on the committee. The family biographer, Edward Earle, was the latter's son, and wrote of the two men: 'The two brothers were strangely unlike each other in temperament. My father was a serene, kindly man, slow to anger, tactful in his dealing with others. My uncle, on the other hand, was a true martinet, a self-assured, uncompromising dictator, capable of fighting tooth and nail against anyone – be he prince or pauper – who dared to go contrary to his wishes. It was not long before he had taken the reins of the Association firmly unto himself.'

H. M. Dorling was accused often enough of being ultra-conservative and reactionary. Even the *Daily Telegraph* once brought itself to say that his policy seemed to be based on the principle of what had satisfied once would always satisfy. From his reign we can expect much strength, but less vision; organization rather than innovation. For the time being, however, Henry Mayson Dorling was not in the seat of power. He was the junior member of the five-man EGSA committee still chaired by Francis Knowles, who now became sole managing director at £1,000 a year. He was to enjoy thirteen years of solo power, and he made the most of it.

Just before the annual meeting of the EGSA in 1874, which marked the end of his first year in this position, the usual committee meeting was held to finalize the report that would be presented to the shareholders. This one was attended by only three members (Dorling and John Barnard were missing), one of whom was the chairman. It was resolved that the committee should present Mr Knowles with 250 guineas 'to be expended by him in the purchase of a piece of plate by way of testimonial on the part of the shareholders of their appreciation of his indefatigable exertion in the management during the period of the last thirteen years of the affairs of this Association'.

The matter came before the shareholders in even richer terms: 'The favourable financial position of the Association being in the opinion of your committee considerably due to the untiring energy of your managing director, Mr Francis Knowles, your committee recommend that this meeting should authorize them to present him, out of the funds of the Association, with the sum of 250 guineas, to be expended by him in plate or in some other suitable manner, as a testimonial from the shareholders of their appreciation of his services, both as a member of the committee during seventeen years and latterly as managing director, considering that much of the present prosperity is owing to his exertions and ability in guiding your affairs through the many difficulties of the past few years'.

Such praise would have been hard to read out publicly unless the reader really believed it. It was in fact read by the chairman, Francis Knowles, who also moved its adoption!

The new Lord of the Manor of Epsom was Lieutenant Charles Vernon Strange, R.N. From him Knowles had swiftly obtained a new three-year lease of the non-racing ground (£1,500 a year again) and of the Stewards' Stand (£50 a year). Barnard and Langlands rented the land again from the Association at the same price, but this time Knowles insisted that they should increase the donation to the race fund from £500 to £1,800.

Derby day, 1875, was a memorable one, and an expensive one for the EGSA, but before it there were two other occasions when the committee was moved to dip into the funds. In January it contributed £10 to a trust fund for the family of a racing journalist who had died, leaving his widow and children unprovided for; and in May, £20 to the mother of a jockey 'unfortunately killed while riding at the spring meeting'. A few days later it had to shell out forty times that figure to accommodate royal visitors at the Derby.

The Association had expended £200 in fixtures and fittings for Queen Victoria's visit in 1840, since when she had not returned; and after Albert's death in 1861, her retirement from public life made the possibility of a visit even more unlikely. Her eldest son 'Teddy', was, however, extremely keen on the turf – he won the Derby with Persimmon in 1896, possibly the most popular victory Epsom has ever seen – and took many opportunities, during his long wait to become Edward VII, to enjoy it. On this occasion the Prince of Wales sent a message to Epsom saying that he would require accommodation for a large party of the royal family only a fortnight before the Derby. The committee were plunged into a temporary panic: a brace of royals, a handful of equerries and a bundle of Windsor Castle servants they could cope with, but there was no place in the grandstand where a large party (which could involve dozens of attendants) could be accommodated in suitable style. It was not just a matter of persuading the tenants of a few private boxes to vacate them on the one day of the year when they really want to be there: there was also the problem of finding retiring rooms, dining-rooms, and a separate kitchen.

To plead lack of time was unthinkable; the builders had to be brought in and put to work to construct, in 14 days, the necessary suites over the weighing rooms which Mr Briscoe had let them build between the grandstand and Barnard's stand. The builders made it in time 'only by the dint of very great exertion', and knew there was nothing the committee could do but pay the bill of £810 19s. 6d. It was all worth while, apparently, as Mr Knowles was later able to assure shareholders that His Royal Highness 'sent for your chairman and expressed himself as highly pleased with the efforts that had been made to carry out his wishes'.

The turn-out was most impressive: five of the Queen's children and their spouses – as well as Edward and Alexandra, Alfred the Duke of Edinburgh and his Duchess, (he was the only man to hold this title before Philip), Prince Louis of Hesse and Alice, Prince Christian of Schleswig-Holstein and Helena, and the Marquis of Lorne and Louise – and the Queen's cousin, the Duke of Cambridge, son of the seventh son of George III. Cambridge had married an actress, Louisa Fairbrother (who was known as Mrs FitzGeorge) but she was not in the Derby party.

Honoured though it was by the royal visit, it was particularly galling that the EGSA should have had to spend so much on a temporary addition to the stand when, as the committee knew, it was on the verge, at last, of winning from the Lord of the Manor the land it needed on each side to make a considerable and permanent extension. Knowles had been negotiating this with Lieutenant Strange for some time. A lease was signed in April 1876, retrospective to the previous June, for 43¼ years at £61 a year – twice as much ground rent, incidentally, as had been paid for the entire original grandstand acre – plus a free box for six in the grandstand.

Over the next three years, at a cost of £4,172, a large east wing extension and a lesser one on the west (Barnard's side) were built. For an extra £1,400, the whole of the balcony tier of boxes in the main stand was rebuilt, with a new floor and permanent roof to correspond with the balcony tier in the east wing. The many small iron columns in the front of the main stand, which supported the tiers, were replaced by single substantial columns – 'and the whole now presents a handsome architectural appearance'. The cost took the total expenditure on the grandstand to nearly £34,000, and the Association had also to agree to allow Strange free access to the Clerk's rooms, a box for six, and six tickets to the paddock.

In the summer of 1877, the year Victoria was proclaimed Empress of India and Edison invented the gramophone, a death took place at Hyde Park Gardens, which, to the EGSA, was of far greater significance than any other event of the year: that of Edward Studd, Lord of the Manor of Walton-on-the-Hill. He left £160,000, but directed his trustees to sell the Walton estate to pay his debts and funeral expenses. Catalogues of sale were prepared the following year, but before the property reached the market, it was acquired, to the Association's intense frustration, by one Henry Padwick of Horsham for £25,000. It immediately began negotiating with him, not just for the section of the racecourse that crossed Walton land, but for the entire 728-acre estate. Padwick apparently agreed, or so the committee thought, to sell for £30,000, and on that it deposited £1,000. The committee suggested it should pay Padwick £3,500 in cash, £4,000 in promissory notes at 5 per cent, and take out a mortgage for £22,500. All seemed to be going well when, on 19th September, 1879, Padwick announced that he required the whole £30,000 within 10 days or the deposit would be forfeit.

'I think we must attribute this circumstance to his severe illness,' wrote the Association's solicitor. 'I must therefore advise you to abandon all thought of the purchase.' Thought was not abandoned, but, for the time being, hope was. Padwick died a few days later, but it was not until after his widow's death that the question of the sale was raised again.

While the Walton endeavours were in hand, the committee learned that James Stuart Strange, who had taken over the manor from the lieutenant, was contemplating pulling down the old Prince's Stand and replacing it with a much larger one, 'quite double the size'. The late Reginald White, an Epsom historian whose mother, Jane, was one of Henry Dorling's many daughters, was in 1944 able to recall that his first memory of Prince's was that it was empty and locked up even on race days. This, he said, was in about 1870.

His recollection, which had been considerably doubted, is now supported by some interesting circumstantial evidence. In 1841, 4 years before Henry Dorling took the lease of the grandstand, the Lord of the Manor – in whose freehold Prince's had always been held – leased 'that brick-built cottage commodity called the Prince's Stand' to Edmund Clives for 21 years. Clives was also the lessee of the Rubbing House hotel, and most probably used Prince's as a store. Both leases were taken over by the Pagden brothers, who held the Rubbing House when it was destroyed by fire in 1857.

Briscoe offered to lease a new hotel and Prince's to the Pagdens for 40 years – the stand at £10 a year. Pagden's do not seem to have taken up the offer of Prince's, thus confirming Mr White's memory of its disuse and explaining Mr Strange's intention to pull it down and rebuild in 1879. Seeing yet another threat to its monopoly, the EGSA committee promptly resolved that it did 'disapprove of the contemplated erection'. Knowles was despatched to tell Strange of this, and to suggest that the proposed alteration would be contrary to the covenant against permanent buildings contained in the Association's lease from the Lord of the Manor. Strange was not greatly moved, and the new Prince's Stand was put under way forthwith. It still bears the date of the transformation on its balcony wall: 1879. There is no record of whether the original stand was completely demolished or only extended. Certainly the 'new' Prince's bears little resemblance to the old, though subsequent repairs and alterations have disclosed some very old woodwork within, and there is still a cellar there which is certainly of much earlier origin.

At this moment H. M. Dorling, as Clerk of the Course, notched up his first major negotiation. He succeeded, where chairman Knowles had failed, in persuading the Earl of Egmont to lease to the Association a chunk of land to the north of Tattenham Corner – part of the Nork Park estate, in Banstead. This included what is now the first furlong of the five-furlong straight, before it is cut by the Tadworth Road. Dorling took five-and-a-half acres from Egmont for 21 years at £200 a year, and had in addition to pay £116 compensation to the tenant of North Tadworth farm, who was cultivating it at the time. (Ten years later the Earl sold the whole of the estate, and the EGSA was able to buy the freehold of its interest for £2,000.)

Knowles was further discomforted in 1879, by a letter from the Jockey Club complaining that the Derby accommodation afforded them at the grandstand was inadequate for their requirements. Though the west extension had only just been completed, it suggested it should be rebuilt on a much larger scale.

The Jockey Club could not be ignored, and the committee had plans drawn up to suit them, but Strange objected to them. The Jockey Club then approached him directly, suggesting that the Association should build on the site of Barnard's Stand a completely new one 'to be mainly devoted to the use of the Jockey Club and the upper classes'. Barnard, who still had four years to run on his lease, obstructed that idea by agreeing to surrender only 100 feet of land, for which he demanded a premium of £4,000 and £300 rent. Gazumping had hit the Downs.

Two years later Strange wrote to the EGSA solicitor: 'After a good deal of pushing we have got Barnard to state his terms about his stand at Epsom. He says that other members of his family have a share in the stand, and they will not allow more to be given up than so far as the winning post.' (Barnard's, which existed long before the grandstand, was beautifully positioned at the finishing line.) 'This, although they know that the lease will not be renewed if the Grand Stand Company remain in the same mind as at present.' Strange suggested that plans and leases for the new stand should be prepared so that operations could commence as soon as Barnard was out.

The Barnards were a family whose history one cannot long escape when looking into the story of Epsom Downs. Like the name of Dorling, that of Barnard appears on the original deeds of the EGSA in 1829; and the Barnards were considerably older as an Epsom family, pre-dating the grandstand by more than a century. As we know, their temporary stands were on the course long before the grandstand, and in a somewhat condensed form were still there nearly two hundred years later.

On the death of John Barnard in 1897, the family sold the whole lot to the EGSA for £350 – including 'platforms, roof cloths, back cloths, shutters, glass windows, five pay boxes, iron railings, mouse traps, etc.' That much is a fact, though the senior Barnard at the time of writing, Mrs Gwendolen Burns, believes that John's brother Ted kept the business going. Certainly her mother (John's daughter) took a lease of the site from the EGSA in 1906. Barnard's Stands – seven of them – were flourishing again, and continued to do so until the rebuilding of the grandstand in 1926.

Not until that event was the EGSA entirely happy about the Barnard situation, which it had always regarded as over-privileged, nor was this feeling unique; in his *Atlas and Review of British Race-Courses*, F. H. Bayles in 1911 had this to say of the Barnards: 'Under what conditions Barnard's Stands are held I am unable to say, but, to my mind, some attempt should be made to remove some of the authority which empowers this family to monopolize the most advantageous part of Epsom race course, which I contend should be occupied by others who have more right to this principal position. It is provoking to see the Royal enclosure, not to speak of the professional and other qualified element who pay large fees for boxes etc., deprived of a proper view of races at Epsom, whilst this plebeian enclosure, "Barnard's", is indulged with a perfect view of the last 60 yards of the most classic events in our racing annals.'

The new extended stand left the family with only a small patch of ground between Prince's and the end of the Club Stand, mean enough to satisfy the strongest opposition but still near enough the winning post to appeal to the customers. Today, the site is largely occupied, for the spring and Derby meetings, by two temporary stands built on scaffolding, and the name of Barnard still echoes across the Downs.

The family firm is now called Barnard and Hill. It occupies the Derby Stables, a stone's throw from the back of the grandstand, and also leases Prince's Stand from the Association. John Barnard did have a son, Herbert, an amateur jockey. He died of pneumonia following a chill he caught while riding, and the name of Barnard is perpetuated in the firm by sentiment rather than by fact.

While waiting for further deaths and delivery from leases to enable grand developments to proceed around the racecourse, spare an eye for a few odd, insignificant details. Some will appear again. Strange, for instance, renewed a 20-year-old agreement with the 3rd Surrey Rifle Volunteers to use a piece of the Downs for target practice and musketry instruction; permitted the London, Brighton and South Coast Railway to erect a flagstaff by the Downs station; and licensed James Lock, pork butcher, to rent some waste ground by the station for three months each summer 'in order to set up or put or place on the said premises . . . one stall or booth for the sale only of Ginger beer, lemonade, and other refreshments of a non-intoxicating nature, and one stand for four swings and two lots or rows of cocoanuts'. His £8 a year enabled Mr Lock 'to break the soil of such portion of Epsom Downs' between 14th June and 15th September – not the racing season.

In 1884, when Barnard's lease had expired, Strange offered the Jockey Club the lease of a piece of land 50 feet wide immediately west of the grandstand, at £100 a year. The Jockey Club informed the EGSA, but when it approached Strange he at first asked for £300. He later relented, and the Association took the extra land on lease for 33½ years. On it, and on the land occupied by the existing west extension and weighing rooms, it put up, for £8,930, a Club Stand, the members of which were to be elected by the stewards on payment of an annual subscription. A three-storey job, crowned by an odd little tower, it was, they told themselves, 'a handsome and commodious building, which has added greatly to the popularity of Epsom Races among the influential supporters of the Turf'.

While it was being built (it was completed in seven months, but for papering and painting, in good time for the spring meeting of 1886), the committee had a bit of architect trouble again in the person of Hatchard Smith. He attended a meeting to complain of a letter from the Association's solicitor alleging that the mortar used in the erection of the walls 'was of an improper character'. He would, he said, examine it closely after fourteen days and if it proved to be in any way improper he would pull down the walls and rebuild them. The committee terrified at the thought of the walls collapsing while the stand was loaded with Jockey Club members, the nobility and maybe the Prince of Wales and – 'without raising any doubt of the talent and ability of Mr Smith' – resolved to splash out £3 a week on a clerk of works to supervise the building in the architect's absence.

Before it was finished, the EGSA was engaged in yet another rates battle, the biggest to date. The rateable value of the stand had increased horrifyingly; since their 1868 appeal, it had gone up to £4,600 in 1877, and £6,000 in 1879. In 1883 it trebled to £18,000, but was reduced on objection to £10,200. They also appealed against this sum knowing that worse would come when the Club Stand was up.

Though the Association that year made a profit of nearly £12,000, and its average since 1880 had been slightly higher, it was at pains to point out that they were in a risky business. The profits depended on the staging of open-air entertainment on six days a year only – two in April and four at the beginning of June. A bad spell of weather in Derby week could be ruinous, and it had, after all, snowed on Derby day in 1839 and again in 1867. Whatever the weather, it had to guarantee £10,000 a year to the race fund, pay £1,000 to the police, £500 to course officials, and another £500 to catering staff. (Students of domestic economy may care to note that the grandstand employed a catering manager at £85 a year and 161 temporary hands at a cost of £429 18s: 3 superintendents, 9 cooks, 45 barmen, 32 waiters, 30 porters, 35 women and 7 boys.)

The main outside contributions to the race fund were £300 from the Lord of the Manor, 200 guineas every second year from the Queen as a plate to be run for, and £50 each from the two railway companies. Since the Association held no lease of that part of the racecourse that lay within the parish of Epsom, it always had to face the awful possibility that there might one day be a Lord of the Manor who disapproved of the whole business, leaving the EGSA with a stand that would comfortably allow 50,000 to sit and contemplate the empty Downs.

By 1884, the Association was paying out £2,541 a year altogether for the right to use various bits of the Downs and neighbouring land – and did not, incidentally, even hold a licence to stage horse races; that was granted personally to the Clerk of the Course, at the time H. M. Dorling. The parish of Epsom rate assessment of more than £10,000 a year was rather steep in the circumstances, for the rateable values of the racecourse stands elsewhere were much less: at Newmarket, with its 484 acres of heath, £5,100; Doncaster, £6,103; Ascot, £3,400; and Goodwood, £1,595. (As a matter of interest, Lord's was then rated at £1,000 and the Oval at £479; the Albert Hall at £4,160 and the Lyceum Theatre at £4,076.) The EGSA's appeal was, however, dismissed and the assessment confirmed.

Shortly afterwards Francis Knowles, who must have been very tired of playing a leading part in such battles, sold most of his large shareholding in the Association and resigned as managing director, chairman and committee member. Another era had ended. He was succeeded in the chair by Henry Mayson Dorling, an obvious choice, since, for the past eight years the committee had voted him and his brother Edward an annual £250 bonus 'for their exertions in attending to the concerns of this Association'.

Already Clerk of the Course since the death of his father, and now chairman, Henry Mayson and his brother were also appointed joint managing directors at £500 a year each. Even his father had not had such power; and the son was to retain it for 33 more years.

CHAPTER ELEVEN

Feuding and fighting

It is almost beyond belief, but it seems to be true, that for sixty years the EGSA thrived on the profits of the Derby and the Oaks without contributing directly to either race. The Association could not even say that it provided the racecourse: that was there long before it was. What it had done was to put its back and its money into providing accommodation for spectators who wanted to see the two greatest horse races in the world. The entrance fees it kept to itself.

The situation could only be equalled today if the owners of Wembley Stadium were to pocket all the profits from staging the Cup Final, leaving nothing for the Football Association nor the competing clubs. Inflation notwithstanding, the change of attitude is well reflected in the fact that the Epsom proprietors today (the Horserace Betting Levy Board) contribute £40,000 to the Derby stakes alone, out of the total prize money of £94,000.

In his *Blue Riband of the Turf*, Louis Curzon, in 1890, tore into the EGSA with unparalleled ferocity. 'Despite its wealth,' he wrote, 'it is the most niggardly racing corporation in the kingdom, and not only do they not give one shilling to the Derby or the Oaks, but not so long ago they had the impudence to make the winner of these races pay the salary of the judge and the police expenses for keeping the course, and also £50 for champagne.'

To get it straight, winning owners were required, from 1831, to pay £100 towards the salary of the judge – though for the whole of the meeting in 1847 we know the EGSA paid the judge only £10. In 1848 the Jockey Club decided that this sort of thing had gone on long enough, and issued this notice: 'The Jockey Club, having learned that it has been an ancient practice for winners of the great stakes to make presents to the Judge, are of the opinion that such practice is, in principle, objectionable, and that hereafter, a fixed sum should be paid out of certain large stakes, in lieu thereof, and that the Judge should be precluded from receiving any presents whatever from winners of races.' It resolved that the Derby winner should pay £50, and it was nearly twenty years later before it removed such an obligation from the winner and placed it entirely on the promoters of the meeting.

There is no doubt that towards the end of the 19th century, racehorse owners were so appalled by what Curzon called 'the avariciousness of the Epsom authorities', that serious representations were made to the Jockey Club to have those two races taken away from Epsom. At least, Curzon said, the Jockey Club should consider telling the EGSA how much money it must add to the stakes for those classics, and 'how they ought to be remodelled as to admit of the owners of horses obtaining something more than their own money from a company which was reputed to be making £20,000 or £30,000 per annum . . .'

His was not the only public suggestion that Epsom should be forced to surrender the most precious jewels in its crown. A much-respected racing journalist had written a year or two earlier that 'the Derby might flourish if it were not run at Epsom, and the funds derived from the various sources of revenue were devoted to other uses than the enrichment of the persons who own the grandstand and lease the racecourse'. He could not see why 'the gentlemen of England' should subscribe some £10,000 in entry fees, to be competed for on Epsom Downs so that the members of the EGSA should grow fatter. Meanwhile, as the sniping went on, the Association quietly and relentlessly pursued its policy of land-grabbing.

The whole history of the racecourse, reduced to a line, is a wide-screen spectacular of land-grabbing. What else could it have been, when nothing but the acquisition of land would allow the full potential of the Downs to be exploited for racing? One's interpretation of the situation depends largely on one's point of view: did the EGSA consist of baddies cheating the public out of their historic rights, or goodies fighting giant landlords for territory so that the public could be entertained and occasionally rewarded?

So on and on the EGSA went, grabbing where it could, and occasionally holding back for fear of antagonizing the locals. In 1887, for instance, the committee felt it could not accede to H. M. Dorling's recommendation to fence the course 'as they feel it would tend to exasperate the crowd and perhaps cause a riot if the public were excluded from a privilege which they have always enjoyed'. A few months later it did agree to 140 yards of iron railings along the course, opposite the grandstand.

In 1886, an October meeting had been re-introduced after a

break of about 50 years, but again it was not a success, and only lasted three years. Profits for 1886–7 were more than £13,000 – rather less than Curzon thought, but 'satisfactory in the face of keen competition, unfavourable weather, and the acknowledged badness of the times' (this was the time of Gladstone's third and briefest administration, defeated over the Irish Home Rule Bill, which split the Liberal Party; of the early stirrings of George Bernard Shaw and the Fabian Society; of Jack the Ripper; and of 'Bloody Sunday', when there were more than a hundred casualties in a Trafalgar Square battle between police and public).

John Barnard was still a member of the committee, but did not attend in December, but he sent a cheque for £50 as his donation to the race fund of the autumn meeting. The committee responded by expressing its regret that he could not see his way to sending a larger amount. In 1890, he resigned from the committee, and offered to take again a lease of the non-racing Epsom land (held by the Association at £2,500 a year) for 5 or 10 years at £2,800 a year. The committee regarded the offer as inadequate. Barnard offered £3,300 a year for 3 years, but this, too, was turned down. The only settlement reached between them was for him to take Barnard's and Langland's stands, either side of the grandstand, at £2,400 for only a year.

By then Dorling had made his massive pounce on the Walton estate. Mrs Susan Padwick had died in 1886, leaving the bulk of the family fortunes to her son Henry. Two years later he sold to Dorling, for the Association, '205 acres of boldly undulating land including the famous galloping or training ground for flat races distinguished as Six Mile Hill and a portion of the Derby Racecourse adjacent to the far-famed Tattenham Corner.' It saved the Association a rent of £1,000 a year, but cost it £20,000.

It was at about this time that two substantial legal actions for encroachment were taken against the Association and the Lord of the Manor of Epsom. Messrs Horne and Birkett took theirs against the EGSA and Strange; Messrs Buller and Jay against Strange and the EGSA. Both pairs of plaintiffs had similar grudges, both believed they were acting for their fellows. Buller and Jay seemed the most effective and implacable, and organized some influential opposition to the Association, which became known as the Buller committee. They alleged that by the running of horse races on the Downs, by the building of the grandstand and its recent extension, the Club stand, and by the granting of land for shooting to the army, there was an illegal interference with the commoners rights to walk, ride, and exercise their sheep thereon.

The Association pointed out that, apart from the short-lived autumn meeting, racing took place on only six days in the year; that the right of the public, if it existed, was simply a right of passage, and that there were still several points at which the public's passage across the course was unimpeded; that the railing along the course was high enough to allow sheep to graze beneath it; that the EGSA now contributed a fifth of the entire rates of the parish; and that such activities as it pursued over the common lands of Epsom were by the permission and the licence of the Lord of the Manor. Though the papers in the cases were presented to the High Court, neither appears to have been tried.

The objection of Epsom residents in general was not so much to any interference with commoner's rights, but – as it still is – to the noise, mess, damage, and general chaos caused by those who attended the races. The worst complaints were against the nuisance caused by the 'gipsies and other vagrants' on what was known as 'Show-Out Sunday' – the Sunday before Derby week. This was without doubt a day of riotous assembly and disorderly scenes took place on the Downs and elsewhere, and it was largely to control and suppress such carryings-on that the Association took from Mr Strange in 1890 a lease of the whole of Epsom Downs, with the exception of the Downs Hotel, still occupied by Strange's tenant.

This was granted for 29 years at £2,595 a year. The lease would expire, as would all other leases held by the EGSA from the Lord of the Manor of Epsom, in 1918. Negotiations immediately commenced for a fresh lease to cover all the Epsom land that the EGSA used, and it was hoped that Strange would grant this in 1902 for 106 years at a rent of £3,000 a year, and for the somewhat staggering premium of £25,000. Meanwhile, the lease of the Downs enabled the committee to take resolute action 'to the great satisfaction of the inhabitants of Epsom'.

The ground would be let for the purpose of erecting refreshment booths only, it announced in the local press: 'No illegal betting or unlawful games will be permitted on any part of the Downs, and notice is further given that during Sunday, the first day of June 1890, being the Sunday next before the Derby and commonly called or known as Show-Out Sunday, no roundabouts, swings, steam engines, rifle galleries, circus displays, nor any objectionable or noisy trade or business whatsoever will be allowed . . .'

The purchase of Six Mile Hill allowed the Association to get more order into the matter of training charges. Henry Dorling, shortly before his death, had instituted an annual charge of a guinea to all trainers using Epsom Downs. The leading local trainer, John Nightingale, then took Six Mile Hill for £140 a year plus the cost to the Association of keeping the turf in order; another trainer, John Jones, had training rights on Epsom manor land under a £10-a-year agreement with Strange. After Nightingale's death in 1891, by which time the EGSA had the lease of the Downs, the Association gave Jones notice for not fulfilling his covenants (to 'quit and peaceably and quietly leave surrender and yield up unto them . . .'), and devised a new plan for use of the training gallops.

The fixed rent would remain at £140 and £10 plus costs, and all dues would be apportioned among trainers *pro rata* according to the average number of horses from each trainer's stable using the exercise grounds during the previous quarter. It was a mutual agreement, but there were always some trainers who objected strongly enough to refuse to pay their share. One of the first of these was E. Sawrey Cookson, who declined to pay £9 14s on the grounds that he was as entitled as any Epsom man to ride horses on the Downs: the court found for the Association with costs, agreeing with it that no rights existed which permitted damage to, or destruction of, the turf – an inevitable consequence of training race horses there. Some years later, the EGSA obtained an injunction preventing another trainer from exercising his horses on the Downs: it did not apply for costs as he had no visible means of paying them. Shortly after the case against Cookson, incidentally, the committee noted that 'considerable damage has been recently done to the furzes on Six Mile Hill by some evilly disposed person or persons'.

Occasionally there were, and still are, private individuals passionate and determined enough to take a stand against authority for what they believe to be their rights on Epsom Downs. One of the most tenacious and energetic of these was, in 1892, 'a person named Applegarth', who claimed that none could stop him taking exercise on the Downs whenever he chose, and none could force him to pay for such a right. In support of his stand he obtained most favourable opinions from three extremely influential local residents: Lord Rosebery, by then the owner of Durdans and, as such, in the process of a considerable private quarrel with the Association himself; the Attorney-General, Lord Russell; and Mr T. T. Buckwill, QC, MP.

'It seems to me,' wrote Russell, 'that if the Grand Stand Association do not take care, they will raise many questions about their own uses of the Downs which it is in their interests to let sleep.'

Buckwill was more forthright: 'I have never heard of such a right on their part, or on the part of the Lord of the Manor, to prevent persons riding all over the Downs. If the Association attempt to prevent you riding over the Downs by treating you as a trespasser, I shall be very glad to subscribe towards the expenses of fighting the question, and I have no doubt that many others will do the same.'

Applegarth, with such support, was entitled to feel smug: 'Fortunately these gentlemen reside in the neighbourhood and occasionally use the Downs themselves,' he wrote to the EGSA. 'I suppose after the opinions I have forwarded to you, those like myself may take their healthful exercise without being troubled about the question of right, and left to subscribe voluntarily if they feel disposed to do so.'

The committee was sufficiently put out to send him a solicitor's letter, giving him notice not to ride on the Downs again: 'The Grand Stand Association have never done, and have no intention of doing, anything to prevent the public at large using the Downs in a reasonable manner for the purpose of exercise or recreation, but the Association cannot admit that any persons have a right to gallop horses on Walton Downs (of which they are the owners), or Epsom Downs (of which they are the lessees), when and while they please, and the objection of the Association applies with greater force if the persons riding or driving across the turf do damage to it by cutting it up.

'Permission is given the Epsom trainers to use the Downs for training racehorses, and these persons contribute towards the repairing of those parts of the turf which they use, and those only. Our clients consider you are attempting to raise a false issue in the minds of the Local Board (of Health) and the public. They say you were upon Walton Downs, using the part set apart for gallops, almost daily in the autumn, and your case is totally different from that of persons who ride across the Downs occasionally, and with whom the Grand Stand Association do not wish to interfere in the slightest degree.'

By then, the 21-year lease that the Association had taken on the Durdans paddock had expired. Rosebery followed the Heathcotes there, and in 1892 the Association took the lease for one more year at his figure of £1,200, with free use of balcony box number one. By the end of the year, the committee informed him that it was not disposed to renew the tenancy on the same terms, and sent Dorling to negotiate. Rosebery expressed apparent unconcern as to whether the Association rented the paddock or not, but if it did, it would be on the same terms as before. If it did not, and instead tried to make a new saddling paddock nearer the grandstand, the Earl warned Dorling he would oppose any such further encroachment on the Downs, and if it were intended he would again join the Buller committee.

It was, reported the outraged Dorling, 'a distinct threat to do all the harm in his power'. Rosebery also made it plain that if the Association did not renew the lease of the paddock, he would build a wall round it and return it to his park, and that would be the end of the matter.

A fairly tense correspondence ensued, to which the customary civilities were nevertheless appended ('Believe me, Yours truly, Rosebery.' 'I am, Dear Sir, Your obedient Servant, H. M. Dorling'). At the end of it the committee offered to take the paddock outright for 26 years, and Rosebery insisted on optional clauses. The EGSA had to agree.

With Applegarth, Cookson, and Rosebery, 1892–3 was not a happy year at Epsom. But more ominously, the profits, which had risen to £18,000 in 1892, dropped sharply a year later. 'Not to be wondered at,' commented Dorling gloomily, 'considering the great depression in trade that has existed for some time.' In the past five years, in Europe as well as in Britain, the rumblings of a suppressed and totally discontented majority had broken out in a few ugly snarls. The London dockers went on strike, for a month, to get sixpence an hour; London busmen struck, till their employers agreed to allow them only a twelve-hour day; there was a national mining strike; Keir Hardie reached Parliament. While wages were slowly rising, prices were fast falling, as Britain was hit by competition from both the Continent and America.

By now, too, Sandown Park (1875) and Kempton Park (1878) had joined Ascot in providing hefty competition for Epsom. The Derby, the Oaks, and the City and Suburban were unlikely to suffer, but Dorling warned shareholders that it would be necessary 'to keep up the high character of the sport by liberality in the way of added money, even if it should ultimately be at the expense of the dividend'. The Derby then offered 5,000 sovereigns to the winner, and the Oaks 4,000, to which the Association was, at last, contributing a little. As Curzon grudgingly put it in 1890: 'This year, impelled no doubt by the force of public opinion, the authorities at Epsom have so far accommodated themselves to the spirit of the times as to have ventured on a new departure in respect of the monetary and other considerations which shall in future govern the great race.' One would not say he was entirely satisfied, since he concludes his chapter on the financial situation at Epsom thus: 'The persons who derive so great a profit from the Derby and the Oaks should be compelled to disgorge a larger portion of it than they seem inclined, to those who in reality provide the sport.'

Another boom was on the way, but while fortunes were low the committee was glad to pick up a little extra where it could. It took £2,000 out of the bank and lent it to the Epsom Rural District Council at 3½ per cent, let the Prince's Stand for one year at £78, the Old Stewards' Stand for one year at £250, and accepted a tender of £750 for the right to run the grandstand wine cellars and supply refreshments. After the death of John Barnard in 1894, it kept the land he had leased, but let the plots beside the stand to W. G. Langlands for £1,000 a year. E. J. Dorling died in 1896 (to be succeeded on the committee by Walter Dorling), leaving H. M. the sole, undisputed, and majestic boss of every aspect of the racecourse.

He was instantly confronted with a small problem that exposed his worst faults and landed the Association in a petty and most unfortunate court case, in which it was successfully sued for breach of contract. The plaintiff, a Mr F. G. Haines, had paid for admission to the stand on the first day of Derby week, and later bought another ticket, for £2, which entitled him to enter the reserved lawn (in front of the stand) on the four days of the meeting. He put the second ticket in the lining of his hat, but on the next day – Derby day – found that he had put on a different hat.

Haines explained his predicament, but was refused admission. He bought another ticket for the lawn, and on the third day brought both of them to the grandstand and asked for his money to be refunded on one of them. The request was refused. Dorling, regarding the matter as a test case, pointed out that among the conditions in small print on the back of the ticket was one that under no circumstances would any application for the return of admission money to the reserved lawn be entertained.

It may have been petty, but the judge was puzzled. There was no law which precisely governed the dispute, and he could not find any precedent to guide him. The defendants were no doubt justified in making Mr Haines pay for another ticket on the second day, but not, he thought, in refusing to return his second £2 when he produced both tickets. He found for the plaintiff and added a wounding rider: Mr Haines had been known at Epsom for twenty years, and was a man in every way above suspicion; having regard to all the facts, the Association, in making him sue for the return of £2, had behaved in a very unsportsmanlike way.

The Association could not afford the slur on its reputation, but it could afford the costs. Prices were rising, owners of capital growing fat again, and the profit at Epsom that year was £18,000. The committee voted itself an extra £500 bonus, and recommended a dividend of £3 15s on each original £20 share. By the end of the century, the annual profit was up to nearly £24,000, the reserve fund had risen to £28,000, and the committee felt able to make an examination of the basement and roof of the grandstand 'with a view to an installation of Electric Light'. The Epsom Urban District Council was asked in 1901 to quote for the supply of sufficient electricity for 200 lights of sixteen candle power, and to work a passenger lift, which it proposed to instal in the Club Stand for the use of the king and queen. The lift cost only £388, but the Association had to pay the Council £1,675 to lay on the electricity.

The royal lift was sure to be well used. With Edward VII newly on the throne, the Derby, at least, was certain to receive his attention – he had, after all, won the race as an owner twice in the previous four years. In 1896, in what *Racing Illustrated* described as the most memorable Derby of modern times, the Prince of Wales had entered Persimmon. This was a remarkably impressive but somewhat unpredictable horse, whose form had been so disappointing a little earlier in the year that it had had to be scratched from the 2,000 Guineas.

Persimmon was trained, with the rest of the royal stable, by Richard Marsh at Newmarket, who described the animal as the best he had ever had. In more specific detail: 'Behind the saddle he was indeed wonderful in the remarkable length from hip to hock, and from hip to the round bone. I should be correct in saying that he was just a trifle slack in his back ribs, but he girthed rare and well.' Marsh had to travel in the horse box with his temperamental treasure all the way from Newmarket.

Prince Edward brought another large royal party to Epsom – five princes and princesses, five dukes and duchesses – on a day that was gloomily overcast until shortly before the Derby. Even if it had been pouring, the rain would have made little impression on the crowd's burning enthusiasm; Persimmon won at 5–1, beating the odds-on favourite by a neck. The racegoers went mad with delight.

In due course, the news reached the old Queen at Balmoral. She sent her son a telegram to Epsom, to which he replied: 'Most grateful for your kind congratulations. The scene after the Derby was a most remarkable and gratifying sight. Albert Edward.' Marsh, for his pains, received a bonus of £500.

Nor was that all that was memorable about this Derby. Though *Racing Illustrated* did not mention it, the race was filmed, and was shown that night to an amazed and wildly jubilant audience at the Alhambra Theatre, Leicester Square. Their enthusiasm was such that they demanded, and got, a second showing, and then a third, of the historic event. The Prince was present, and his delighted supporters filled in the long minutes of re-winding by hearty renditions of *God Bless the Prince of Wales*.

Four years later, it was the turn of Diamond Jubilee, a horse so wildly-behaved that only one young and inexperienced jockey, Herbert Jones, was able to manage it. With Jones up, Diamond Jubilee won the 2,000 Guineas, started at 6–4 in the Derby and won it by half a length. The crowd were so moved that the national anthem swelled spontaneously over the Downs. The news, when it reached South Africa, was said to have greatly heartened the loyal participants in the Boer War.

Within months, Edward was on the throne, but his involvement in racing did not decline. He won the Derby again in 1909, with Minoru, and continued to give a tremendous boost to a sport which, at that time, was far from being accepted in the middle-class circles. On his death, a contemporary racing journalist wrote of 'the Herculean pillar lost to our manly pastime, against which, if I am not mistaken, the irons will be heated again to burn holes in its structure and existence'.

As well as paying for 'the Electric Light', there was enough in the kitty at Epsom at the dawn of the century to take out the new lease on all the Epsom Manor land used by the Association. At a rent of £3,354 a year, it was to run for 106 years from 29th September, 1902 – with that initial payment to Mr Strange of £25,000. This gave the EGSA, for the first time, the control of Epsom Downs and (almost) everything on it – including the Stewards' Stand, the Prince's Stand, and the Downs Hotel. For himself and the Clerk of the Course (*his* Clerk, as the lease makes clear), the Lord of the Manor reserved free use of offices in the grandstand and right of way to the paddock; for himself, 'certain sporting rights' on the Downs, and a grandstand box for ten.

The Association was bound to hold races on no more than six days a year, in not more than two meetings, not to enclose the gallops, to maintain the Downs in good order, and to continue to provide free space for spectators on foot on the south side of the course. The Tattenham Corner enclosure known as Epsom Gate was to remain freely available during race meetings to 'any and every person (either with or without a carriage or other vehicle) who may be a freehold or copyhold tenant or commoner of the Manor of Epsom'.

The existing buildings, to which the Association was not allowed to add without Strange's permission, were covered by the usual painting and good repair clauses. The lease ends with three or four pages on the massive question of what was to happen if, by order of the Jockey Club, racing was to be stopped at Epsom, or reduced below six days a year. Those clauses were to be invoked all too soon, with the outbreak of the Great War.

(Rather curiously, though beyond the scope of this story, James Strange, in 1906, mortgaged the freehold of all the land that he had leased to the Association, for the sum of only £1,500. The mortgage was not lifted until 1911, three years after his death. Economists and accountants may understand this better than historians.)

The profits of the Association thereupon – and quite irrelevantly – went into a disastrous slump, falling from the £24,000 of 1899 (at which the rateable value of the property rose to £14,500) to £15,000 in 1902, £14,000 in 1903, and £10,000 in 1904, the year the Association was registered as a limited company. At the same time, the money guaranteed for prizes was rising almost as fast, and reached £28,600 in 1904 – when the Derby was guaranteed £7,100 with £2,480 added.

At this stage, a third Dorling (another Henry) joined the committee, giving the family a majority vote. He resigned five years later, to be replaced by Edward Earle Dorling: at the annual meeting confirming his appointment, another two Dorlings were present, Francis and Lionel. Henry Mayson Dorling was still carrying on the printing business, and doing so well with the race cards that he volunteered, in 1904 to pay the EGSA £200 a year from the profit they brought him.

In 1906, the shareholders heard of the plight of the family of George Moore, their Downs foreman. He had died suddenly, leaving a widow and daughter 'who by reason of bodily affliction were unable to support themselves'. The chairman was authorized to apply the sum of ten shillings a week to their benefit 'so long as he considered it necessary to do so'. The next business was to give hearty thanks to the five members of the committee for their hard work during the year, and a bonus of £500 for their benefit. Six months later, the committee heard of an accident to one of their labourers, George Cates, as a result of which his right arm would be permanently disabled and he would be unable to work any more. The chairman arranged with Cates to accept a sum of

£62 8s in full satisfaction of any claim which he might have under the Labourers' Compensation Act.

At about this time, the EGSA lost another court battle, one of the oddest ever to arise from a race meeting, and Epsom's most celebrated case since Lord George Bentinck unmasked the ringer sixty years earlier. The judges were again the stewards of the Jockey Club, the matter before them was the sale of a horse named Star of Malta. The three-year-old filly was entered in a selling plate, the Horton Handicap, at Epsom in June 1904. The idea of such events is that the runners are sold by auction after the race, the owner receiving his asking price, if it is reached, and the racecourse authority receiving the difference between that and the sale price.

Star of Malta, which was owned by a Mr William Stevens, won the Horton, and was bought by James Hickey for 310 guineas. Stevens handed the horse over to Hickey, though the Epsom executive had not at the time received the money, nor did it ever. Shortly afterwards Hickey was certified insane. He claimed to have bought the horse as an agent for Spencer Gollan, to whom he had delivered it. Gollan admitted possession, but denied that Hickey had any authority to buy for him.

William Stevens, meanwhile, had died. His widow, two years after the race, was without either horse or money. Epsom could not give her back the animal, since her husband had given it to someone else, and declined to give her the £100, since it had never had it. It was May 1908, four years after the race, before the Jockey Club pronounced that the EGSA must pay up.

Despite the ups and downs of financial fortune, the Association's policy of acquisition and expansion under H. M. Dorling proceeded inexorably. It was now paying £100 a year for a long narrow strip of land south-east of Tattenham Corner, which it was able to add to the racecourse and along the boundary of which the owner insisted they erected 'an unclimbable iron railing'. In 1910 came another burst of buying and building: two lavatories under Barnard's Stand; 37 acres of Walton land from the Earl of Egmont, for 14 years at £45 a year; and The Warren, the hunting box with a 25-acre estate built in 1666 by Charles II on the south side of Epsom Downs. It included the original Derby saddling paddock, and the freehold cost the Association £9,000.

The following year it nibbled away another piece of Walton: three acres bought from Lady Russell, widow of the former Lord Chief Justice, for £200; and acquired a 14-year lease of a training gallop off Epsom Lane for £10 a year. The Association now had so much land on the Walton side of the course that it had to build a cottage for a bailiff over there. The slump, however, was over. Profits were back to over £20,000 by 1912, with better to come, and the Association went ahead with its plans for what is still known on the course as the Great War building – the rectangular lump at the back of the grandstand. It was to contain, basically, dining-rooms, kitchens, and dormitories for temporary staff and stable employees. At the end of the year a tender of £14,000 was accepted, and building was completed in six months.

We have just passed a Derby that must be recorded, and we are about to come to one that will never be forgotten. Both, oddly enough, involved King George V – the first only insofar as it was held on the day of his coronation in 1911 (when his granddaughter's turn came, the Derby moved to a Saturday to avoid it).

The Derby favourite that year was Sunstar, which had reached 6–4 when, the week before the race, it strained a ligament and went lame. The trainer, Charles Morton, told the owner that the leg was so swollen that it would be impossible for the horse to run: if it did, it would never run again. Jack Joel, the South African millionaire who owned Sunstar, mindful of the vast amount of public money and interest in the horse (and perhaps of his own as well) ordered Morton to get the horse to the post and run it. Morton wrapped the injury in cabbage leaves, inducing a heavy sweat, reduced the swelling and got the horse to the post. Such was the secrecy of the operation that the odds had only lengthened to 13–8. Sunstar ran, and won, but never ran again.

With no knowledge of the international disasters that were to come so swiftly and so tragically, all would have seemed exceptionally rosy on the Downs in 1913, but for the sensational tragedy that marred the Derby that year – still perhaps the most shocking and best-remembered incident in the history of British racing.

As the field, by then considerably spread, thundered round Tattenham Corner, a woman stepped out from the crowd at the rails into the path of the horses and was knocked down by Anmer, King George V's runner. More than that cannot be absolutely certain, as the incident happened so suddenly that accounts by spectators and even the jockey – Herbert Jones, who later won on Diamond Jubilee for Edward VIII – were confused and often contradictory. Some say she placed herself in front of the King's horse with her hands above her head; some said she seized the reins. The horse fell, turned head over heels, and rolled with the jockey underneath. Anmer was not much hurt, and quickly sprang up again. As one of Jones's feet was still caught in the stirrup, he was dragged a few yards along the course. He was picked up unconscious and taken by ambulance to the Jockeys' Room, where it was found the door was too narrow to admit a stretcher. He was left outside until he could be taken to hospital.

His injuries were found to be not serious, but the woman never recovered consciousness. She was later identified as Emily Wilding Davidson, a militant member of the Women's Social and Political Union, whose colours she wore round her waist. Her history of exhibitionist law-breaking was extravagant, and it was this that soon caused the tragedy to be regarded as an attempt by a desperate woman to draw attention to the suffragette cause. She had been imprisoned six times: for causing a disturbance, throwing stones in Manchester and in Radcliffe, breaking a window in the House of Commons, setting fire to pillar boxes in Westminster, and finally for assaulting, in Aberdeen, a Baptist minister whom she mistook for Lloyd George. Each sentence was ended after a few days, since Miss Davidson always refused to eat in prison.

She died in Epsom hospital the following Sunday, a martyr to the cause of democratic rights for women. Her actual hopes and intentions at Tattenham Corner were never proved, but popular history has it that she flung herself to death under the hooves of the King's horse. This at least can be disproved. One man, near her in the crowd, thought that she was trying to cross the course, seeing a considerable break in the runners, and was appalled to find more were coming. Herbert Jones himself spoke of the look of horror on the woman's face.

It is certainly unlikely that she could have picked out the King's horse deliberately, perhaps the aspect of the incident that ensured its survival in history. On all the evidence that is now available, one tends to think the act was deliberate, but only insofar as she hoped to disrupt the Derby by forcing a horse out of the race. She perhaps saw herself hanging on to the bridle till the horse stopped, then herself leading it down the finishing straight, in front of the grandstand and the royal box: complete domination, supreme exposure. Understandably, public sympathy reached out to her, but though Queen Alexandra sent a messenger to the hospital, Miss Davidson did not seem to have concerned the King much.

In his private diary that night he wrote: 'As the horses were coming round Tattenham Corner, a Suffragette (Miss Davidson) dashed out and tried to catch Anmer's bridle. Of course she was knocked down and seriously injured, and poor Herbert Jones and Anmer were sent flying. Jones unconscious, badly cut, broken rib and slight concussion; a most regrettable, scandalous proceeding.'

By extraordinary coincidence, it was not the only scandal of the race. In the grandstand, where the occupants were not aware of anything more than some sort of disturbance at Tattenham Corner, they were much more concerned with the finish of the race. Craganour, the favourite, passed the post first, but an objection was immediately lodged by the rider of the second horse, Aboyeur, a horse considered so little worthy of serious attention that it started at 100–1. The stewards found that Craganour 'did not keep a straight course', and the horse was disqualified. Though the crowds on the Downs were greater than ever before, it was, as King George recorded, a disastrous Derby.

CHAPTER TWELVE

The big buy

The outbreak of war did not immediately bring racing at Epsom to an end. Its first effect was negligible: the War Department hired one room in the bailiff's cottage near Tattenham Corner for ten shillings a week; its second, in February 1915, was that the EGSA agreed to let the new building be used as a war hospital, without charge, on the rather odd condition that three floors must be vacated during race meetings. There seems to be no record as to whether or not the temporary evacuation involved patients, but the news of it caused considerable ill-feeling within and without racing circles. Among those who believed that wounded soldiers were going to suffer for the benefit of the Association was the Duke of Portland, whose public condemnation of the suggestion produced fire and fury from the Earl of Durham at the next meeting of the Jockey Club: 'He accepted, or hypnotized himself into believing, that the Stewards of the Jockey Club and the Stewards of Epsom, and the racing community in general, would commit the unspeakable atrocity of ill-treating wounded soldiers because they were interfering with the ordinary usages of portions of racecourses. Without any inquiry and without any evidence he wrote a letter to *The Times* maligning the upholders of a sport from which he had derived almost unexampled success and benefit.' The Duke was indeed a winning owner of great substance, with one Derby under his belt. In spite of his and other objections, the two-day meeting was held in April as usual. Exactly a month later the Stewards of the Jockey Club cancelled all meetings, except Newmarket, for the rest of the year. Epsom went out of business for the first time, and though the continuity of the Derby was somewhat unsatisfactorily preserved by running it at Newmarket (where Steve Donoghue had two of his six wins), it brought no credit to the Association. By the end of the year it was in court again, sued by the Lord of the Manor's widow for arrears of rent of £2,604.

The terms of the lease were that £750 of the rent had to be paid on 25th March, each year, and the remainder of the £3,354

E   125 on 24th June. It was agreed that if racing were cancelled by the stewards after the spring meeting and before the summer one, the Association should pay only £750, providing it gave not less than one month's notice.

The summer meeting had been called on 20th May, 1915, only three weeks before the races were due, but the Association declined to pay the full balance. The High Court ordered it to do so, and to pay the costs of the case; the plaintiffs agreed to accept only half the rent as long as racing was suspended. It was a bad year for the EGSA; which lost £3,600, and, by mid-summer of 1918, its losses totalled £10,500 – more than £8,000 of it had gone to Mrs Strange, and most of the remainder in ground rent to its other landlords.

Within a year of the cancellation of racing, it had taken out bank loans of £5,000, but even this was not sufficient to meet its obligations. H. M. Dorling advanced a further £500 (at 6½ per cent), but, by summer 1917, it had to think about selling some of its assets. The most immediately negotiable was the wine stock, worth nearly £1,700, and this was disposed of in June.

A year later the Association was broke again; Dorling lent £1,000 (at eight per cent), and arranged for a further £1,000, on the same terms, from a Mr Ralph Dennis. The chairman then proposed Mr Dennis's election to the committee. There was unanimous agreement.

Unusual activity was meanwhile taking place on the Downs. In July, 1916, the Army set up camp south-east of Tattenham Corner station. In August, the Association caught a man cutting grass on the Downs and prosecuted him: he was fined £1 and ordered to pay £1 for the damage. The following May, at the same time that the Army took over the grandstand, the Board of Agriculture and Fisheries wrote to ask that the Epsom Golf Club (who had played on EGSA-leased land near Epsom Downs station since 1893) should give up its course to hay. Charles Oughton, the Association's secretary, replied that it could not co-operate, firstly because of the copyholders' right to graze sheep on the manorial waste, and secondly because the Army was using part of the golf course for machine-gun training.

Later that year the War Agricultural Executive ordered the Association to break up 68 acres of Walton land for cultivation. Dorling lost his appeal, and then wrote to say that since the Association had no funds, no labour, and no instruments, it had no means of complying with the order. The land was therefore taken over by the Surrey Agricultural Committee, who immediately began cultivation. After a while the EGSA committee realized they were throwing away a natural asset and, like the wicked man two years earlier, it cut the grass – though to do so it had to buy a two-horse mowing machine.

The Association's buildings were by this time insured for an annual premium of £2 os 6d against 'destruction or damage directly or indirectly by Aerial Craft (hostile or otherwise) or Shots Shells Bombs or Missiles from or used against Aerial Craft'. Surprisingly enough, there was no damage.

Racing returned in 1919 with a glorious swoop; within two years the Association had made a profit of £63,000, an increase of 50 per cent on the last two pre-war years. Attendance at the spring meeting, however, was far from being a record, despite the war break. On the Sunday before the meeting, several inches of snow lay over the Downs, and there were still patches on the course when racing began in cold, windy, and overcast conditions. *The Times* reporter noted that probably no living person had ever before seen snow on the course during a meeting (a false assumption, since, though it had been 80 years since snow fell during the Derby, it was falling shortly before the race in 1867 – and that was in June, not April), and it so displeased the Jockey Club that Dorling, as Clerk of the Course, was fined £50 for not clearing it away. (He had also been fined in 1882, when a piece of paper blew on to the course and caused a horse to shy.)

Despite the fact that cars had largely replaced donkeys as the basic means of transport to the Downs, the cheerless weather kept most people at home. *The Times* man commented that there were more people in the grandstand in 1914, and he had seen more in the paddock at Sandown during the winter in a snow-storm. Tattenham Corner was deserted 'but for less than a dozen cars, two bookmakers, and a man, with an undisguised face, playing a banjo'.

No doubt many decided to save themselves for a splendid outing to what was being called the Peace Derby. Unfortunately, it rained on and off for much of the day, and the crowd, though immense, was not as dense as had been anticipated. People were, however, determined to celebrate, and, despite the rain, thousands of them thought that for such an occasion umbrellas and coats would be inappropriate. It was also a full-blooded royal occasion. King George and Queen Mary brought their three eldest children: the Prince of Wales, then 25; Prince Albert, later Duke of York; and Princess Mary, later Countess of Harewood. Henry (Duke of Gloucester) and George (Duke of Kent) were still in their teens, and their father was not one to allow them days off school; their youngest child, John, was incurably ill and died a few months later. The royal party travelled by train from Victoria to Epsom Downs station and drove in three carriages to the course, where it met the king's uncle, the Duke of Connaught.

Though it had been 80 years since the line was first opened to the Downs, rail travel for the commoners – even the first-class travellers among them – was not always an attractive experience. The racing writer F. H. Bayles, after one of his journeys to Epsom, put pen firmly to paper: 'It is simply abominable to experience the coercion that is imposed . . . in their excess rates, not to speak of the disgraceful time that is generally occupied in travelling twelve or fifteen miles, and the undesirable element that is tolerated to gather on the platforms at every meeting.'

Accommodation in the town was scarce, and many occupants vacated their houses for the week since a good profit could be made by letting them to racegoers. The local council tarred most of the roads leading to the Downs in order to reduce the dust that usually rose in suffocating clouds on race days – it was one hazard that few can now remember; that it was real and ghastly is demonstrated by the fact that, on this occasion, Epsom council arranged for a supply of water pails and soap to be placed along the main racecourse routes to prevent pedestrians washing in the horse troughs and thus defiling the water for the horses.

Although the favourite faded, with Donoghue up, and came only third, it was a happy day, and a surprisingly well-behaved one. The magistrates only dealt with 26 charges – including one for 'Welshing', fourteen for playing at crown and anchor, but none for drunkenness.

It was to be Henry Mayson Dorling's last Derby. He had been Clerk of the Course for nearly half a century, and it was 33 years since his appointment as the Association's joint managing director. He was, by now, 84 and on 6th November 1919, Walter Dorling reported to the committee that H. M. Dorling was very seriously ill. His condition was critical for a week before he died. It was as if the grandstand itself had fallen. He was without question a most remarkable man, with a great independence of mind and an obstinate refusal to be swayed by criticism that often made him difficult to work with.

Even his family agreed that, to outsiders, he was not a very likeable man, never going out of his way to be pleasant to people. His nephew, in a biography of his uncle, quoted H. M.'s proud boast: 'Everyone hates me, and I like it.'

His death meant the total reshaping of the committee of management, one by-product of which was that the committee minutes – for nearly half a century sparse and often non-existent beyond recording time, date, and list of attenders – suddenly flowered into comparative models of their kind. For the first time in 15 years, the Dorlings were not in a majority, though the two that remained retained a great deal of power.

Walter and Edward Dorling, respectively step-brother and nephew of H. M., became joint managers of the Association at a salary of £600 each. The appointment of Edward Earle Dorling was remarkable; he was not only a schoolmaster, but a minor canon of Salisbury Cathedral and lately curate at Ham Common. Walter was also appointed joint Clerk of the Course with Walter Langlands (worth another £300 a year, plus fees), Charles Oughton, whose salary was raised to £300, joined the committee, which was completed by the wealthy Mr Dennis and Mr R. G. Pulleyn as chairman.

It was soon clear that there were two major objectives for the new management: the acquisition of the freehold of Epsom Downs (already held on a 106-year lease), and the rebuilding of the grandstand, now 90 years old and quite inadequate for current needs. Lord Rosebery was no more co-operative about the paddock than he had been with H. M. Dorling, refusing to sell and limiting his leases to seven years at a time. With the ever-rising cost of the races – the Jockey Club suggested in 1920 that £3,000 should be added to the Derby stakes, and £2,000 to the Oaks – the grandstand's earning potential had to be increased if it was to survive as a profitable enterprise. Indeed, unless it could be improved there was some doubt as to how long racing would be allowed to continue with or without profit.

At the spring meeting in 1922, there were some protests at the grandstand about the unsatisfactory balance between the price of admission and the facilities offered. They led to an extremely critical report in the press, the cutting of which is still in the Association's possession, though its source is not recorded: 'Even with £2 to pay the stand on Derby day will be packed beyond reason and the enclosure impossible of penetration. I do not consider that £2 is an unfair charge, but I do think the Association ought to limit the number of people whom they allow into the enclosure and stand. It becomes robbery almost with violence to take £2 from people who arrive after the place is already filled. Theatrical managers do not do it, and the gates are often closed at professional football matches and at Lord's.'

Following this, the Association admitted, in a letter to the Strange trustees, that both the Jockey Club and the Epsom Urban District Council had warned that 'unless we make some alterations and improvements it is a serious question whether or not we do not lose the licence to run races at Epsom'. The man appointed to investigate the problem in detail was Charles Oughton, the first strong secretary the Association had had. Only seven months after his salary had been increased to £300, it was raised again, to £500.

In August 1924, he and Walter Dorling met the Jockey Club's Epsom stewards, and Oughton's summary of their plans – which depended on permission, from both the UDC and the Strange trustees, to put up additional permanent buildings – came down to these five points:

1. Remove Barnard's Stands (which had, since Barnard's death, belonged to the Association) to ground at the other, east, end of the grandstand, at that time let to Mr Langlands.
2. Build a new Club Stand where Barnard's was.
3. Extend the grandstand westwards over the present Club Stand and weighing rooms.
4. Replace Barnard's with a permanent stand.
5. Move the course 20 feet south, giving more room to the grandstand enclosure.

After obtaining the committee's approval, Oughton put the proposals to Mrs Strange thus: 'In view of the possibility that unless we carry them out, racing will no longer be allowed at Epsom, we submit that it is desirable that your Trustees consent to these improvements . . . My directors, in view of the large outlay that these improvements will cost, consider that a demand for an increase of rent by the Trustees of the late J. Strange would be fatal to the proposals . . . In the present critical position it is urgently necessary that both you and the Association should be unanimous in our endeavour to preserve Epsom Races. Our interests are identical.'

Mrs Strange's reply has sunk without trace, but it may have contained the first suggestion that the trustees would be willing to listen to proposals for the outright purchase of Epsom Downs. The possibility was certainly being thoroughly discussed within three months, and the first formal opening came from the Strange solicitor, Sir John Oakley, in February 1925 – at almost exactly the same moment that Stanley Wootton, a local landowning farmer, intimated that he would be interested in buying the gallops on Six Mile Hill, the former Walton Manor property, and leasing some of the gallops on Epsom Downs.

The committee immediately offered £55,000 for the Epsom Downs freehold, and asked Wootton for an offer for the Walton land: he bid £35,000. Less than 40 years earlier the Association had paid £20,000 for 205 acres of Walton, including Six Mile Hill and a slice of the racecourse. They promptly accepted Wootton's offer, for only 188 acres, and from that time he administered the training gallops as a commercial undertaking.

The committee's offer for Epsom Downs was not well received by Oakley. It was increased to £57,500, plus a grandstand box for life for Mrs Strange, and, by the summer, a sum of £58,000 was agreed. The land was conveyed to the Association in November 1925, its most important transaction since leasing that first acre almost a century earlier.

Despite the £35,000 from Mr Wootton, the EGSA – needing a huge sum for the new stand – had to mortgage all its Epsom properties to the National Provincial Bank, which thereupon agreed to provide such sums in future as the Association might from time to time require. When all the negotiations were completed, Edward Dorling wrote a glowing letter of thanks to Oughton, and asked that it should be placed on record.

The purchase of the Downs, he said, was 'the result of a very long series of negotiations carried through by you with great courage, and unfailing patience and tact, and a devotion to the best interests of the Association for which all shareholders, both now and in the future, will owe you an immense debt of gratitude. I am sure that, without your persistence and capacity, this matter would never have been brought to its triumphant conclusion.'

Walter Langlands had died in August 1924, and since then Walter Dorling had acted alone as Clerk of the Course. In December 1925 he died, thus leaving two places to fill: Charles Langlands was appointed Clerk, and Oughton became joint manager with Edward Dorling.

Now that the EGSA owned the freehold, it was able to abandon Oughton's schemes for shifting stands here and extending them there, and determined to build anew. It advertised its intentions, and received tenders ranging from £168,000 to £196,000 – something of a blow, since the Association was determined to keep the cost down to £100,000. However, it accepted the second cheapest, at £173,658, and its architects, in consultation with the builder, achieved a reduction of £50,000. By reducing the length of the main stand and increasing that of the simpler east stand, by cutting back on requirements for gas, electric light, and plumbing, the cost was further reduced to £113,078. However, through no fault of the contractor, this proved one of the most sensationally inaccurate estimates in British building history: the total cost, not finally reckoned until two years later, was nearly a quarter of a million pounds.

CHAPTER THIRTEEN

A ghastly monument

All the work on the stands, including demolition, had to be carried out between the end of the Derby meeting in 1926, and the opening of the spring meeting ten months later. It was planned that the first stage, the steel erections for the new Club Stand, would be started in July and that the builders would proceed eastwards so that the open stand would be completed by the end of November. But the General Strike in May was followed by a protracted and disastrous dispute in the coal mining industry, which was not resolved until late November, thus temporarily wrecking the British steel industry.

Precise specifications for girders soon became no more than a dream. The contractor scoured the country for any steel stocks that he might make use of. This involved material heavier than necessary, much of which was in uneconomic lengths and required acetylene cutting which caused wastage on the site; ultimately he had to turn to the Continent for supplies, with a consequent huge increase in transport costs.

This meant that the original schedule was abandoned, and work had to proceed on the two end stands at the same time, leaving the main stand till last. Four times the anticipated amount of erection machinery and plant had to be used at the site, and the work fell desperately behind. At the beginning of September the committee remarked on the slow rate of progress on the stand; by October the chairman noted that the advance did not seem all that could be desired.

The men were already working 'extraordinary and exceptional overtime', and unexpected charges were also piling up at Tattenham Corner railway station. The EGSA's specification had assured prospective contractors that the station was available for goods traffic, but when it came to negotiation, the Southern Railway Company was reluctant to allow the contractors to use the station at all, geared as it was to dealing with little more than the influx of passengers during two weeks of each year.

Not only could the railway company not deliver goods from

the station to the site, it proposed to charge the contractors rent for use of a crane (one that proved far too small to unload such heavy materials), rent for storage of materials between unloading and removal, and a percentage of the bill for the increased staff which the work necessitated.

By December 1926, the days were so short and the weather so bad that it was made clear to the committee the stands could only be completed in time if work went on day and night without interruption, and that would mean expense on a scale hitherto unparalleled. The committee had little choice but to authorize this and from then on, between 400 and 500 men worked round the clock, seven days a week. A hundred and fifty of them actually lived on the job, in the remains of the old stand, and it was there that Lord Lonsdale entertained more than three hundred of the workers to dinner in a splendid effort towards good industrial relations.

In January the steel erector alone estimated that his costs would rise ultimately by at least £40,000: even that proved insufficient and his account eventually amounted to £104,000 – only £9,000 less than the contractor's total estimate for the completed stands. (Long negotiations by the architects persuaded him to reduce that to £90,000 in June 1928, for 'a speedy cash settlement'. By the end of July the oustanding balance on the entire account was still £57,000 – more than a year after the work was finished. It was paid by the end of the year, and then the Association was faced with architects' fees of nearly £14,000, being six per cent of the new grandstand's cost of £232,188.)

It had long been apparent that the new stands could not be ready in time for the 1927 spring meeting, but an astounding effort did enable the building to accommodate 12,000 spectators for it. 'The new stands are as yet far from complete,' a reporter noted, 'but it is already obvious they will be really excellent when finished.' That happy moment could not have come closer to the deadline: carpenters, plasterers and painters were still at work on the evening before the Derby meeting, but all was well on the day – the largest if not the most handsome racecourse stand in Europe, was ready to receive its 20,000 visitors.

It is difficult to envisage any grandstand of economic size and structure that would not be an eyesore in that setting, and Epsom's grandstand is a ghastly monument to man's sense of values. It is only from within, looking out, that the stand feels magnificent, and only when thronged, teeming with the traffic of excited racegoers, that it is acceptable.

It should be recorded, however, that on 30th May, 1927, *The Times* reporter commented that, from the far side of the course, the new stand presented 'a bright and picturesque appearance', with its red roof, white concrete, and blue girders. He drew the public's attention to the fact that the most intense wind pressure hurling itself across the Downs and into the gaping mouth of the new stand need cause the occupants no alarm, as a careful analysis had been made of such stresses on the Forth Bridge over the past twenty years, and an ample margin of safety allowed in the strength of the Epsom structure.

The British Broadcasting Corporation had such faith in the stand that it permitted two of its men to be boxed up on its roof for the first radio commentary on the Derby: 'The race will be read by Mr Geoffrey Gilbey,' it announced, 'and Mr G. F. Allison will describe the scenes.' An early radio critic reported that 'the delay at the start was very well described and the details of the race itself were given with great clearness.' The transmission was relayed to listeners in South Africa with only 2 seconds' delay, and to Australia with only 3, but His Majesty's loyal subjects in China had to tap their heels for 51 seconds before the Derby commentary reached them.

The more elegant and less active members of the crowd on the course packed proudly into the new stands: more than a furlong of steel and concrete, from the open, single tier in the east, through the massive central stand, topped by 215 private boxes, each with its own bar and luncheon room, to the elite Club Stand in the west. Here the Queen's party can sit, twenty strong, at a 20-foot dining table, for lunch prepared in the adjacent royal kitchens and served by the royal staff; before advancing to view the races from the wide, flower-decked terrace.

Within range of an elegant nod were the Jockey Club box, the directors' box, and the gallery for trainers and the press. Below and immediately to royalty's left, there is now a glass-fronted box built onto the front of the main stand. Here the McAlpine suite outshines even Her Majesty's quarters. There is a private kitchen here, too, and a dining table to seat 35; an elegant withdrawing room; and a viewing lounge in which nobody has to stand: tiered, plush seating faces the course, fronted by electrically-operated windows.

Such refinements were not available in 1927. In fact, the lifts were not installed in time for the Derby meeting, and it is a very long climb to the top deck of boxes. Every step must have hurt members of the management committee all the more for the colossal bill they knew awaited them. It was paid, of course, leaving the Association with an overdraft of £145,000, half as much again as the bank had agreed to allow it.

At such times the committee's penny-watcher, Ralph Dennis, leaped into action. He had, some years earlier, drawn attention unsuccessfully to the high sum of money paid for the management of the grandstand, and, in 1927, he proposed that the managers' salaries should be reduced, but he found no seconder. In 1928, on discovering that the caretaker at the Warren Stables earned £2 15s a week, he proposed, and the commitee agreed, that the man's wages should be reduced to £1 15s, in addition to the occupation of a tied cottage. At the annual meeting in July neither Mr Dennis nor Arthur Read, who had succeeded Pulleyn as chairman, were re-elected to the committee by the shareholders.

The Association had meanwhile negotiated a loan of £140,000 in the city, but, at the end of the 1920s, its vast financial problems were compounded by another drop in profits: from £27,000 in 1928 to £21,500 in 1929 and £19,500 in 1930. Disaster struck with the Depression. The national financial crisis, which brought down Ramsay Macdonald's Labour government, led to the National Economy Act and a ten per cent cut in all salaries. The EGSA's profit in 1931 was only £12,500; in 1932, £5,500; and in 1933, £8,500.

On the eve of the Depression, the shareholders called for a special general meeting at which they received a report on the recent financial dealings of the Association, and considered its future policy. Their spokesman was a Mr Lewis E. van Moppes, a canny diamond merchant. The shareholders insisted that he was added to the committee, in exchange for which Mr van Moppes 'agreed not to raise other matters'. He remained on the committee – which almost immediately became the board of directors – for more than 40 years.

There was, however, more than its overdraft to worry the EGSA. Apart from a strong complaint in the press at the 'entire absence of any organized attempt to keep the Downs and the course clean' (Ascot apparently was like a new pin each morning, while Epsom grew, day by day, more like a garbage heap), two spectres had arisen that could not be ignored – the gipsies and the Council. Now that the freehold of Epsom Downs had passed into the hands of the Association, there was no public watchdog to safeguard the rights of the people – a role that the lords of the manor had hitherto played. From this time on, the local Urban District Council began to concern itself more with the EGSA's activities, and, for the most part, the Association did not welcome its interest. 40 years later an objective assessor was to repeat that relations between the two bodies 'had existed on a disturbed and bitter basis for many years'.

Until 1927, their skirmishes had largely been over the rates, which was the only direct benefit that the Council could derive from the presence of the grandstand and the existence of the Association. The councillors shared with most of the townspeople the general resentment against the chaos and upheaval caused by the race meetings in general, and the Derby in particular. 'Great care is taken by the Urban District Council to prevent infectious diseases from being imported into the town during the incursion of the unholy mob.' But now the UDC was poised for further action.

While the new stands were going up, the EGSA applied to the Ministry of Agriculture and Fisheries for permission to erect a large, two-sided number board on the Hill in which to display the names and numbers of the jockeys. The UDC objected, not so much because it was opposed to a new number board, but because, now that the Association held the freehold, the Council was determined to assert the right of common on the Downs. It agreed to the new proposal only on condition that the new £2,000 board should be subject to architectural approval by the Council; that it should replace and not complement the two existing smaller boards; and in compensation to the people for the common land that they would lose by the building, the EGSA should give the UDC a portion of The Warren estate for use as a pleasure ground. The Association appealed against this, but the Ministry heeded the UDC and permission was given for the new erection on the conditions laid down by the Council. The precedent was a most significant one; the Council still holds that portion of The Warren grounds (now used as a school playing field), and the principle that the EGSA should compensate in kind for any additional land it requires to improve the amenities of the race course still stands.

In the same year, the UDC first proposed the establishment of a body of Conservators to control and legalize activities on Epsom and Walton Downs, and to preserve the natural beauty of the Downs in the face of all intrusions, though it was to be eight years before that proposal was taken any further.

One of the major headaches that the Conservators would face were the gipsies, who turned up in their caravans for every Epsom race meeting, and in enormous strength for Derby week. They had done so since long before the old stand was built, indeed, before the Derby was ever run. In 1927, and until the

Second World War, their presence was, by and large, welcome, at least from a distance, and the Romany caravans certainly contributed considerably to the gaiety of the scene. Those who came in close contact with them, however, shared a good deal of disgust about their unhygienic habits, and local residents suffered additionally from the customary requests for buckets of water for their horses. The gates of co-operative householders were marked and they soon found themselves providing water for quantities of horses. In addition, the gipsies became bolder with the years, and by the summer of 1927 had taken to roping off areas of the Downs as car parks, and charging for entrance to them. To the dismay of the racing correspondent of *The Times*, the police stood by and took no action; the unofficial park keepers, he said, were 'unpleasant-looking folk whose language and behaviour, unless their demands are met, becomes unpleasant in the extreme'.

As public reaction against gipsies, and caravanners in general hardened, the somewhat eccentric Rosebery daughter, Lady Sybil Grant, rose to their defence. Herself a caravan-dweller and a hawker, (though between whiles she occupied Durdans) she proclaimed defiantly that she was going to prove that 'we' could be as clean and tidy as any householder. In the 1930s she instituted awards of baskets of groceries and plaques with enthusiastic messages to those caravanners who left their sites on the Downs in the very best condition. In the spring of 1937, to her dismay, the gipsies were successfully banned from the Downs by the authority of a by-law made by the Conservators. After the war, however, the growing determination of the gipsy brotherhood to hold on to its rights rendered the by-law almost impossible to enforce, despite the help of a uniformed security patrol, and the EGSA was eventually forced to set up a caravan camp.

The Epsom and Walton Downs Regulation Act, which established the Conservators, became law in 1936, after being moved in the Commons by Chuter Ede, later Home Secretary in a Labour government, then an alderman of the Epsom and Ewell Borough Council. The Act is worth examining in some detail.

What follows is merely a summary of the main aims and achievements of the Act, which is possibly of some help to those with no stomach for the thirty pages of the official version.

The Act is an attempt to regulate the use of Epsom and Walton Downs in such a way that the business of the owners – then the EGSA and Stanley Wootton – could be satisfactorily carried out without entirely abandoning the ancient rights of public access for air and exercise to those Downs. To preserve the peace among all the interested parties, and to see that none of them spoilt the Downs, the Act set up a body of Conservators, with somewhat vague but extremely wide-ranging powers.

The expenses incurred by the Conservators are met by a common fund provided by the EGSA, Stanley Wootton, and the Epsom and Ewell Urban District (now Borough) Council. The ten Conservators are appointed by those three constituent bodies – six by the Council, all of them to be members of the Council and to serve for three years each; three by the EGSA and one by Mr Wootton, the latter four to serve indefinitely, or to the requirements of those two constituents. The funds are provided in the same ratio of 6:3:1.

The first duty of the Conservators, according to the Act, is 'to preserve the Downs so far as possible in their natural state of beauty with due regard to the rules of good forestry'. Towards that objective, and within their domain, the Conservators are as strong as a local authority, with power to make by-laws and the authority to remove physically from the Downs those who break them.

They may prohibit and prevent parking, camping, sleeping, digging and the playing of organized games; they can regulate 'other means of recreation and the assemblage of persons on the Downs'. And may take down or remove 'any unauthorized enclosure building shed tent or other structure any unauthorized photographic cart show exhibition swing roundabout or other like thing or any horses cattle sheep pigs goats or other animals unlawfully on the Downs'. The Act firmly extinguished all rights of common or pasturage in and over the Downs, and those who lost such rights were compensated under the Act.

Stanley Wootton's right to preserve and maintain the training gallops on Walton Downs (Six Mile Hill) were protected; he had bought this land from the EGSA in 1925, and 30 years after the Act, he relinquished his hold on it in favour of the Horserace Betting Levy Board, by then the owner, in practice, of Epsom Downs.

The EGSA's rights take up, as you might expect, a major portion of the Act. Reducing them to simple sense, it recognizes the Association's obvious rights to maintain its own buildings and exclude the public from them; to control access over the Downs to the racecourse on the days when racing is on; to arrange for and allow, in specified areas, car parks, advertisement hoardings, stands, sideshows, swings, roundabouts, public conveniences and certain necessary fences: all of which temporary intrusions must be removed within ten days of the end of a meeting.

On the age-old problem of when and where the Association may prevent the public from crossing the course, the Act is firm and not particularly generous to the Association. The public may be excluded from the whole of the race course 'so far as may be necessary to enable racing to take place', and, in addition, during any race meeting and for fourteen days before it, the public may be excluded from the finishing straight, providing passages to a width of four feet are maintained during the preliminary period opposite each end of the grandstand. The most easterly of these passages has now been replaced by a pedestrian tunnel; that on the west is seldom used as it is more convenient to use the Rubbing House crossing.

There is still a public road across the main racecourse at two points, where the Old London Road used to run from the direction of Epsom Downs station across to Walton. These crossings, covered with matting and cut grass on race days, are still open to vehicular traffic – though it is not actually encouraged – except 'for such interval or intervals of time between the hours of one and five in the afternoon on any day during the racing period'.

That much noted, we must now step back to pick up a couple of points that were left behind, one of much consequence, the other of none. We will deal with the second first: after the Derby of 1930, Major B of Ebury Street London SW, summoned Sir Basil C, of Cadogan Gardens, London SW, for common assault on top of a bus.

Major B, having paid for a ticket to view the Derby from the top of an open bus, took up his place in the gangway between the two front seats. This caused some displeasure to the gentleman in the seat on his left, Admiral Sir Henry Y, and to Sir Basil C, sitting behind him, both of whom complained that he was obstructing their view. At the end of the Derby, there was some dispute over the winner, and Major B mounted the front seats, astride the gangway, to see better. At this point he fell forward (or was he pushed?) to the front of the bus, and, on regaining his footing, turned angrily on the Admiral.

Thinking the Major was about to strike the Admiral, Sir Basil rushed forward and punched him in the face, blacking his eye and cutting the inside of his cheek on his false teeth. Major B, who was a big man, then caught Sir Basil's head and held it under his arm until his struggles subsided. Sir Basil, who told the judge that the Major had tried to pull his ear off, said he thought it his duty as a gentleman to prevent an unjustifiable assault on the Admiral. He did what any decent Englishman would have done, and did not regret it. The judge did the sporting thing and dismissed the case without costs.

There was no such entertaining nonsense the next year, but on Derby day, 1931, John Logie Baird, the father of the television, made the world's first attempt at an outside broadcast transmission of a topical event. With the co-operation of the BBC – who, ultimately, did not adopt the Baird system – his company broadcast a transmission of scenes from the Derby, including the preliminary parade in front of the grandstand, and shots of the winning post during the race. There were some who saw a mystical connection between Baird's activities and the fact that, an hour or two later, an aeroplane flying low over the Downs, caught its wheels in the telegraph wires at Epsom Downs station and landed without ceremony on the railway lines. The pilot and his two passengers were not much injured, and a few railway workers soon hauled the plane off the track and let the racegoers continue their journey to London.

Baird was pleased enough with his efforts, which he repeated at the Oaks, to try again the following year. At the Metropole Cinema, near Victoria Station, London, a large and enthusiastic audience assembled for the first public showing of a TV outside broadcast. This time, with sound, he attempted to show the actual finish of the race, and one of the audience later commented, with amazement, that the bunch of horses was clearly seen as it flashed past the camera.

It was another six years before the BBC had improved its outside broadcast techniques sufficiently to announce, in January 1938, its intention of televising the Derby. It had good reason to hope, it said, that the transmission would prove successful. Nine days later came an announcement from the EGSA: it had not yet been approached by the BBC, but would not, in any circumstances, give their permission to the televising of any races on Epsom Downs.

Those opening shots in the battle between Epsom and television – and the BBC in particular – were typical of the salvoes that were exchanged sporadically for the next quarter of a century. On one side, there was aggravating assumption that what television wants, it must have; on the other, immediate suspicion, unreasonable obstinacy, and a determination to be obstructive. This time, it took the BBC only 2 months, and a cheque the size of which was habitually undisclosed, to persuade the EGSA to withdraw the embargo: the Derby would be televised. The news caused *The Times* man to observe, flatly, 'I have no idea how it is going to be done'.

Done it was, however, and seen not only on the few hundred TV sets then in domestic use, but again in the heart of London, at the Tatler News Theatre on a screen 8ft 6in square, with the projection apparatus close to the screen. The response expectedly enraptured. 'More than two hundred persons were present in the theatre,' a reporter noted, 'and to many it seemed to be as thrilling as being in the grandstand at Epsom.' An accurate comment, since there was little to be seen of the runners rounding Tattenham Corner, 'but the last quarter-mile was splendidly shown . . . the audience in the theatre could not refrain from bursting into applause'. It was not only the race that captivated them, but the preliminaries: 'It was fascinating to see each horse appear on the screen as it was described in the parade'.

In the same year, another innovation caught the imagination of the public: a totalisator office on the Downs. It took twenty minutes to reach the front of the queue, at which point many were astonished and alarmed to find the minimum stake was two shillings.

The following year even the most politically gullible racegoers were aware that war could not be avoided. At the Derby meeting, trouble from the IRA and its supporters was also anticipated; as the official communique had it, special secret precautions were taken to prevent the success of any attempt by Irish political extremists to interfere with racing. The outbreak of war in September was, however, an interference that could not be countered. In January 1940, all racing at Epsom was abandoned for the year – and, as it proved, for 5 years in all. A substitute Derby and Oaks were to be run at Newbury, but that meeting, too, was called off, and the classics were run, as they had been in the first world war, on the straight, flat acres of Newmarket Heath.

So Epsom was vacated one more, and left to the devices of the military, whose officers used Prince's Stand as a mess. There was the same fight between the EGSA and the national food producers as there had been in the previous war, but in 1943 the Surrey War Agricultural Committee agreed to forego its claim to plough up the gallops. The most strenuous equine exercise in the area during those years was a meeting organized by the local Pony Club on the Epsom Recreation Ground: there Eph Smith won the 'Derby' (run over a quarter of a mile) for Lord Astor, Gordon Richards won the 'Great Metropolitan Handicap' and Steve Donoghue came out of retirement to take the 'City and

Suburban'. The Oaks was reserved for female riders only and contested by members of the Pony Club – a precedent that, without such a rigid qualification, might well be followed in earnest now racing silks are sometimes so sweetly filled.

CHAPTER FOURTEEN

Intermission III

For 364 days in the year, wrote Charles Dickens, a cannon ball might be fired from one end of Epsom to the other without endangering human life: 'on the 365th, or Derby Day, a population rolls and surges and scrambles through the place that may be counted in millions'. He was writing in 1851, with a journalist's flair for colourful exaggeration. Today it is even less accurate, but in spirit it approximated to the truth then and still does.

Epsom has never let itself become a hum-drum suburb. Enough signs of 18th century glory still remain to make it a remarkable little town, but it is little different from comparable small towns – until the first week in June. Then, up on the hill, many forms of hell break loose and some of them spill garishly down to soil the propriety of the valley. In the days when the Derby was run on the second or third day of the meeting, the locals had the time and opportunity to prepare themselves for the most violent invasion: the Derby outing. Those who want value for money in terms of mass, colour, life, and excitement, save themselves for that day, and have done for a long time. 'The whole world was at Epsom yesterday,' reported *The Times* after Derby day, 1829 – the first with a grandstand. 'Independently of the numbers of visitors who, having arrived on the preceding day, ventured to remain a night in the town notwithstanding its dear and bad beds, London and the surrounding country sent out fresh hosts in the morning.'

Few need to sample the beds now, thanks to the marvels of modern transport. The roads to Epsom are smoother and faster flowing, but more polluted and infinitely less colourful. In 1829: 'Equipages rolled on wave upon wave almost in one unbroken stream from eleven o'clock till the hour for commencing the racing had nearly arrived. The scene was peculiarly striking and animated, from the moment when the carriages descried at a distance, winding their way through various roads leading to the Downs, seemed like so many glittering toys, till they came upon the eye in their full proportions, gay with rich liveries and brilliant colours flaunting in the beams of the morning sun. Horsemen came in clouds, and foot travellers not a few.'

Nowadays, it is much the same; in fact, since some start heading for home again as soon as the great race is over, there is scarcely an hour in mid-afternoon on that devastating Wednesday when the A 24 is not rasping, gasping and totally nauseating.

Unlike Ascot, Epsom is not thought of as a week, but as a race, and on Saturday there is another race. The social obligations of attending Ascot scarcely exist at Epsom: one goes, actually, for the sport, for that gripping, throbbing run up the last two furlongs, when the good horses give way to the great ones and, somewhere up in that stand, a fist is clinching inside one owner's stomach and a heart is wondering which way to beat next. It's not just the £63,000 prize money, but the everlasting honour of winning the world's greatest race that is at stake; of owning a horse which in some men's minds, will give its name to the year. Ah yes, that was Nijinsky's Derby, and that Mill Reef's, like Newcombe's Wimbledon, or Drobny's.

But the excitement is not limited to the owners, it also grips those clutching bookies' tickets on the rails, as if the winning of a few pounds will alter life significantly. It is, enough, though, to set the crowd jumping, screeching and beseeching, as the runners hurtle into vision and out again. That glorious, irreplaceable, unforgettable moment makes every discomfort worthwhile, every frustration tolerable. A man who has not felt the hail of scattered turf has not really been racing.

Save possibly at Goodwood, there is no sight in the whole of British racing to equal that from high up in the Epsom grandstand. The splendour of the empty Downs is quite breathtaking; thronging with the Derby crowd, they have to be seen to be believed. On The Hill and in The Dip are enough people to fill a large town. It is their day. To quote the owner of the 1972 Derby winner, Roberto: 'Anyone who doesn't consider the Epsom Derby one of the greatest sports events in the world must be out of his mind.'

Its greatness lies not only in the acuteness of the test and the desperation of the chase, but in the enthusiasm of the people. As Hugh McIlvanney wrote in the *Daily Express*, it is one of the last genuine folk festivals left to us; no lens is wide enough and no screen big enough to capture its real essence. One can see the race well enough on television, but one is deprived of participation. 'In contrast with the priorities at Ascot,' wrote McIlvanney, 'the people matter more than the clothes at the Derby. It is an occasion with sweat under its armpits.'

As early as dawn there is an astonishing sense of impending excitement. Driving up through the damp and silent golf course one is always, and always suddenly, aware of the overwhelming openness of the place that lies in front. Huddled tight against the trees on the right is the fairground community: rows of sleeping caravans, not white and bulbous like those in the camp a mile over the course, but hard and grey and shiny. Tethered close by, two little Shetland ponies stand unblinking under a tree, knowing full well what the day holds in store for them. On the corner site, to which it has been banished from The Dip, is packed and wrapped the fair itself. Outside, the generators that will later cough life into the buzzing, whirling machinery within.

There is no sound as one pads through the passages of grass, already massacred by four evenings' brisk business, save the occasional flapping of a canvas corner stirred by the breeze. Neon strips poke over the screen around the bingo stall, and peeking through the cracks, one can see the nasty prizes. The coconut shy is open, but nutless. In the next alley one surprises a perky mongrel peeing on the ghost train. He sniffs his patch and scratches before scampering off, hairless legs criss-crossing double quick, past the helter-skelter and unerringly between the naked, knife-ringed lady and the boy with the elephant face, as if he had an assignment, in these private moments, with the two-headed dwarf. Carlos is asleep, just inside the bend at Tattenham Corner, in his orange tent beside his orange hamburgers, oblivious to the promise of the day. Over the track, in Six Mile Hill car park, the first bookie's stand is already up from the previous day. Close by, though it is barely past six o'clock, two men are hunched behind the windscreen of their little van, hard against the rails, peering up the course to catch sight of the first of the morning gallopers.

They usually come in pairs, sometimes in threes, drumming out of the mist, round the outside of the course, on a dummy run for the day's great event. Motoring back to cross the course by the track just on the stand side of Tattenham Corner, it is as well to remember that other road users are already up and about: at 6.25 on the morning of Derby day 1972, a Daimler crossing towards the heath was suddenly confronted by two racehorses coming full tilt round the outside of the bend, straight for his bonnet. The driver popped smartly into reverse, slamming into the front of a flashy yellow Fiat that was following him. The odds against two cars colliding on a racecourse before breakfast must be gigantic, but it happened at Epsom!

Following the cars across the course and round the road that runs inside the great bend to the top of the Hill, one is surprised at the amount of activity. There are already a dozen or twenty cars up there, and a good scattering of pedestrians besides. Down the chalky lane that runs towards Walton, on patches of heath between the scrubby copses, schools of horses parade primly, circling their trainers. On their backs, under the saddles, each horse has a blanket with the trainer's initial bold and clear in two corners. Thus 'our course correspondent at Epsom' can survey the field at this early hour, drawing his own conclusions from their behaviour, condition, and speed, in time for the early editions of the evening papers.

If those who lean knowledgeably on the rails up there are not course correspondents, they may be stable staff, trainers' wives and children, even the odd owner or two. Some, incredibly at that hour, are devoted spectators, carrying flasks of coffee and packets of bacon sandwiches. Many are very short, elderly men in gum boots and flat caps, no higher than a horse's shoulder – where, no doubt, they have spent most of their lives.

The dawn riders are seldom those that will be seen later in silks. They are stable lads and lasses, wrapped up against the cold, most in quilted jackets and none with whips. When their turn comes for a gallop, they edge their snorting mounts on to the course. Some of them are already frothing with agitation, white flecks scattered in the wind as they toss their impatient heads. They chunter and champ, stamp and shuffle, as long as the body in the saddle is hauling the bit back, but when his turn comes, no urging is necessary – the wrists on the reins relax, and like a dog from a trap, the beautiful beast is off.

By eight o'clock the sound of hammering from the north side of the Hill has become insistent. So too, if the wind blows that way, is the smell of sizzling oil. Down there one finds a hundred stallholders banging away, preparing for the folk festival. Soon they will be ready to sell almost anything that catches the eye and might tickle the fancy – handbags, dresses, blankets, toys, dolls, shoes, umbrellas, coats, hats, and souvenirs – at every turn there will be hot dogs and hamburgers, bottles of pop, lollies and ice cream; but just now only the most efficient are operating, including a fish and chip stall, outlined by garish illuminations, which has been open for an hour or two.

The bookies are about too, scurrying over the Hill with their Gladstone bags and placards, seeking a good pitch. Rows of them are already in line – Honest Joe, Jolly Jack – though there's nothing to bet on at the moment, except how many times it will rain before the start.

This transient city has long been a sore point with the Conservators, but its presence during Derby week is so deeply established that any attempt now to turn away the vans would probably cause a riot. Whole families meet here every year – perhaps their only meeting – and have done for generations. Their persistence can cause a good deal of trouble at the beginning of the week, when the first arrival from one family will attempt to secure large areas of the park for his relations.

Dotted around are some monster caravans, refrigerated, air conditioned, luxurious. One regular arrives with his mobile palace behind a new Rolls-Royce: 'What do you think of that, then? £26,000 that lot cost me.' He has made his fortune out of caravan parks in the west country. Now, annually, he joins this one. Why, with his money, does he suffer the cramped discomforts of Epsom Downs on Derby week? 'When my dad was a kid, his father brought him here every year. When we were kids, the same. Never missed. It's gone on like that with all of us, the whole lot. We meet here every year, different bits of the family from all over England. Half of them, it's the only time I ever see them. But we wouldn't miss it for the world, and I hope our kids don't, either. As for holidays, well, I'm one of the lucky ones. We have a couple of months in the South of France. But do you know, I'd sooner give that up than Derby week on the Downs.'

The money doesn't always stay in the caravans. Prowl around and you'll find, wherever two or three are gathered together, there's a blanket on the ground between them. You can keep your coins in your pocket: these characters are only interested in notes, and usually fivers at that. The big boys go much higher, and there are racecourse people who have seen £1,000 change hands on the turn of one card. It must be painful enough, but if you are going to lose, better to do it that way than at 'toeing the line'.

This primitive form of gladiatorial combat is as beastly an exercise as man has devised for himself. A line is scraped on the turf, one man each side. Each puts down £100, on which a third party puts his foot. In turn, each man hits the other. The feet may not be moved, nor the hands used in defence. Bob and weave and take it. Crunch. Then his turn. Crack. The breath is sucked under the front teeth of the watching ring. First man to fall loses his stake. It doesn't last long.

Then there are the fortune-tellers in their caravans, nine or ten such, most of them claiming to be descendants of the Gipsy Lee of Devil's Dyke. One of them, indeed, announces on her board that she is the original Gipsy Lee; another is just Gipsy Lee; Gipsy Lee's grand-daughter Priscilla is prepared to solve our problems while we wait. Nancy Lee is the great-grand-daughter, she says, of Old Nancy Lee; like Madam Lee, Gipsy Rose Lee, and Zeta Lee, Emily Lee has already been consulted by the crowned heads of Europe and two Aga Khans, with Victor Mature as her unexpected bonus!

Such delights are seldom sampled by the grey ghosts from the Club Stand, and not often by the merrymakers on the open-topped buses, which now lend the occasion its only eccentricity of transport. In that respect at least, the Derby has changed for the worse in the past 150 years. Before the industrial revolution made rail travel the most sensible way of reaching the Downs, the infinite variety of transport for racegoers was not abandoned out of sight of the course, but used throughout the day: 'Coaches, carts, waggons and every other description of vehicles, were drawn up along the Race-course, and converted into temporary stands,' reported *The Times* in 1830. 'The line drawn by them extended for full three-quarters of a mile in a direction from the winning to the starting post at either side of the course, and for a considerable distance they were placed four or five deep.'

On Derby day these open-topped monsters bring their revelling to the course at mid-morning. They park, at extraordinary expense and to the dismay of thousands on the grass behind them, along the lower side of the finishing straight. Those at the winning post end have as fair and comfortable a view of the race as any patron in the stands opposite, except when it rains. To make up for that, the best-organized of the bus hosts see to it that the inner man is superbly catered for: the cunning and intrepid gate-crasher may hope for Pimms and cheese straws at midday, champagne with his lunch of salmon mousse and straw-berries and much comfort from a bottle of Scotch through the hardships of the afternoon.

After the last race is over, the fairground becomes insufferably crowded. It's the time to be out of it, back to the course where you began your wanderings twelve hours earlier. Still magnificent, despite the pummelling it has taken, but no longer beautiful. It is marred now by the ugly mass of rubbish that fringes it: the cans and bottles, the plastic cups, pie packets, rejected sandwiches, greasy bags, and banana skins; the sheets of newspaper that, released from the grip of a million feet, now scud over the turf and cling to the fences, or whirl giddily in the wind before the stands:

> *Five hundred tons of paper,*
> *Three miles of broken glass;*
> *And what with bags*
> *And packets of fags,*
> *You can hardly see the grass.*

It's a disgusting way to end the Derby, but nothing could change it now.

CHAPTER FIFTEEN

Post-war debits

After the Second World War, nothing could ever be quite the same again, and though post-war Epsom did its best to carry on from where it had been so rudely interrupted, it didn't quite manage it. Neither the course nor the buildings were in very good condition after the long intrusion of the army and the brief but violent one of a bomb that bounced off the front of the stand and exploded in Tattersall's enclosure. When the Welsh Guards did move out, Epsom was faced with the same restrictions that beset us all in the immediate post-war years: the war damage commission was slow to settle and building licences were hard to come by. Worst of all, the EGSA suffered five consecutive wet Derby days.

However, overwhelming the dreariness came the post-war boom – that explosive need to spend and to enjoy that possessed the nation on the day of liberation. The Association's trading profit was £34,000 for 1946, £35,000 for 1947, and £39,000 for 1948 – each one a record. It was unlikely to last, and it knew it, but while warning the shareholders of grey days to come, the directors, reasonably enough, took the opportunity to remunerate themselves for all those bonusless war years.

On the morning of 5th June, 1946, the wind blew fiercely and the rain fell in frequent and heavy showers. The gathering crowds, denied petrol and short of trains, nevertheless remained optimistic and scavenged what food they could from the booths, in the luxurious knowledge that they could do so without handing over their coupons. Ten minutes before the start of the Derby the sun broke through and shone for the rest of the afternoon, bringing an instant boost to the bookmakers, who find people are much more inclined to part with their cash when they are warm. From the height of the stands, the immediate difference between this Derby crowd and any other of our lifetime lay in the large number of service uniforms that peppered the Downs, from the brass buttons and peaked caps in the members' enclosure to the drabber khaki clusters to the south of the course, where wooden boxes on the rails were in great use. In both areas there was language used that would have meant nothing in 1939: on all sides, as *The Times* man observed, you could hear the phrase 'I've had it' or 'You've had that' – the one in disgust, the other in cheerful jibe.

By the end of 1947, building licences worth about £16,500 had been granted, 85 per cent of which was recoverable from the government. The War Department had paid £18,000 for occupational damage, so it wasn't the difficulties of rebuilding that depressed the racecourse authorities. They grunted and groaned under two clouds; one of them they knew would pass, the other they were afraid might not.

Though the total ban on motoring for pleasure must be seen from this distance in the context of the comparatively small number of cars that could anyway have been on the roads, the petrol restrictions did deaden other forms of transport too. Taxis and hire cars were restricted to a radius of twenty miles – fortunately the distance from Epsom Downs to central London was within the limit – and in 1947 there was a 12½ per cent cut in petrol for coaches. On top of that, in 1947, 1948 and 1949 the Derby, by order of the government, had to be run on a Saturday rather than a Wednesday, to reduce the risk of industrial absenteeism. Epsom's great day thus conflicted not only with rival sporting attractions, but with the coach companies' usual heavy week-end commitments; in addition special trains to race meetings were banned in 1946 and 1947.

Nevertheless, even in 1947, the profit from car park fees was more than £9,000 – nearly three times what it had been before the war. What really worried Epsom, and racecourse managements everywhere, was the entertainment tax, for these were the days of austerity.

For entertainment tax purposes, the government declined to regard racing as a live sport. Every admission ticket to the stands was subject to a 46 per cent tax (48 per cent in 1947), which meant that the EGSA was paying more in one year than it had done in the six before the war put together. The racing industry as a whole was paying something like £1,800,000 tax a year – £400,000 more than the total stake money – and by 1950, at least twenty courses were running at a loss.

The emperor of the Downs was by now Charles Langlands, who had been Clerk of the Course since 1924 (succeeding his father) and managing director of the EGSA since 1926. As chairman, he spoke of the outlook for 1948 as being 'difficult and unpredictable', pointing out that the public had the government's blessing for spending five days at Lord's, a week at Wimbledon, or a fortnight at Wembley (for the forthcoming Olympic Games), but it appeared to be the government's view that the public should be denied the opportunity of seeing the Derby except on a Saturday afternoon.

Between the spring and summer meetings of 1948, the basic petrol allowance was restored to the long-suffering population, but the number of vehicles on the Downs still remained at less than two-thirds the pre-war average. The royal limousines managed to make it to the Derby, despite the fact that a tree was blown across the Reigate Road at Ewell. The convoy was diverted through a farm, to the considerable surprise of the farmer. This was the Derby that was won by My Love, whose odds dropped to 100–9 when a rumour spread over the Downs an hour before the race that he had dropped dead in his box. He might well have dropped dead on the course, incidentally, had not Langlands discovered a garden fork on the track a few minutes before the start.

It was the Derby during which it was announced – but not from Epsom – that Princess Elizabeth was pregnant, and the Derby for which Moss Bros gave heartfelt thanks to Buckingham Palace, for King George asked, through the EGSA, that as many racegoers as possible who used the Club Stand should wear morning coats, though service dress or lounge suits would be tolerated. This inspired the incomparable essayist, Robert Lynd, to write in the *News Chronicle*: 'It must be admitted that England has never been the same since man became more and more neglectful of the duty of putting on a morning coat and a top hat before setting out for the day's work or enjoyment. First they left off their top hats, and not long afterwards hundreds of thousands of them ceased to wear any hats at all, so that at present you can see men who ought to know better going about bare-headed like savages in the jungle.'

Food was still rationed in Britain, and people were so conditioned to scarcity by then that the appearance of a mobile restaurant on the Downs, serving 1,500 hot meals in 90 minutes, seemed a miracle to equal that of the loaves and fishes. One worthy alderman, at a meeting of the Epsom Food Committee, complained of the number of licences issued for the sale of food at race meetings, and the amount wasted, while in the same week a letter to *Sporting Life* pinpointed the hardships of austerity: 'Refreshments of a sort could be obtained provided one did not object to partaking of them in surroundings which were irresistably reminiscent of a public air raid shelter. I sighed for the lovely lawns, comfortable and roomy stands, and clean and attractive restaurants which are at the disposal of racegoers in other countries for less than an Epsom car park fee'.

Someone from the *Manchester Guardian* attended, and obviously hoped for worse than he found: 'Where were the gipsies and the spivs, the narks, the touts, the wide boys, the broken jockeys, the fine old riffraff of the turf? I saw only a vast collection of middle-class people so respectable, so reserved, so innocent of mien that they might have been transported here straight from the Chelsea flower show.' But if there were complaints in 1948, that was also one massive compliment. An Australian newspaper owner, Sir James Joynton Smith, came to England for a holiday and liked the look of the Downs so much that he made a cash offer for them, reckoning to run the Grand National there as well as the Derby. (Rebuffed at Epsom, he later turned his attention to Hyde Park, which he thought had the makings of a decent racecourse.)

As Langlands had forecast, the bubble burst the following year. Entertainment tax was still being levied, and profits dropped from £39,000 to £23,000. But the last of the bomb damage was repaired – much to the relief of patrons of the ground floor bar in Tattersalls, who had, for the past three wet years, suffered much from leaks through cracks in the steps above.

The shadow of what was to be the King's final illness, not yet publicly known, fell dimly on the Downs in 1949 when it was learned that he could not attend the Derby. His consort, Queen Elizabeth did, however, and at the last minute the management realized it did not possess a Queen's Standard to fly over the grandstand. A hectic dash to Buckingham Palace and back succeeded in getting one to the Downs a shade ahead of the royal party, who were, in racing terms, barely distanced. The only other off-course skirmish worth recording was that of the *Daily Mail* reporter who scored eight direct hits on sideshow coconuts. Only one fell off, and when he got that home it was bad.

By now television was well in the hunt, and a long-running battle had begun between the EGSA and the BBC. The Derby was televised in 1938 and 1939, but the service then was both experimental and limited to so small an audience that the potential effect on live attendances was hardly worth considering. Ten years later there was not exactly a mass audience for television, but sports promoters were acutely aware of its significance. The medium then appeared to be designed for live outside broadcasts rather than eternal soap operas, and it was clear that a spectacle like the Derby was going to be a high-priority programme.

In 1946 the Association for the Protection of Copyright in Sport was formed, and Langlands was the Racecourse Association's representative to it. When the BBC wanted to televise the Derby in 1948, Epsom stood firm and asked for a fee of £10,000. 'With other promoters of big-time sport,' explained Langlands, 'the EGSA are protecting their interests against the inevitable development when television is certain to be rediffused on the cinema screens.' The idea that the Derby, or the Cup Final, would one day be seen by 25 million people in their own homes was then unthinkable. The danger, promoters thought, was that TV cameras would transmit live to cinema screens.

The APCS, said Langlands, believed that the promoting organization was entitled to a return in revenue to compensate for the televising of what was, after all, their own production. Until the BBC agreed to reasonable terms, they proposed an absolute and immediate ban on the televising of all sporting events. As a result, the Postmaster General convened a conference between sports promoters and the BBC, at which he undertook to set up a committee to analyse the effect of live television on sport, if the promoters would agree to an experimental period during which they would make a hundred events available for television.

The promoters agreed, with the provision that there would be no compulsion to make available any one given event. Predictably, the EGSA was then put under strong pressure to allow the televising of the Derby (in 1950). It refused to be swayed. It was not the policy of the directors to be obstructive, said Langlands, nor to cast themselves in the role of Canute, but until the whole position had been clarified by the government it was extremely unlikely that the Derby or any other race at Epsom would be televised.

The government committee's report was published in 1952. It agreed that the promoters were entitled to protect their interests, but declared that the performing rights in a sporting spectacle should be vested in the broadcasting authority rather than the promoter. The EGSA was not too happy about the committee's conclusions, which did not recommend any legislation to prohibit a broadcasting authority from televising a sporting spectacle against a promoter's wishes, from a site outside his control. This could obviously be achieved on Epsom Downs, and the directors maintained their opposition to the whole business. 'The key to the whole problem is money,' chairman Langlands told the annual meeting in 1953. 'It is apparent that the funds of the BBC, who so far have been getting sporting events on the cheap, are insufficient to enable them to pay the full value of the major events they would like to televise.'

Let's leave that one simmering for a bit, as indeed it did, and catch up with other events of the early 1950s. In 1951, the government changed, and entertainment tax on racecourse admissions was reduced from 49 to 32 per cent, compensating for the considerable fall in attendance at Epsom in 1952 – by which time the Court was in mourning for the death of King George. Lester Piggott came in second on Gay Time in the Derby that year, and was responsible for one of the race's most hilarious incidents. After a tight finish, one of the four French jockeys asked Piggott who had won.

'Tulyar,' he said.

'Who?'

'Tulyar.'

'Who, please?' said the Frenchman.

Piggott leant nearer, shouted 'Tulyar, Tulyar,' and fell flat on his face.

His liberated horse took off through the paddock and galloped in the direction of Epsom. It was caught by a stable lad and returned just in time for the weigh-in, which the jockey had to perform in the wrong colours, dressed as he was, by then, for the next race. This, in fact, broke the rules, but in the circumstances Piggott was allowed to get away with it.

Two more Downs problems arose in 1952, both the result of the difficulty of finding a satisfactory compromise between the individual's rights on common land, and the need of the Association to maintain discipline during meetings. The authorities had long been aggravated by the habit, indulged in by certain sharp characters, of delivering to the course on Derby day a lorry load of orange boxes. These were hired out to the public on the south side of the finishing straight ('the free strip') at £2 a time, or £5 for two and a plank. Thinking no doubt that it was a small step from two boxes and a plank to a temporary stand, the EGSA wanted the boxes prohibited. It had some support from the Epsom and Walton Downs Conservators, whose concern was not to stop people standing on boxes for a good view, but to prevent them blocking the view of those behind.

Despite the encouragement of both bodies, the police declined to take action against the box touts, since the law as it stood had no relevance except unless nuisance or obstruction could be proved. Since the fine for such offences was no more than could be recouped by hiring out one box, offenders were undeterred. It took much pressure from Epsom before the Home Office agreed to impose a maximum fine of £5 on those found guilty of being 'likely to cause an obstruction'.

An extraordinary, possibly unique, civil action also began after the August Bank Holiday meeting that year. Bookmaker Joe Lee (whose name was, in fact, Herbert Knight) set up his pitch on the Hill, but refused to pay the 30 shillings fee demanded by the Association. The rights of bookies were defined by the Epsom and Walton Downs Regulation Act of 1936, under which the EGSA was empowered to set aside places on the open Downs for bookies and to make a charge for their pitches, providing such charge did not exceed the amount charged for a pitch in the East Stand enclosure during the corresponding meeting in 1936. The complication in 1952 was caused by the fact that there had not been an August meeting in 1936.

The case was first heard at Epsom that November, when the County Court judge ruled for the bookmaker. The Association immediately lodged an appeal, which was heard in the Court of Appeal in January, 1953. The County Court judgment was upheld, and leave to appeal to the House of Lords refused. It left the EGSA in the unreal situation of being allowed to charge for pitches only in April, May, or June, but not in August or any other month when a meeting might be held.

But British justice usually finds a way of sorting out such anomalies. Though the Appeal Court ruled that there should be no appeal to the Lords, the EGSA petitioned the judicial committee of the Lords for leave to appeal to that House, and in March the petition was granted, with the proviso that the Association should pay the respondent's costs. In July, the Appellate Committee of the House of Lords sat to hear the case, but on the second day one member was too ill to attend. The Committee decided that the appeal must be re-argued, and this could not be arranged until February 1954. Judgment was eventually given in favour of the EGSA in March – 20 months and 5 hearings after the offence. The cost of recovering those 30 shillings had been immense, but its value to the Association was inestimable.

While the case was dragging on, Epsom enjoyed the boom that Coronation year, 1953, brought to all festivals of its kind. The race meeting profited more than most, since it opened the day after the Coronation. Wednesday's weather was gloomy, with a cold wind, but by the time Derby day dawned on Saturday there was brilliant sunshine. The Club Stand was festooned with flags, banners, shields, bunting, cords and tassels, gilded lions' heads, and 2,000 hydrangea plants, at a cost of £1,300. There was vintage champagne, at £2 12s 6d a bottle, for those who did not bring their own, but in Tattersall's one could still buy a four-course lunch for eight shillings.

Thirty trains an hour arrived at the Downs and Tattenham Corner stations, and 2,800 vehicles an hour were pouring out of London. A crowd of 30,000 massed outside Buckingham Palace to see the royal party leave on the short hop to Victoria Station, and tickets for the Epsom stands were as hard to find as they had been for Westminster Abbey on the Tuesday, Coronation day. It was a great day, except for the bookies and occupants of Prince's Stand, the roof of which had been stripped of lead the previous night.

The bookmakers were faced with two exceptional horses – Aureole, belonging to the Queen, and Pinza, ridden by the newly-knighted Sir Gordon Richards. Money was piled on these two in unprecedented amounts, and overnight they were joint favourites at 5–1. On the course, the public's loyal hopes for a royal win were overcome in a surge of support, both emotional and logical, for the mount of the man who had been 25 times champion jockey, but at 49 had never won the Derby. Aureole dropped to 9–1, and came second to Pinza. The bookies paid out £1 million.

There was a grey patch on the turf at Tattenham Corner that day – the ashes of a racing man, scattered there by his widow that morning. If there was any other sadness, it was in the town of Epsom, through which the Queen did not drive on her way to Windsor in the evening, disappointing a huge crowd that lined the streets in confident expectation.

The year brought the Association profits of £37,000, and the directors paid shareholders a 7½ per cent dividend, plus a Coronation bonus of 2½ per cent. Charles Langlands had retired from all his positions of power the previous year (Lewis van Moppes had been appointed chairman, and Major Watts Clerk of the Course), but was nevertheless delighted to find that the bank overdraft – which had stood at £180,000 when he took over, had at last been eliminated from the balance sheet.

The Board's attitude to television altered slightly with the retirement from the chair of the implacable Langlands. In 1955, the first occasion on which Van Moppes addressed the shareholders, he said: 'The time is approaching when Epsom will revert to the 1939 practice and permit at least its main event to be televised'. The overriding fear of the EGSA that television would result in the decimation of attendances at the meetings was somewhat assuaged when Van Moppes discovered, on a visit to New York, that the American racing associations actually encouraged TV companies to visit their courses as they had found that television had a beneficial effect on attendances.

Though the opposition in principle to the live televising of races was thus softened, in the matter of adequate fees the American trip had slightly hardened Epsom's heart. Van Moppes returned with the conviction that it was 'grossly unfair to the promoters of sporting events to suggest that the fee for the televising of the events which they promote should be arbitrarily reached and expressed in terms of guineas. The true measure is obviously the number of people who view and it is, in the opinion of your Board, proper that the fee to be obtained from the televising of racing at Epsom should be upon the basis of a fixed sum per head of the viewing public'. At the same time, and for the first time, the EGSA nodded heavily in the direction of ITV, newly set up in 1956 – small wonder in view of their experience of negotiations with the BBC.

It was, indeed, the commercial network that in 1960 – six years after Van Moppes' American experience – landed the Epsom contract. That year, despite an increase in expenditure of £30,000, there was an increase in profits over the previous year of some £21,000. The chairman was quick to point out that there was no relation between this figure and the television fee. Though the latter was never disclosed, it was believed to be £50,000. Epsom seemed satisfied with the negotiations. But in December 1964, the Racecourse Association instructed all members to hold out for a collective bargaining arrangement for TV, and until it was agreed, no racecourse was permitted to sign a TV contract for more than one year.

The Racecourse Association informed the TV companies that, from the end of 1966, any racing agreement would have to be negotiated with the Association. Both the BBC and ITV declined to be a party to such negotiations, and as far as Epsom was concerned, ITV signified that it was not interested in an agreement for one year only. 'The impasse appears complete,' said Van Moppes, 'and neither side is willing to give way.' The chairman of the Doncaster Race Committee had, by then, declared firmly that racing would disappear from the TV screens altogether unless a realistic fee was forthcoming, and Van Moppes himself had come round to the idea that TV was responsible for declining attendances at Epsom.

This decline was real enough; from the record pre-tax profit of nearly £79,000 in 1961, it fell to £57,000 in 1962 and £40,000 in 1963. The question was whether Epsom could afford to hold out. In deference to the Racecourse Association's directive, it had already, painfully, rejected ITV's offer of £130,000 for three years: but before the end of March, 1965, it succumbed and unilaterally negotiated a four-year agreement. Profits leaped to £74,000.

On and off over these post-war years, the slings and arrows of outrageous fortune had caught the EGSA an occasional clip on the ear. Blows like the deluge Derby of 1956, when even the bookies packed up and went home, were forgotten by the next sunny meeting. Criticisms it withstood, and often ignored. After the spring meeting of 1950, for instance, the correspondent of the *Sheffield Star*, an evening paper, suggested that the time might have come to take the Derby away from Epsom. It was ludicrous, he said, that the country's greatest race should be held on a course which was crossed in seven places by public rights of way – including a main road a hundred yards from the five furlong starting gate, and a much-used path a furlong from the winning post. And what kind of a racecourse was it, he asked, where it was a quarter of a mile, without shelter, from Tattersall's to the paddock?

These were complaints of which the EGSA was well aware, and which it undoubtedly would have liked to rectify. Some, in due course, it did. Meanwhile, the royal apartments were modernized and reconstructed in 1957 ('Her Majesty expressed herself as charmed by the effect – a sentiment which was later conveyed in writing to us by the Keeper of the Privy Purse'), and the following year – one of record profit – £18,000 was spent on renewing the motors of the five lifts in the stands. The same year, 1958, the chairman was able to tell shareholders that the ground staff had produced 'a racecourse about which no criticism has been levelled; in fact, the contrary'.

At the close of racing in 1959 (Entertainment Tax had been removed from racing in 1957, and there were record receipts, though not a record profit), the East Stand was demolished. This had always provided, and still does, the cheapest accommodation of any of the grandstand buildings, but it had long been clear that its appalling lack of facilities had become intolerable. A new single-tier stand, the Rosebery, was built for £60,000. It was opened by the Earl of that name the following spring, and gave what was then better value for money than any comparable enclosure in the country.

In the same year the freehold of the nine-acre Paddock was at last acquired from the Durdans estate, thanks to the intercession of Lady Halifax. Plans were approved for an important development there – a single-storey block of stables with 100 loose boxes and sleeping accommodation for 90 stable lads and 20 girls, at a cost of nearly £50,000. Work began at the end of 1961, and the Association looked shamelessly to the newly-formed Horserace Betting Levy Board for financial assistance.

Throughout Derby week that year the going was rock hard. Epsom Downs comprise too thin a layer of soil – albeit topped with that magnificent turf – on a vast bed of chalk. Even a heavy rainfall can drain out in hours, and most jockeys and trainers, including Sir Gordon, were much in favour of artificial watering. The opposition was crystallized, soon after the Derby, in an article in *Horse and Hound* written under the pen name of Audax by the well-known journalist-jockey John Lawrence. It must have shaken Epsom considerably:

> Unlike the Grand National, the Epsom Derby is not, in itself, a spectacle of unique interest or excitement. The atmosphere and prestige of the great race spring almost entirely from its long-established claim to be the supreme, ultimate test of the three-year-old thoroughbred racehorse. And that claim, make no mistake, is fast becoming as empty and useless as a broken beer bottle . . .
>
> The first, most pressing question is not whether the watering of racecourses is theoretically desirable but whether, without watering, the Epsom Derby can keep its place in the fast developing fabric of international racing. And the answer, surely, is no . . .
>
> More and more foreign owners are coming to regard the Derby as a pointless, dangerous free-for-all in which their horses run considerable risk of permanent injury on ground much harder – and hills much steeper – than anything they are likely to meet at home or elsewhere.

The very next Derby, in 1962, was a disaster. Seven horses fell at Tattenham Corner, including the favourite, Hethersett. Six horses finished riderless, the seventh – Ryan Price's King Canute II – was destroyed on the course. Six jockeys were taken to hospital and four detained. It was generally thought that the chaos was caused by the unusually large number of horses falling back as they reached the corner, thus meeting those that were then closing up. After an enquiry, the Stewards 'accepted the view with regret that so many horses which had no right to be in the field were allowed by owners and trainers to start'.

Though the incident rated not a word in the chairman's annual statement, he did say it had been 'undoubtedly a difficult year for racecourses generally'. Profits fell heavily, but the EGSA managed to maintain the dividend of 15 per cent to which it had climbed in 1960 – a figure that critics rated as extraordinarily high in view of the work that needed to be done on the course.

CHAPTER SIXTEEN

A new master

The sixties, which were to be the most momentous decade in the history of Epsom racecourse, opened with a splendidly clear example of the malaise that threatened the EGSA: its pre-tax profits in 1961 soared to an historic total of nearly £79,000; and at the same time, its pride was bruised – or it should have been – by professional allegations that racing conditions were sometimes so deplorable that Britain's greatest flat race was becoming something between a rodeo and a donkey Derby.

In 1962, the year of the Derby's Tattenham Corner chaos, profits fell by more than £20,000 – assisted by unfortunate August Bank Holiday weather. The chairman, Mr van Moppes, could see no cause for pessimism, however, and recommended a continued dividend to shareholders of 15 per cent, which amounted to a payout of nearly £24,000. Two extra days were added to the racing programme in September, 1963, but profits fell to £40,000 – just over half what they had been two years earlier. The dividend was cut to 10 per cent.

During the year, the new paddock was completed, and the pedestrian tunnel under the course at the east end of the Rosebery Stand was installed. This extremely useful adjunct, of equal benefit to horses, jockeys and spectators – the crossing on the course was closed – cost £13,000 and immediately attracted the local practitioners in graffiti, which it continues to do. A *Sporting Life* correspondent noted at the first meeting of 1964 that most of the messages seemed to be written by stable lads ('More pay for the lads'), at least three of whom were in love with the same girl.

The tunnel, eighty yards long and twenty feet deep, was topped with two feet of earth and turf. The rainfall in March was so heavy that the turf did not knit as well as was expected, and 10 days before the spring meeting, the stewards refused to sanction racing without a further inspection. If the course had not improved sufficiently, Kempton Park was to take over the fixtures; the Press speculated about the possibility of having to relay the turf, and the consequential fate of the Derby, with a record £80,000 at stake? Mr van Moppes blanched at the thought, but, as it happened, all was well.

The Clerk of the Course, John Watts, spent £144 in May on powdered seaweed in an attempt to keep the course damp, and experimented with foundry sand instead of peat on the road crossings, those irksome stretches of tarmac at which, however disguised, a galloping horse is still liable to jump. The following year, with greater success, he turned to coconut matting spread with cut grass at the Mile Post crossing, and this was later adopted at all necessary points, at a cost of £3,000.

By now the Horserace Betting Levy Board, chaired by Lord Harding, had begun to interest itself in the modernization of race-courses. In January, 1964, it announced a subsidy of £106,000 for Epsom; consisting of a grant of £13,000 for the completed pedestrian tunnel and a loan of £93,000 to cover the purchase of the paddock freehold from the Durdans estate, and the building of the stables. Lewis van Moppes was able to assure the public that, among other improvements planned at Epsom, the grand-stand was to be rebuilt at a cost of £2 million.

The EGSA had another, non-racing development up its sleeve too; it wanted to demolish Tattenham Corner stables, which had been in use since 1925, and to erect a modern housing project on the 4-acre site. Now that the paddock stabling was complete, the Tattenham Corner block was obsolete. It was, in any case, hopelessly out of date for modern requirements, and structurally was in such a bad condition that it was unsafe. Three alternative plans were submitted to the Borough Council – 23 detached houses, or two nine-storey blocks of flats, or three three-storey blocks. All were rejected.

The EGSA appealed, pleading that the land could be spared from its present use and would make a useful contribution to meeting housing needs. It got nowhere. The forces ranged against it were immovable, from the Town Clerk to the Surrey Trainers' Association. For the trainers, Walter Nightingale said there was no doubt the premises could play a very important part in the future of the racehorse industry in the borough; he was thinking, no doubt, of the future already looming when the trainers with establishments in Epsom town would be forced by the huge rise in the value of their land to sell out to property developers. The Tattenham Corner site would be ideal for a trainer. The Borough officials were not moved at the thought of all those extra homes; the development of the land, they said, would be prejudicial to the amenities of Epsom Downs, and could completely destroy the character of that part of the course.

Many people feel much the same about the caravans that now threaten to engulf much of the Downs during Derby week. This is a running battle at Epsom, and it's probably not over yet. As in 1937, the caravans had been driven off at the spring meeting in 1963, when the numbers were not particularly excessive. In 1964, the Conservators announced that all unlicensed caravans – that is, those that were not a part of the fairground battalion – would be turned away. At the same time, the Conservators ordered the mechanical part of the fair to shut down at 10.30 every evening, and the whole site to be cleared 72 hours after the race meeting ended. They employed eight officials, and the Association three, to deal with the caravan parkers, but it was a daunting task. There was nothing they could do when owners either refused to give their names or gave false ones, as 72 did, and it was perhaps a bit rough of the Surrey Downs Association to say later that the Conservators made no attempt to prevent unauthorized parking. Thirteen summonses were issued and there were nine prosecutions; the fines amounted in all to £19, causing the EGSA secretary to remark that the caravanners were better off than when the Association allowed them on the Downs and charged a parking fee.

At the meeting of the Conservators the following spring, their Clerk, Edward Moore (also the Epsom Town Clerk), put the blame firmly on the EGSA: if it let the sites to caravans and sideshows, it must control them. The Conservators as a whole were in favour of the EGSA putting an end to the Downs fair altogether, tantamount to curing a septic finger by chopping off the hand. Their chairman conceded that the old horse-drawn Romany caravans were very much part of the Epsom scene: 'but these glittering motorized things charge up like tanks and are part of nothing'.

In Derby week the *Epsom and Ewell Herald* joined in. 'Contempt', an editorial considered, 'is not quite the word to describe the mood of the citizens of Epsom for those two classic races, the Derby and the Oaks, of which they are such close neighbours, but familiarity brings its problems.' Why did not the Conservators ban, it wished to know, 'the obviously undesirable types of man and motor that explode on to the Downs to the annoyance of the local inhabitants and the apprehension of the health authorities?'

Thirty years after the Epsom and Walton Downs Regulation Act of 1936, a joint committee, formed from four local residents' associations, led by the Epsom Protection Society, produced *The Downs Report*. It was an interesting and constructive assessment of the current effectiveness of the Act, and was not short of suggestions as to how it might be better implemented. This, too, deserves summarizing here – a task a good deal easier than it was with the Act, since the Report is written in language both lucid and sharp.

Its preface declares immediately that 'the steadily deteriorating condition of the Downs is the subject of increasing concern to the public and particularly to those sections of it who, living nearby, make most frequent use of them for fresh air and exercise'. The Act, the committee believed, was now clearly outdated, and many of its provisions obsolete or irrelevant: it called for its outright repeal, and its replacement by a new and simpler Act designed for contemporary conditions.

The task of the Conservators had become increasingly difficult as they endeavoured to perform their duties in circumstances which were not envisaged at the time of the Act. Consequently many provisions of the Act were not being complied with and breaches of the law were being condoned in the process: 'This is a state of affairs that cannot be accepted. Either the law must be upheld as it stands, or it must be changed.'

The report makes two early and relevant points: first, that despite the very considerable geographic and personal interest which the Urban District of Banstead had in Epsom and Walton Downs, that local authority was not represented on the Conservators; secondly, that the Act places no limit on the number of race meetings that could be held in any one year, and indeed, since the Act, the number had increased from two to four. Since it was permitted to erect temporary stands up to six weeks before a meeting, the committee could see the possibility of the temporary becoming virtually permanent. It suggested no more than sixteen weekdays, and the substantial curtailment of the preliminary period in which such structures could be erected.

The committee wanted 'the gallops' precisely defined, to leave an adequate area of downland accessible to the horse-riding public; and a re-examination of the restrictions imposed on traffic during race meetings, with a view to lessening the inconvenience to the public. It recommended far stricter control over the fairs, and the restriction of caravan parking to that housing the fairground population. Because the Act was drawn up at a time when cars were a comparative rarity, the committee thought that the provisions relating to motor vehicles needed drastic alteration: the Downs should be preserved, it said, as an open sweep of downland on which people could roam and play at will, without the hazard created by motor traffic or the unsightly intrusion of large groups of parked vehicles. Except during race meetings, parking should be greatly restricted and as unobtrusive as possible.

The Grandstand Road (which runs across the golf course towards Buckles Gap) should be closed altogether, and all roads across the racecourse and Walton Downs should be permanently closed to vehicular traffic – a move which it rightly thought would be welcomed both by local residents and the racecourse management. It supported the building of an underpass for Langley Vale Road by the Paddock (since accomplished), and also of one at Tattenham Corner.

On the matter of the constitution of the Conservators and their officers, *The Downs Report* is most pertinent: the method of appointing the Clerk should be reconsidered – he was then, and still is, the Clerk to the Epsom Council; of the six Conservators representing the Borough, not more than three should be aldermen – at the time of the report, all six were aldermen, and, as such, not accountable to the electorate at the polls for their actions as Conservators.

The difficulty the Conservators had in executing their authority on the Downs was recognized, and the committee suggested an increase in the numbers of the keepers (whom it preferred to call rangers), and a strengthening of their powers; some might be mounted on horseback, and a permanent post should be set up on or near the Downs, from which their activities could be con-ordinated and controlled.

In 1967, when summonses for illegal camping were served by the Conservators on 40 families, the secretary of the Gipsy Council was quick to defend their rights. He estimated that a thousand families, a quarter of the gipsy population in Britain, met on the Downs for Derby week, and had done for nearly two centuries. From every angle, that seems an exaggeration; certainly an examination of the recent Derby caravan sites reveals not many genuine gipsies. A large number seem to be what could be more harshly called itinerant tinkers or other tradesmen; Lord Wigg dubs them the travelling people.

Two years later, the Conservators handed the job over to a security company, which provided 24-hour patrols on the Downs to warn unauthorized campers that action would be taken against them, and to provide the necessary evidence to enable proceedings to be taken. The gipsies, if that is what they were, had spent a particularly harassed winter and did not take kindly to their new opponents. If they were prevented from camping, they said, they would stop the Derby by driving their caravans across the racecourse. On the first day of that week, two hundred caravans arrived and parked as usual, with the security men doing their best to take names, addresses and vehicle registration numbers. Another hundred settled in the next day, and the campers announced that victory was theirs, hands down. On Derby day 160 summonses were issued, but the race was not interrupted: 'We did not stop the Derby,' said the gipsies' president, 'because we have won. We are on the Downs.' By the end of the week only 29 summonses had been served, and 27 proceeded with; each brought a £3 fine for trespass, with three guineas costs.

It is not the end of the caravan problem, but let's go back to 1964, where we left the EGSA frustrated in some of their development plans, and optimistic on others, and when the *Daily Mail* noted, it is relevant to recall, the Clerk of the Course had improved the Epsom turf almost out of recognition, but there was still nothing to prevent hooligans from invading the track at any time and sabotaging the races. Shortly after that complaint, John Watts resigned after ten years as Clerk (he had succeeded the formidable Charles Langlands in 1954, there had thus, until that time, been only five Clerks of the Course in 125 years). Watts was succeeded by Peter Beckwith-Smith, the first Clerk with any experience of the job to be appointed at Epsom: he had held the same position at Lingfield, a course owned by his family. The new man's credentials were impeccable: Eton and Sandhurst, Major in the Welsh Guards, a JP and Deputy Lieutenant of the County of Surrey.

The Press continued its compliments the next spring, by which time the Rosebery Stand had been considerably refurbished, and, for the first time, its patrons could buy hot meals. 'Epsom has been given the most marvellous £50,000 face lift,' said the *Sporting Life*. Looking past it, the *Sporting Chronicle* reckoned that the EGSA had realized the reason for the diminishing attendances could be given in one word – discomfort. 'Those who considered that in return for their entrance money they were entitled to a view of the racing, good food and drink well served in attractive surroundings, were forced to look elsewhere for their entertainment.' The *Mail* acknowledged that the Rosebery Stand was now better value than any other cheap ring, but believed that at least £1.5 million was required to modernize the course.

Derby week that year attracted its usual delightful variety of recordings of the scene by Fleet Street, including an updated version of Charles Dickens' *Household Words* feature on the catering: the order was now for half a ton of salmon, half a ton of turkey, a ton of beef, 900 eggs, 7,000 punnets of strawberries,

168

3,000 bottles of wine and 240 dozen bottles of champagne (fish and chip quantities unspecified). The Queen came to the Derby, and *Queen* magazine was there to see her: 'What a cheer the crowd each side of the course gave our dear Queen when she arrived with Prince Philip, looking radiant in a very pale green silk coat and hat to match'.

There was another of those merry scenes past the winning post on the first day, when a horse called Tumidora threw its jockey, dashed down Chalk Lane and along South Street till it reached the forecourt of the Marquis of Granby, where it jumped over a car into the arms of a former jockey who happened to be passing.

Such diversions apart, the EGSA had determined, and had embarked, on a policy of gradual modernization, without which racing on this most majestic of courses was in danger of being laughed off as an anachronism. An automatic watering system was at last installed, but doubt was deep rooted as to whether the EGSA, whose policy had for too long been to allocate a large part of the profits for the payment of dividends at the expense of maintenance and development, was determined enough to set the matter right. This was Epsom, Epsom of the Derby. The mightiest racing men of the world came here, and found, for instance, that to stay in the paddock till saddling was complete meant a somewhat undignified scramble back to the stand before the field was at the starting gate – a scramble of a full furlong that involved crossing a public highway.

On this point at least action was promised, and here comes the extraordinary tale of the Langley Vale Road underpass. Just after the 1965 Derby, the EGSA announced that it hoped work would start, in the autumn, on a tunnel to take that road under the racecourse. Negotiations had been in hand for three years, and the cost was expected to be between £80,000 and £100,000. The secretary, Alan Crego-Bourne, then relieved himself of the immortal phrase, 'much water must pass under the bridge first'.

Charles Langlands had first suggested this tunnel in 1948. No doubt due to the lack of money and lack of building permits at that trying time, no action had then been taken, and it was now costing the Association £1,000 a year to cover and police the crossing during meetings. The tunnel idea seems to have been taken off the shelf and dusted down in 1962, when its estimated cost was £50,000. In June 1963, an estimate of £60,000 was obtained for the work, at which point the Levy Board encouraged the Association to go ahead. No progress was made, however, until 1965, a quite extraordinary year, at the end of which the

EGSA had made a pre-tax profit of £74,000 and increased its dividend to a phenomenal 21 per cent.

As exactly as it is possible to place events during that year, this was the way things went. In March, the underpass estimate rose to nearly £100,000. In April a holding company, United Racecourses Ltd., was formed by the EGSA directors and others; that had no particular relevance to the underpass, completion of which was expected by spring 1966; and the EGSA made it known that since the tunnel would benefit racing at Epsom, but not the shareholders of their Association (to whom at the end of the year they made a present of £32,000) it was most reluctant to contribute anything at all to its cost, which it thought should be borne by the Levy Board: it was not even prepared to apply its annual improvement grant from the Board to that purpose.

By the beginning of August 1965, the expected completion date had moved to the spring of 1967, but the work had not even been put out for tender. By the end of the month it was agreed that £100,000 would not cover it, and in September the official estimate was £139,000. As winter rolled on the EGSA reiterated its refusal to pay for it, the Levy Board put it on its 'low priority' list, and United Racecourses announced the acquisition of Sandown Park, the Esher racecourse some of the directors of which had been anxious to sell for housing.

So underpass matters remained in abeyance for another long period. The EGSA was still nominally under the chairmanship of Lewis van Moppes, while United Racecourses was chaired by Sir Brian Mountain, chairman of Eagle Star Insurance. The financial arrangement between the companies was that the EGSA each year paid a lump sum to the holding company, which itself paid the dividends to shareholders. At the end of their full year of association, 1966, the EGSA paid UR £34,000, and UR paid dividends amounting to £45,000. In each of the next two years, the EGSA transferred £35,000 and UR paid out £42,000 to shareholders. There can certainly have been little cause for commercial complaint when, in 1967, the Association had to turn its attention to the thorny problem of Stanley Wootton.

Mr Wootton, an Australian who had come to England in 1905 and had been a successful trainer and jockey, held Six Mile Hill and other Walton Downs land on lease from the Association, and administered it as summer training gallops. Since neither Six Mile Hill nor the gallops on Epsom Downs were viable for all-year-round training, the Association decided that the two areas should be united under one management. Wootton's lease was due to expire in June 1969: the EGSA, whose relationship with the lessee was far from amicable, failed to make satisfactory progress with him on the matter, and in November 1967 gave him notice to quit on expiry of the lease.

Notice of opposition came from his lawyer in December, and in March 1968, Wootton applied to the County Court for a new lease, and to the High Court for a declaration that the leased property was an agricultural holding, in which case the lease was not determinable under normal landlord and tenant procedure.

The battle won, that most astute of landowners and accomplished of strategists deftly donned the mantle of national hero by offering the spoils of war to the people – in April 1969 he offered the 206 acres of Walton Downs gallops to the Levy Board, on lease for 999 years 'at the rent of a peppercorn if demanded'. This magnificent and irrational gesture, coming so soon after his determined fight to retain the land, was in effect presenting the nation, or at least the racegoers in it, with the bulk of Walton Downs for posterity. To those who knew anything about Stanley Wootton and the history of his relationship with the Epsom authorities, it was unthinkable that he would consider giving the land to the EGSA, but he did not hesitate to give it to the Levy Board – or, significantly, to the safe keeping of the Levy Board chairman, Baron George Edward Cecil Wigg.

Lord Wigg will probably be pigeon-holed by historians, when the sad time comes to shove him aside, as a controversial figure. A soldier for 30 years, and an MP for 20, George Wigg took his peerage and the chairmanship of the Levy Board in exchange for the Paymaster-General's office, and, outside the Jockey Club, nobody in the racing business can have a day's regret about that – except perhaps the bookmakers, whom he so successfully levied when most around him said it could not be done. But most relevant to this story, he is a man who loves racing in general and Epsom in particular, and what he has achieved there may possibly have given him greater satisfaction than any other act of his life.

From the moment of Wootton's offer – or perhaps before it, the Levy Board went to work to acquire Epsom Downs as well as Walton Downs. By the end of April, the Board had made a public offer of 25s for each 10s United Racecourses share – a bid for the firm amounting to about £1.1 million. Infinitely the largest shareholdings in UR were held by Evelyn de Rothschild and, jointly, Sir Edwin and Robin McAlpine; with Charles Langlands, the former EGSA chairman, and Sir Rex Cohen the only other notable shareholders.

Evelyn de Rothschild, in the customary pattern of such

financial dealings, said there was no question of an agreed take-over at that figure. Shares of UR jumped from their depressing 5s to 29s in the expectation of a further bid, at which point it seems that Rothschild and Cohen increased their holdings. Mid-way through May, the Levy Board raised the bid to 30s a share, which Rothschild called 'a fantastic deal'. It put a value of £1,360,000 on the firm, and about £160,000 on Mr de Roths-child's own holding.

Regardless of finances, it was a takeover that made sense. Epsom and Sandown both needed a lot of money spent on them – an underpass here, a grandstand there – and, as Lord Wigg said then: 'We want racing at both courses for all time.' Sub-sequently the Levy Board, through its newly-established arm, Metropolitan and County Racecourse Management and Hold-ings Ltd., also bought the half-derelict Kempton Park. Sir Brian Mountain remained as chairman of UR, but among the changes at Epsom were the resignation of Alan Crego-Bourne, secretary for the past 20 years, and the appointment of Frank Coven, first as general manager and, 6 months later, as managing director of UR. (In 1972 Air Commodore Brooks took over as managing director, Coven moving up to become vice-chairman.)

The Levy Board takeover dated from early July, 1969. With that accomplished, the deal with Stanley Wootton could proceed. It involved not only the usual interminable legal procedures relevant to the transfer of the ownership of Six Mile Hill, but a compensatory cross-transfer of sixty acres of farmland owned by the EGSA, of which Wootton was the tenant, and the planning of the future management of the combined Epsom and Walton Downs gallops. The Levy Board took possession of the Walton gallops at the end of the year, and soon afterwards a board of management was formed, appointments to which are in the hands of the chairman of the Levy Board, Mr Wootton, the Surrey Racecourse Trainers' Association, the Conservators, the Borough Council and the County Council – reflecting the overwhelming importance of the proper preservation of the gallops.

The administration is largely in the hands of Jos Hall, a former divisional commander of the Metropolitan Police in the area, whose ceaseless task it is, as Conservation Officer, to allo-cate ground to the many trainers in the area (some 500 horses train on approximately 250 acres, summer and winter), to main-tain it in the best possible condition, and to keep an eye on the 'hackers', the horse-riding members of the public who are allowed to use parts of the Downs. His constant contact with representatives of all the interested parties has also done much to assure a better relationship between factions which, in the past, had found it hard to shake hands without trying to crack each other's fingers. His job of maintaining the winter gallops on Epsom Downs, within the curve of the racecourse, was made much easier by the Levy Board's decision, in 1970, to remove the fair, and the caravans that went with it, from its traditional site in The Dip to a spot out of sight of the grandstand, between it and Epsom Downs station – a move that was received with much thanks by the trainers, but with some sadness by the race-goers.

But what of the infamous underpass, on which the last action worth recording had been in the autumn of 1965, when the Levy Board and UR had put a ceiling target cost of £145,000 on the project? The matter now passed rapidly from low to high priority in the Levy Board's rating, but, in November 1969, the estimate had risen to £203,000. It was finally completed in April, 1971, at a cost of £216,000 – more than four times the original estimate 9 years earlier, and nearly as much as it cost to build the grandstands in 1927. At the same time £83,000 was spent on the new parade ring and its Tote and bar, to all of which the grandstand patron can now take a walk which, if still as long, at least is no longer in competition with passing traffic.

CHAPTER SEVENTEEN

Epilogue

Four years after the authors of *The Downs Report* had suggested new legislation to replace the Regulation Act of 1936 – on which the entire Epsom Downs operation hinges – the Conservators asked the Borough Council to consider promoting a Private Bill for that purpose. With reasonable alacrity a working party was set up, under the chairmanship of Edward Moore (Clerk to the Council and to the Conservators), 'to study in depth and to report in due course on the existing Regulation Act and the question of the promotion of an amending Private Bill'. The working party was composed of representatives of the interests most directly concerned with the future of the Downs (the Levy Board, the EGSA and the Surrey Trainers' Association), plus the Conservation Officer and three senior Council officers. The Chief Superintendent of police at Epsom also attended.

They first met in December 1970, and produced their report in May 1972. The conclusions were unexpectedly negative, due apparently to two main and largely predictable obstacles: the reluctance of the police to become more closely involved in the enforcement of the Conservators' by-laws, and the reluctance of the Town Clerk to recommend the Council to promote a Bill that brought any diminution in the rights of the public. Understandably, the Levy Board and the EGSA, as owners and operators of the racecourse business, had several ideas for new legislation that could not strictly be said to be in the public interest (the general rather than the racegoing public), and this seems to be an essential ingredient of a Private Bill.

The Borough Council's parliamentary agents, having studied the working party's deliberations, could see no compelling reason, at that stage, for promoting legislation to amend the 1936 Act. The Town Clerk said there was nothing to justify the Council taking such a course, but pointed out that this did not prevent the EGSA from promoting a Private Bill. With such lack of support from the public's representatives, its chances of success would be slight, but the possibility does make it important to look carefully at the racecourse authority's suggestions, as published in the report.

The one that caught the eye of the local press was the mention by Gordon Hadden of the Levy Board that, in any rebuilding of the grandstand (planned, you may recall, in 1964), facilities should be incorporated that allowed a much wider use of the site – indoor tennis courts, for example, or an indoor athletics track. This idea, vigorously promoted by Dr Roger Bannister as chairman of the Sports Council, is now almost national policy. It is absurd that two or three acres of ground should be taken up by a building complex that is only used nine days a year – particularly one with the structural properties of a stand, under which there are always vast open spaces ideal for indoor sports.

What is interesting is the fact that the EGSA clearly wants bigger stands that will bring it a higher income from increased admissions; by incorporating other sports facilities it will not only engage the sympathy of the Sports Council, but should also become entitled to a development grant. However, bigger stands mean more ground, and here the racecourse executive has to reckon with the public, or worse, those who are the zealous watchdogs of what they believe to be the public's interest. A grandstand that is also a multi-sports centre might well be welcome (if it does not, by its isolation, prove to be a white elephant), but to get it, the EGSA will almost certainly have to give up to public use a slice of land elsewhere.

What likelihood there is of the Levy Board providing four or five million pounds for a super-grandstand when at the moment the only worthwhile profit comes from one race meeting a year, and almost entirely from one day of that meeting, is another question. For the moment lesser matters concern the EGSA, which made it clear to the working party that it would seek provision in any new Act to close the 'free strips' that run along the finishing straight in front of the coach and car parks, and to establish in their place, during meetings, enclosures for which there would be an admission charge. The Association still clearly resents the fact that the public can watch racing at Epsom without paying; the public, with its long memory, might find it more convenient to reflect that, until the EGSA put up the grandstand a mere 150 years or so ago, there was nothing to stop it enjoying 'its' Downs in peace, and it had done so for centuries.

The racing executive would also like to close the racecourse track to the public at all times, except for suitable pedestrian crossing points, but was advised by the working party that this suggestion, too, would surely be countered by a demand for an equivalent piece of Epsom Downs to be handed back to the public for 'air and exercise,' In the face of this, the EGSA is likely to reduce its demand, should new legislation be promoted, to the closure of the track for two weeks before any meeting.

The concern expressed in *The Downs Report* over the period during which the temporary stands are allowed to remain up was also discussed by the working party. While it was agreed that the time allowed for erecting them could be reduced, no conclusion was reached as to the possibility of shortening the period between meetings during which they can remain (at present ten weeks).

The fact is, though it was not publicly reported, that the cost of erection and dismantling is now so high that, were the owners forced to do it more than once a year, it would probably be un-economic to continue their leases. That would probably not upset the Association too much in the case of Barnard's Stand, a thorn in its side it would pay good money to be able to pluck out.

Fairs and caravans, a joint problem without solution that has come up so often in the history of the racecourse and the writing of this book, received a good deal of pretty fruitless discussion by the working party. Local residents found the experiment of combining the Dip fair with the off-course fair on one large site at Tattenham Corner Road was one that gave them even more offence than before – it was all much closer to them. Their objections were swamped by the benefits derived by the EGSA and the Conservators from the new scheme: greater control over the fair and less damage to the training gallops. The combined fair is there to stay.

As to the caravans, the future of this problem was discussed in the chapter dealing with the activities of the police on the Downs. The Conservators' by-laws give them power to control or ban caravans: without the complete support of the police, the by-laws are impossible to enforce. The working party was unanimous in suggesting that provision should be made in any new Act for the police to be given authority to work with the Conservators to enforce the by-laws, and Edward Moore regarded this as the chief item of public interest in any proposed new legislation. He submitted a memorandum to the Commissioner of Police at New Scotland Yard, and discussed it with an Assistant Commissioner and the divisional Commander. The result was disappointing; while the police were willing to offer such assistance as they were able, they preferred to do so within the limits of their existing powers. That effectively put an end to any proposed legislation, since there is not the slightest chance that a Bill affecting the police could become an Act without their prior consent. With the Commissioner's decision to oppose any measure designed to widen the police's power on the Downs, the interests of the public in a Private Bill virtually disappeared.

Beyond that, as Moore pointed out, most of the more important and fundamental issues considered by the working party were concerned with the interests of racing and not of the public. 'Although the Borough Council would not be unduly concerned with the interests of racegoers and restrictions applied to the general public at race meetings,' he said, 'they (the Council) could not reasonably be expected to foot the bill, or the greater proportion of it, for promoting such proposals.'

That, of course, does not mean there can be no changes in the regulations currently controlling the use of the Downs. Under the Local Government Act of 1972, a local Act such as the Epsom and Walton Downs Regulation Act will cease to have effect at the end of 1984. Once the new law relating to local government comes into force, in April 1974, an application can, and no doubt will, be made to the Minister to extend the life of the 1936 Act beyond 1984. He has powers to do not only that, but also to alter the provisions of such an Act: any amendments he is prepared to include could be vitally important to the future of Epsom racecourse.

That it has a future is without question. Thanks to Lord Wigg and Stanley Wootton, Epsom now belongs to the nation. Barring catastrophe or demonic decisions, there will be racing on the Downs well beyond our time.

'I stood up there,' George Wigg said, 'and I looked over that marvellous hill and over the trees on Walton Downs and there was Headley Church standing up, tiny against the sky: and I thought, "Why not for ever?" and by God we've done it.'

The Derby

Though this book does not pretend to be any sort of a history of equine achievement, the story of Epsom racecourse would be monstrously incomplete, even for those readers who have not been within a furlong of a track, without a passing record of the Derby.

Before we get to the starting post, it is worth remembering that entries for this, the greatest of all flat races, close more than a year before the race, and it used to be even earlier. In practice, this means that a potential Derby runner must be spotted as a yearling – before he has ever raced. This results in hundreds of entries every year, the vast majority more in hope than expectation. As the race gets nearer, most of the original entries are withdrawn, and the later the date of withdrawal, the greater the forfeit paid by the owner. These entry fees form the stake money, and it was long a complaint against the Epsom authorities that they formed the only stake money. Now they are more than doubled by what is known in the business as added money, usually contributed by the promoters – or, in other races, by the sponsors.

To take 1972 as an example, there were 647 entries at the closing date, 24th March 1971. Each owner had then paid £25. Those who had not withdrawn by 16th November paid another £50; by 18th April, 1972, another £25; by 23rd May, another £50. Finally, those declared to run four days before the race (24 in all) had to pay another £250, making a total entry fee of £400. Stake money that particular year amounted to about £45,000, to which £50,000 was added. More than £63,000 of that total went to the winning owner.

And so, briefly, to the bones of the matter. Bones that have formed the skeleton of Epsom racecourse for two centuries: without them, it would certainly have collapsed. Those who want to explore every interesting shred in the life of the race should turn to Roger Mortimer's tremendous *History of the Derby Stakes*, a work to which I have constantly had recourse while writing this chapter, which gives brief year by year accounts of the Derby.

1780: won by Diomed at 6–4, ridden by Sam Arnull, owned by Sir Charles Bunbury.

As earlier chapters made clear, organisation and finance of the order which developed were not envisaged when the 12th Earl of Derby and his friends (including Bunbury) set up the first Derby Stakes, in a further attempt, like the founding of the Oaks the year before, to break the monotony of racing in heats. The prize money, however, was quite generous for the times: 1,125 guineas, derived from a 50 guinea stake from 36 entries, including 27 which withdrew, forfeiting half their entry fee. There is conflicting evidence as to whether this was the only Derby run over the straight mile course, or if that practice continued for the first three years.

1781: won by Young Eclipse at 10–1, ridden by Hindley, owned by Major O'Kelly.

This was one of three Derby winners sired by the great Eclipse, about which much has been written earlier (both the second and third in the first Derby were its foals). O'Kelly later became a colonel, though his military service was somewhat questionable. He was considered a typical Irish rogue, who progressed from debtors' prison to immense wealth, thanks to his ability to spot a talented horse.

1782: won by Assassin at 5–1, ridden by Sam Arnull, owned by the Earl of Egremont.

Lord Egremont had a tremendous stable at Petworth, where some said the management was so lax that several four-year-olds were Derby runners, and two of them Derby winners (Egremont had five winners in all). Though the earl was not married, the family name of Wyndham was perpetuated and a descendant was granted a peerage in the name of Leconfield.

1783: won by Saltram at 5–2, ridden by Hindley, owned by Mr Parker.

A socially remarkable Derby, since only one of the owners of the six runners was a peer, at a time when the aristocracy dominated racing. Mr Parker, however, wasn't far removed from this elevated category: an MP for 20 years, he became a baron the year after his win, and his son was to be an earl. Saltram was later bought by the Prince of Wales.

1784: won by Sergeant, at 3–1, ridden by John Arnull, owned by Colonel O'Kelly.

Like Saltram, this was another winning Eclipse colt, the third in the first five Derby Stakes. Socially, the balance was now properly restored: the ten owners involved this year included the Duke of Cumberland, the Duc de Chartres, the Earl of Derby, Lord Grosvenor, Lord Cavendish, Sir Charles Danver, and Sir Charles Bunbury. The jockey was Sam Arnull's brother.

1785: won by Aimwell at 7–1, ridden by Hindley, owned by Lord Clermont.

O'Kelly, who trained at Clay Hill, Epsom, had two unplaced runners. It was the winning jockey's third Derby success, and his last.

1786: won by Noble at 30–1, ridden by J. White, owned by Mr Panton.

Long odds for a Derby winner, but no longer than Noble's record would suggest. When retired to stud two years later, the fee was two guineas and half-a-crown for the groom. Its sire, Highflyer, was an oustanding and unbeaten horse. When it died in 1793, the owner, Richard Tattersall, had these words engraved on its memorial: 'Here lieth the perfect and beautiful symmetry of the much lamented Highflyer, by whom and his wonderful offspring the celebrated Tattersall acquired a noble fortune, but was not ashamed to acknowledge it'.

1787: won by Sir Peter Teazle at 2–1, ridden by Sam Arnull, owned by the Earl of Derby.

The only success by the Derby family in their Stakes between 1780 and 1923, and a remarkable one. Sir Peter Teazle and its stable mate, Lady Teazle, were named in honour of Derby's second wife, an actress who had often played in *The School for Scandal*. The colt had never raced before, was retired early and at stud sired four winners of the Derby, four of the St Leger, and two of the Oaks. This was another Highflyer foal.

1788: won by Sir Thomas at 6–5 on, ridden by William South, owned by the Prince of Wales.

There was loyal rapture for a royal win; the support for the unbeaten Sir Thomas was reflected in such odds as the Derby had not seen before. 'Prinny' was on top of the world just now – half-way between the racing debt from which Parliament rescued him, and the Escape scandal that nearly ruined him a second time. Jockey South, by the way, was 54, an extraordinary age in those days for such activity.

1789: won by Skyscraper at 7–4 on, ridden by Sam Chifney, owned by the Duke of Bedford.

This jockey was the same old Sam Chifney who rode Escape for the Prince of Wales when some thought it was not trying, and who consequently came to a sad end in Fleet Prison. His mount was again by Highflyer and owned – as was the second horse this year – by the young Duke of Bedford. The Prince of Wales had two runners, one of which, Soujah ul Doulah, was fourth.

1790: won by Rhadamanthus at 5–4, ridden by John Arnull, owned by the Earl of Grosvenor.

After four Derby seconds in five years, Grosvenor this time made both first and second place, his two runners starting favourite and second favourite. Naming horses is a mysterious business: his runner-up, Asparagus, was sired by a famous horse called Pot-8-os – or more properly, Potooooooos. Third was Lord Derby's Lee Boo.

1791: won by Eager at 5–2, ridden by Stephenson, owned by the Duke of Bedford.

Eager was unnamed when it won, not an unusual event in racing then, but rare in the circumstances of the Derby. It appeared on the card as 'Brother to Fidget, by Florizel', but started second favourite just the same. For the third successive year, the Prince of Wales owned the horse placed fourth.

1792: won by John Bull at 6–4 on, ridden by Frank Buckle, owned by the Earl of Grosvenor.

An interesting example of how a respected owner and a great jockey could shorten the odds, despite an almost unknown horse that only won one other race in its life. Buckle was one of the finest jockeys in the history of racing, both in technique and character. He won sixteen classics, including the Derby five times.

1793: won by Waxy at 12–1, ridden by William Clift, owned by Sir Ferdinand Poole.

Waxy and the runner-up, the odds-on favourite Gohanna, spent much of their racing lifetime in stirring battles on the course. Waxy lived to the age of 27 and had a supremely successful career at stud. A strange feature of this outing was that, though the winner was trained by one of the most gentle trainers of the day, it was ridden by one of the roughest and toughest jockeys.

1794: won by Daedalus at 6–1, ridden by Frank Buckle, owned by the Earl of Grosvenor.

An inexplicably dreary Derby, in which only 4 of the 49 entries finally ran. In these circumstances, it was the more surprising that the Duke of Bedford's Leon, an odds-on favourite, could only finish third.

1795: won by Spread Eagle at 3–1, ridden by A. Wheatley, owned by Sir Frank Standish.

Standish, a member of the Jockey Club, retains a place in racing history as the owner of a horse poisoned at Newmarket years later, for which one Daniel Dawson was hanged. Spread Eagle may well have been named after one of Epsom's oldest pubs, the centre of much racing activity, which still stands at the foot of a road leading to the Downs.

1796: won by Didelot, ridden by John Arnull, owned by Sir Frank Standish.

So little was thought of Didelot's chances that no record was kept of the odds offered against it. The clear favourite was its stable mate, Mr Teazle, at 11–8. However, this Standish horse came nowhere, and never raced again. Sir Frank achieved the rare success that year of winning the Oaks as well.

1797: won by an unnamed colt at 10–1, ridden by John Singleton, owned by the Duke of Bedford.

It was Bedford who had not named Eager till it won the Derby, and this winner ('by Fidget out of a sister of Pharamond') seems never to have been named. It had never run before and only appeared once again. Singleton, the jockey, was intended by his parents to be a surgeon, but ran away to Newmarket to work for Stephenson, who had been Eager's jockey.

1798: won by Sir Harry at 7–4, ridden by Sam Arnull, owned by Mr Joseph Cookson.

It seems unbelievable today that so many horses could have won the Derby without ever having raced before. The absolutely haphazard method of starting races may have had something to do with it; at a roughly suitable moment somebody would shout 'Go!' and it was too bad for those who weren't to hand at the time! Sir Harry was the first Derby winner to be sired by a previous Derby winner.

1799: won by Archduke at 12–1, ridden by John Arnull, owned by Sir Frank Standish.

This was the eighth Arnull winner, and they weren't done yet.

It was the last for Sir Frank Standish, who again had the odd and frustrating experience of seeing his first choice (the evens favourite Eagle) beaten by an unlikely horse.

1800: won by Champion at 7–4, ridden by William Clift, owned by Mr Christopher Wilson.

Champion, a Pot-8-os colt, was the first horse to win the Derby and the St Leger, the Doncaster classic that had started the move to one-heat races. Until rail travel and horse boxes developed, few horses raced in both the north and the south of the country. Mr Wilson, a Yorkshireman with a great love of the sport, was also distinguished for dying at Epsom, without warning, 42 Derby days after winning the event.

1801: won by Eleanor at 5–4, ridden by Saunders, owned by Sir Charles Bunbury.

An historic win; the first filly to win, and one of the few ever to pull it off; also the first to win both the Derby and the Oaks (a race for fillies only). Her trainer's dying message ('Depend on it, Eleanor is a damned fine mare') is chronicled elsewhere. It was Bunbury's first win as an owner since the very first Derby, which he had been so instrumental in launching.

1802: won by Tyrant at 7–1, ridden by Frank Buckle, owned by the Duke of Grafton.

An easy winner for the randy old Duke, though Tyrant never won another race in its life. Grafton, then 66, had been prime minister at 31: as a result of his extraordinarily indiscreet conduct, his first marriage was dissolved by an Act of Parliament, and he then took as Duchess the Dean of Windsor's daughter. They had twelve children. The Duke's grandfather, who was married at nine to a girl of five, was by King Charles II out of Barbara Villiers, mistress and demolisher of Nonsuch Palace.

1803: won by Ditto at 7–2, ridden by William Clift, owned by Sir Hedworth Williamson.

This was the third colt sired by Sir Peter Teazle to win a Derby, and on this occasion the 1787 winner sired the first three to finish.

1804: won by Hannibal at 5–2, ridden by William Arnull, owned by the Earl Egremont.

Enter another Arnull, this one only nineteen years old and Sam's son. The race, which he won easily, was noted for being probably the first about which a report appeared in any newspaper (*The Times*) other than a sporting sheet. It tells us that there was 'severe running' between the horses that eventually finished second and third, until Hannibal took over at Tattenham Corner and won 'in less time than was ever remembered'.

1805: won by Cardinal Beaufort at 20–1, ridden by Dennis Fitzpatrick, owned by the Earl of Egremont.

Another winner first time out, and another second string to beat its stablemate choice; Egremont's Imposter started at 7–4, but was not placed. One runner was brought down by a spectator on the course, an accident that was tragically to be echoed more than a century later.

1806: won by Paris at 5–1, ridden by John Shepherd, owned by Lord Foley.

Only a short head prevented another Egremont win, with Trafalgar. Paris was the last of the colts by Sir Peter Teazle to win the Derby.

1807: won by Election at 3–1, ridden by John Arnull, owned by the Earl of Egremont.

Whatever the strength of the alleged mismanagement of the Petworth stable, Lord Egremont had an uncanny eye for putting the right untried horses into the Derby. Here was another that had never raced in public before, yet still started favourite. Election went on winning, though like many classic winners of the time, its career was never again notable.

1808: won by Pan at 25–1, ridden by Frank Collinson, owned by Sir Hedworth Williamson.

One of the most exciting early Derby races, it looked, until the last breath, like a battle between another Sir Peter Teazle colt, Vandyke and the Prince of Wales's Rubens, when the outsider came up in a great late burst. Collinson, the jockey, is said to have contracted an illness by sleeping in a damp bed on his way south from Yorkshire and died a few weeks later.

1809: won by Pope at 20–1, ridden by Tom Goodisson, owned by the Duke of Grafton.

Mr Christopher Wilson's Wizard, having just won the first Two Thousand Guineas at Newmarket, was 11–8 favourite for the Derby, and was only overtaken a few yards from the post. The following year the two horses met in a match for 200 guineas, which Wizard won, despite conceding three pounds.

1810: won by Whalebone at 2–1, ridden by William Clift, owned by the Duke of Grafton.

To racing breeders, the name of Whalebone is a glorious one. Successful enough as a racer – it led the Derby from start to finish – its triumphs at stud were phenomenal. It was an odd-looking beast, and was sold by the Duke of Grafton and by its next owner. Significantly, Whalebone was bought for stud by the Earl of Egremont, who could never have regretted it.

1811: won by Phantom at 5–1, ridden by Frank Buckle, owned by Sir John Shelley.

Won on the line by a grandson of Sir Peter Teazle. At stud, Phantom sired six classic winners and went blind.

1812: won by Octavius at 7–1, ridden by William Arnull, owned by Mr Ladbroke.

The second favourite, Manuella at 7–2, was ridden by the younger Sam Chifney and deliberately held back. He then backed it at 20–1 for the Oaks the next day, which the filly won.

1813: won by Smolenska at evens, ridden by Tom Goodisson, owned by Sir Charles Bunbury.

A rare win for a black horse, and the first of any colour to win both the Derby and the 2,000 Guineas; but punters may think this race more notable for the fact that his losses on it caused one bookmaker to shoot himself. The great Bunbury, then 73, lived another eight years but won no more Derby Stakes.

1814: won by Blucher at 5–2, ridden by William Arnull, owned by Lord Stawell.

This marked the end of the Derby triumphs of the galloping Arnulls – four wins for Sam, five for John, and three for William.

1815: won by Whisker at 8–1, ridden by Tom Goodisson, owned by the Duke of Grafton.

Old Grafton was dead, but his son far outstripped his father's great racing successes: the winners of 21 classics in nine years were owned by the 4th Duke. Whisker was his only Derby winner and was not much fancied, but stormed home to win at the post.

1816: won by Prince Leopold at 20–1, ridden by Wheatley, owned by Mr Warwick Lake.

Mr Lake was Master of Horse to the Duke of York, the Prince of Wales's brother. The colt was heavily backed by his royal owner, but scantily by the public.

1817: won by Azor at 50–1, ridden by Jem Robinson, owned by Mr John Payne.

None of the fancied horses achieved anything, and two 50–1 shots fought it out between them. This was the first of six Derby wins for the great Jem Robinson, who was later severely injured in a racing fall.

1818: won by Sam at 7–2, ridden by Sam Chifney junior, owned by Mr Thomas Thornhill.

The winner was named after its jockey and trained by the jockey's brother William, both of them sons of old Sam Chifney, who had won nearly thirty years earlier. The remarkable relationship between the owner, a Norfolk squire, and his jockey led to Mr Thornhill leaving his house and stables to Sam in his will.

1819: won by Tiresias at 2–1, ridden by William Clift, owned by the Duke of Portland.

The Duke, who owned part of Newmarket Heath, was the father of Lord George Bentinck, who, as senior Jockey Club steward and virtual dictator of British racing, had more influence on the subsequent development of racing at Epsom than any other outsider.

1820: won by Sailor at 4–1, ridden by Sam Chifney, owned by Mr Thomas Thornhill.

The Norfolk partnership struck again, thanks to a deluge the previous night, which turned even Epsom's hard going into a muddy mess – just the way Sailor liked it. The horse died a few months later, but this race won Thornhill £23,000.

1821: won by Gustavus at 2–1, ridden by Sam Day, owned by Mr J. Hunter.

According to the jockey, he and the runner-up (Frank Buckle) had to wind in and out of the crowd all the way from Tattenham Corner 'like a dog at a fair'. There was not much then in the way of railings to keep the crowd back, and, not for the first time, the efforts of the men hired to clear a way for the runners were insufficient.

1822: won by Moses at 6–1, ridden by Tom Goodisson, owned by the Duke of York.

The Duke was by now said to be so deeply in debt that he could not put much on the winner. His stable was managed at this time by a cousin of Lord George Bentinck, Charles Greville, whose racy diaries acquired such fame that his name was still used as a pseudonym by the *Daily Mail* diarist 150 years later.

1823: won by Emilius at 5–4, ridden by Frank Buckle, owned by Mr John Udney.

The winning horse had an odd life; the following year it was sold to Mr Thornhill, and soon retired to stud. Twenty years later Lord George Bentinck bought it, tottering and weak, and nursed it back to strength only to see it die of indigestion in 1847.

1824: won by Cedric at 9–2, ridden by Jem Robinson, owned by Sir John Shelley.

Jem Robinson distinguished himself by leading in, all in one week, the winners of the Derby and the Oaks and a bride to the altar. He may have been a bit lucky in the first, since there were three false starts in all of which the eventual runner-up covered a good deal of ground.

1825: won by Middleton at 7–4, ridden by Jem Robinson, owned by Lord Jersey.

Middleton shares with Amato, the winner in 1838, the extraordinary accomplishment that this Derby was the only race in which it ran in all its life. The win was in spite of the fact that the stable lad was persuaded to give it a bucket of water shortly before the race. The owner, Lord Jersey, was later Lord Chamberlain to William IV and Master of Horse to Queen Victoria.

1826: won by Lapdog at 50–1, ridden by G. Dockeray, owned by the Earl of Egremont.

Egremont's last Derby, won to the astonishment of all, including its owner, by an unlikely horse and an unlikely jockey, neither of whom was ever successful again.

1827: won by Mameluke at 9–1, ridden by Jem Robinson, owned by Lord Jersey.

Jersey owned the first two to finish, and the second, Glenartney, was much better backed. Perhaps because Glenartney was known to be ridden by a crooked jockey, Jersey's reputation suffered somewhat from Mameluke's win, accomplished after its stablemate was in front, by a comfortable margin, only two furlongs from home.

1828: won by Cadland at 4–1, ridden by Jem Robinson, owned by the Duke of Rutland.

No doubt Charles Bluck was around the course for this one, for by the end of the year he had put in his bid for an acre of the Downs on which to build a grandstand. It was an intensely exciting race, won after a dead heat with The Colonel, the favourite ridden by Bill Scott. At the run-off later the same afternoon, The Colonel was odds-on favourite, but lost by half a length.

1829: won by Frederick at 40–1, ridden by J. Forth, owned by Mr G. W. Gratwicke.

By now the stand was up, and in a fit state to receive company, but incomplete within and without and still partly surrounded by scaffolding. Fittingly, the race was won by two other beginners: Frederick had never run before, nor had Mr Gatwicke ever raced before. His jockey made up for it – he was over 60 years old.

1830: won by Priam at 4–1, ridden by Sam Day, owned by William Chifney.

Reckoned one of the great racehorses of all time, Priam had walked from Newmarket to Epsom with Chifney, the owner and trainer. With the other 21 runners, Priam suffered 14 false starts and a deluge throughout the race. It was beaten only twice in a long racing career, and was rated by some experts as the most perfect racehorse of the century. Despite such a winner, and the new stand, *The Times* commented that the races had not come off with their usual *éclat*.

1831: won by Spaniel at 50–1, ridden by W. Wheatley, owned by Lord Lowther.

An unlikely and apparently unworthy winner of a race which was remembered for the rare presence of a runner belonging to the King (William IV), and for the fact that, for the first time, the winning owner had to contribute £100 towards the expenses of policing the course. The runner-up, which was a 6–4 on favourite, no longer won £100, but only kept his £50 stake. Signs that the EGSA was in operation!

1832: won by St Giles at 3–1, ridden by Bill Scott, owned by Mr Robert Ridsdale.

One of those years that gentlemen like to forget, since the owner and his confederate, John Gully, were rated as black a pair of influential knaves as ever twisted jockeys. The off-course betting was much concerned with the number of riders that year who were in the winning owner's pay.

1833: won by Dangerous at 30–1, ridden by J. Chapple, owned by Mr Sadler.

Lame before and after the race, the winner forgot its affliction while running, and was only challenged by a 100–1 outsider.

1834: won by Plenipotentiary at 9–4, ridden by P. Conolly, owned by Mr Stanlake Batson.

A highly successful Derby, with good weather, a great crowd and a fine winner.

1835: won by Mundig at 6–1, ridden by Bill Scott, owned by Mr John Bowes.

Bowes, a son of Lord Strathmore, was only 21 and a Cambridge undergraduate. Far from being a racing blood, he was a particularly quiet and retiring young man, who later gave up racing and social life altogether. Mundig had never raced before and retired to stud the following year, where he ran amok and killed a groom.

1836: won by Bay Middleton at 7–4, ridden by Jem Robinson, owned by Lord Jersey.

A bad year for the bookies, who were cleaned out by Lord Jersey, Lord George Bentinck, and their friends. A bad year too for the Hon. Berkeley Craven, who lost heavily on the race and shot himself that evening.

1837: won by Phosphorus at 40–1, ridden by George Edwards, owned by Lord Berners.

The first Derby to be started by a flag instead of a shout, it was won by a horse that had so badly sprained a foreleg four days earlier that it remained in a loose box until the evening before the race.

1838: won by Amato at 30–1, ridden by J. Chapple, owned by Sir Gilbert Heathcote.

A great year for Epsom, as Amato was trained on the Downs at what is now Downs House, and used to be known as Sherwood's Cottage. Its owner, Sir Gilbert Heathcote, lived beside the racecourse at Durdans, where Amato is buried, and was a steward of Epsom races. Further excitement was caused by the fact that excursion trains this year came not to Epsom, but within five miles of it – a rare treat for racegoers who were accustomed to walking between eight and fifteen miles for their sport. This was the only race that Amato ever ran in its life, and it died five years later.

1839: won by Bloomsbury at 25–1, ridden by Sim Templeman, owned by Mr William Ridsdale.

Bloomsbury used to belong to Ridsdale's notorious brother

Robert, and Lord Chesterfield, for whom William Ridsdale was trainer, entered the colt for the Derby. The two then parted company, and the ownership of Bloomsbury was in some dispute. This was probably the coldest Derby ever known, and snow fell throughout the race; it was also the first during the reign of Henry Dorling as Clerk of the Course.

1840: won by Little Wonder at 50–1, ridden W. Macdonald, owned by Mr D. Robertson.

The only Derby attended by Victoria as Queen, and won by an unknown colt ridden by a boy. The owner was said to have had no bet on his runner, but his trainer, the wily old Forth, won £18,000. Roger Mortimer tells a delightful story, in his Derby history, of the experienced jockey Bill Scott shouting to Macdonald, as he passed Scott in the finishing straight 'A thousand pounds for a pull!' 'Too late, Mr Scott,' replied the lad, 'too late!'

1841: won by Coronation at 5–2, ridden by P. Conolly, owned by Mr A. T. Rawlinson.

The first favourite to win for five years, Coronation did so in a record field of 29, which was kept waiting an hour and a half for the off.

1842: won by Attila at 5–1, ridden by Bill Scott, owned by Colonel Anson.

Colonel Anson was an old soldier who later became a general and Commander-in-Chief of the army in India. While dining there one night, a telegram arrived to inform him of the Sepoy Mutiny. With unfortunate consequences, he refrained from opening it at the table.

1843: won by Cotherstone at 13–8, ridden by Bill Scott, owned by Mr John Bowes.

Mr Bowes backed his colt to win early, before his victory in the 2,000 Guineas shortened the odds. Lord George Bentinck, whose Gaper was second favourite, backed his own runner to win £135,000, and then covered himself on Cotherstone so completely that he ended £30,000 up.

1844: won by Orlando at 20–1, ridden by Nat Flatman, owned by Colonel Peel.

There was scandal and intrigue that year; first past the post, at 10–1, was Running Rein, later unmasked by Lord George Bentinck – the full story is told earlier – as a ringer: it was in fact a four-year-old, Maccabeus. Colonel Peel, who also owned the runner-up, was a brother of Sir Robert Peel, the prime minister. He later became a major-general without ever seeing active service and was eventually Secretary of State for War.

1845: won by The Merry Monarch without quoted odds, ridden by F. Bell, owned by Mr G. W. Gratwicke.

Though individual odds were quoted for seventeen of the 31 runners, two at 200–1, nothing appears for The Merry Monarch except a job lot of 15–1 for all the horses entered by his trainer. Remembered at Epsom as the first Derby during Henry Dorling's 21 years as lessee of the grandstand.

1846: won by Pyrrhus the First at 8–1, ridden by Sam Day, owned by John Gully.

Interest centred during the race on the runner-up, Sir Tatton Sykes, owned and ridden by Bill Scott, a man given to occasional drinking on a fearsome scale, and the morning of the Derby was one of those occasions. Though with two furlongs to go his horse seemed sure to win, Scott had by then lost control and could not keep a straight course. Sir Tatton Sykes won the Leger that year, and Scott died in 1848.

1847: won by Cossack at 5–1, ridden by Sim Templeman, owned by Mr Pedley.

A record field of 32, and a record time of 2 min. 52 sec. – three seconds faster than the previous year, the only other occasion on which the race had been timed. This was, however, a new course – Henry Dorling's notorious low-level start in full view of the patrons of his grandstand (previously the beginning of the race had been out of sight behind Downs House), which produced the generally unpopular early climb. Also the first year in which the railway line from Croydon reached Epsom.

1848: won by Surplice at evens, ridden by Sim Templeman, owned by Lord Clifden.

Poor Lord George Bentinck; his dearest ambition had been to win the Derby, but two years earlier he had sold his stable – including Surplice. It was while consoling him for his disappointment, tempered as it was by having backed Surplice heavily, that Disraeli coined the phrase 'the Blue Ribbon of the Turf'.

1849: won by The Flying Dutchman at 2–1, ridden by Marlow, owned by Lord Eglinton.

A magnificent horse and a famous winner, The Flying Dutchman brought a record prize of £6,575 for this race to its owner.

1850: won by Voltigeur at 16–1, ridden by Job Marson, owned by Lord Zetland.

Another fine champion, which enjoyed an enthralling rivalry with The Flying Dutchman, Voltigeur died at stud soon after being kicked by a mare.

1851: won by Teddington at 3–1, ridden by Job Marson, owned by Sir Joseph Hawley.

Sir Joseph, later a member of the Jockey Club, was noted in advancing years for his strenuous opposition to heavy gambling. It was believed, however, that he won about £80,000 on this race alone.

1852: won by Daniel O'Rourke at 25–1, ridden by Frank Butler, owned by Mr John Bowes.

Despite the increasing efforts of the Jockey Club to clean up the business, there were few big races without their crooked aspects. This time, the rider of the third placed horse later admitted he had not ridden to win: he had been substituted for the original jockey, who had clearly been nobbled. Nobody lost more on the deal than the horse's trainer, who had backed it to win £100,000.

1853: won by West Australian at 6–4, ridden by Frank Butler, owned by Mr John Bowes.

No quarrel with the quality of the winner here; it won the 2,000 Guineas, the Derby, the Leger, and the Ascot Cup. At the end of its racing career it was bought for 5,000 guineas, and subsequently went to the French royal stud.

1854: won by Andover at 7–2, ridden by Alfred Day, owned by Mr John Gully.

The horse of Gully, bookmaker and former champion prize fighter, was closely followed by that of Baron Rothschild, whose family were later to have a close financial interest in the well-being of the racecourse.

1855: won by Wild Dayrell at evens, ridden by Robert Sherwood, owned by Mr Francis Popham.

Did a horse ever have a weirder, wilder life than Wild Dayrell? Named after a 16th century criminal, sold, resold, bought back and made the subject of one of the most devastating nobbling plots connected with any Derby favourite. No wonder its owner said he never wanted a Derby horse again. The jockey was the son of Ralph Sherwood, the Epsom trainer of Amato.

1856: won by Ellington at 20–1, ridden by Aldcroft, owned by Admiral Harcourt.

Dorling was in some turmoil because of the visit of Prince Albert with Prince Frederick of Prussia, who was about to marry the Queen's eldest daughter, Victoria. With only 24 hours notice, he apparently managed to fill the royal saloon with 'the leading female members of the aristocracy'. Ellington, a colt by The Flying Dutchman, never won another race.

1857: won by Blink Bonny at 20–1, ridden by Charlton, owned by Mr William I'Anson.

Very nearly beaten by a 200–1 outsider, Blink Bonney keeps its head up in history by winning the Oaks two days later. The horse died at the age of eight and its skeleton was displayed in York Museum. The original Rubbing House pub burned down during this meeting.

1858: won by Beadsman at 10–1, ridden by John Wells, owned by Sir Joseph Hawley.

Wells was a considerable character, and was known as 'Tiny' – he had grown from being a very small apprentice into an unusually tall jockey. He won by a length from Toxopholite, owned by Lord Derby: had the latter been successful, he would have beaten by 36 years Lord Rosebery's achievement of being the first prime minister in office to win the Derby.

1859: won by Musjid at 9–4, ridden by John Wells, owned by Sir Joseph Hawley.

It was said that while the brothers Alfred and William Day (who rode the third and fourth finishers) were holding back their mounts and urging on Sam Rogers on Marionette (who was second), Wells extracted Musjid from the close attention of two jockeys down the field and stormed through to win.

1860: won by Thormanby at 4–1, ridden by Harry Custance, owned by Mr James Merry.

The jockey, at 19, was having his first Derby ride, and nearly lost it; on the day of the race he learned that the owner had engaged another, and the matter was only settled in the paddock.

1861: won by Kettledrum at 16–1, ridden by Bullock, owned by Colonel Towneley.

Henry Dorling took some criticism from the Press over this race, for which it was said the course was ill-prepared and the starter even worse. He dropped the flag while three horses were thirty yards from the line and another had its back to him.

1862: won by Caractacus at 40–1, ridden by J. Parsons, owned by Mr Snewing.

The winner was ridden by a 16-year-old stable lad whose name seems then to have disappeared from the circle of popular jockeys.

1863: won by Macaroni at 10–1, ridden by Tom Chaloner, owned by Mr R. C. Naylor.

This Derby was marked by heavy rain and the first visit of the young Prince of Wales (later Edward VII), who became a devoted follower of the sport and himself a winning Derby owner.

1864: won by Blair Athol at 14–1, ridden by Jim Snowden, owned by Mr William I'Anson.

Though the winner had never raced before, it did so well in trials that the owner refused an offer, when it was a two-year-old, of 7,000 guineas. The offer was from a bookmaker, who later bought it for stud.

1865: won by Gladiateur at 5–2, ridden by Harry Grimshaw, owned by Count F. de Lagrange.

A Derby win by a Frenchman was not only unheard of, but very hard to take. The Count's Fille de l'Air had won the Oaks in 1864; now Gladiateur won the 2,000 Guineas, the Derby, the Leger, the Newmarket Derby (by forty lengths), the Ascot Gold Cup, and (in Paris) the Grand Prix and the Grand Prix de l'Empereur.

1866: won by Lord Lyon at 6–5 on, ridden by Harry Custance, owned by Mr Richard Sutton.

The first odds-on favourite since 1835, Lord Lyon only won by a head at the post after one of the most exciting finishes seen at Epsom for years.

1867: won by Hermit at 1,000–15, ridden by John Daley, owned by Mr Henry Chaplin.

The almost impossibly novelletish romance behind this win is given full play in an earlier chapter. The event was a real stunner, which on the track consisted of a sensational win for a horse that, having just broken a blood vessel, was thought by many to have little chance of finishing the race. Off the track, the owner made, and the man for whom his fiancée jilted him lost, at least £120,000.

1868: won by Blue Gown at 7–2, ridden by John Wells, owned by Sir Joseph Hawley.

Favourite was a brilliant filly belonging to the unfortunate Lord Hastings, who had lost so much money in the past two seasons that he had sold most of his estates and his horses. But his temperamental Lady Elizabeth came nowhere, and the Marquis was lost.

1869: won by Pretender at 11–8, ridden by John Osborne, owned by Mr John Johnstone.

For more than a year, the Epsom Grand Stand Association had been in dispute with the new Lord of the Manor of Walton-on-the-Hill over the terms of its lease for that part of the course that ran over his land. He remained intractable, and for a time it looked as though, if there were to be a Derby, the course would have to be changed. In the end, the EGSA paid up. This was the first year in which the racecourse had the use of Sir Gilbert Heathcote's paddock, allowing a straight run out after the winning post.

1870: won by Kingcraft at 10–1, ridden by Tom French, owned by Viscount Falmouth.

Tom French, who was 22 when he rode this winner for the famous trainer Matthew Dawson, died three years later. His death opened the gates to fame for a young apprentice at the stable by the name of Fred Archer.

1871: won by Favonius at 9–1, ridden by Tom French, owned by Baron Rothschild.

A great year for Rothschild, whose filly Hannah won the 1,000 Guineas, the Oaks, and the Leger. By sad coincidence, the venerable Baron, his young jockey, and his winning colt were all dead within six years.

1872: won by Cremorne at 3–1, ridden by Maidment, owned by Mr Henry Saville.

This was the first use of the new course, the only difference being that the opening stages of the race were not run on such a steep climb. Trainers and jockeys had begged for such a change for years. It had nothing to do, as has been suggested elsewhere, with the Walton-on-the-Hill dispute; the part of the course on Walton territory was unchanged.

1873: won by Doncaster at 45–1, ridden by Fred Webb, owned by Mr James Merry.

Doncaster's trainer, Robert Peck, is said to have decided to run the untried colt in the Derby after it had carried his eleven stone most successfully in an informal gallop. He promptly backed it at 66–1, but the racing fraternity remained unimpressed until it was too late. Henry Dorling had died in March that year, after 34 years as Clerk of the Course. He was succeeded by his son Henry Mayson Dorling.

1874: won by George Frederick at 9–1, ridden by Harry Custance, owned by Mr. W. S. Cartwright.

Mr Cartwright, a former solicitor, had the unusual idea of repeatedly mating his mare, Princess of Wales, with the same stallion, and of calling all her offspring after members of the royal family. George Frederick was the fourth of seven, and Cartwright was so sure of its Derby win that he wrote out the telegrams before the race.

1875: won by Galopin at 2–1, ridden by Morris, owned by Prince Batthyany.

The owner was a rich Hungarian prince who had been a member of the Jockey Club for sixteen years. The horse became extremely successful sire as well as a fine racer, producing several classic winners as well as St Simon, one of the greatest horses of all time. The race was watched by a large royal party – led, of course, by the Prince of Wales.

1876: won by Kisber at 4–1, ridden by Maidment, owned by Mr Alexander Baltazzi.

The horse was English born but Hungarian bred, the owner was Turkish born but English bred. He was schooled at Rugby, fell heavily into debt, and made his jockey a most generous award out of the £100,000 he is said to have won on the race.

1877: won by Silvio at 100–9, ridden by Fred Archer, owned by Viscount Falmouth.

The first of five Derby wins for one of the greatest of all jockeys, who most tragically shot himself during an illness less than ten years later. Close followers of the Epsom story may be interested to note that among the owners of unplaced runners was the name of Mr C. J. Langlands.

1878: won by Sefton at 100–12, ridden by Harry Constable, owned by Mr W. Stirling Crawford.

There was nothing remarkable about this win except, perhaps, that the owner's wife, the widowed Duchess of Montrose, a formidable lady unsparing with the face paint and hair dye, was said to have chosen Mr Crawford in preference to Fred Archer. An owner herself, her language at times matched any to be found on the course. After Mr Crawford's death, when she was 70, she was married again, to a man of 24.

1879: won by Sir Bevys at 20–1, ridden by George Fordham, owned by Baron Rothschild.

After this meeting, the Jockey Club complained to the grand-stand proprietors that the accommodation afforded them was inadequate to their requirements, and suggested that the recently-completed small west extension should be rebuilt on a much larger scale, and that it should be 'mainly devoted to the use of the Jockey Club and the upper classes'. Thus was born the Club Stand. The Prince's Stand was also rebuilt that year.

1880: won by Bend Or at 2–1, ridden by Fred Archer, owned by the Duke of Westminster.

Two weeks after this tremendous race Mr C. Brewer, owner of the runner-up, objected to the stewards that, through an early confusion in a change of stable, Bend Or was not Bend Or at all, but Tadcaster. The stewards overruled the objection after an enquiry, but in later years their judgment came to be doubted.

1881: won by Iroquois at 11–2, ridden by Fred Archer, owned by Mr Pierre Lorillard.

The first American Derby winner, and the only one for 173 years, Iroquois would surely have produced something like a riot had it not been trained at Newmarket and ridden by Archer.

1882: won by Shotover at 11–2, ridden by Tom Cannon, owned by the Duke of Westminster.

The favourite, Bruce, lost ground when it shied as some paper blew in its face – an occurrence for which the Clerk of the Course was fined £50 by the Jockey Club.

1883: won by St Blaise at 11–2, ridden by Charles Wood, owned by Sir Frederick Johnstone.

Fred Archer, who rode the third horse home, was alleged to have pulled it, and its owner subsequently sold his stock. The licence of the winning jockey, Wood, was later withdrawn over the same scandal that caused the retirement from racing of a former senior Jockey Club steward, Sir George Chetwind.

1884: a dead heat between St Gatien at 100–8, ridden by Charles Wood, owned by Mr John Hammond; and Harvester at 100–7, ridden by Sam Loates, owned by Sir John Willoughby.

No deciding heat was run in this event, which everybody knew should have been won by that magnificent and unbeaten race-horse St Simon. Sadly its owner, Prince Batthyany, had died the previous year, and by the ludicrous Jockey Club rule then existing all classic nominations for his horses automatically became void.

1885: won by Melton at 15–8, ridden by Fred Archer, owned by the Marquis of Hastings.

This was the next Marquis, brother of the unfortunate young man already mentioned. This one was lucky enough to have Archer, who took Melton ahead at the last stride after a brilliant ride as his jockey.

1886: won by Ormonde at 9–4 on, ridden by Fred Archer, owned by the Duke of Westminster.

One of the greatest and most popular horses of the century, Ormonde won the 2,000 Guineas and the Leger, and there was much unhappiness when the Duke sold it for stud in the Argentine. By then, however, it was a sick horse, and though it fetched a price of £30,000 in 1894, it was destroyed in 1904. The Club Stand was opened for this meeting.

1887: won by Merry Hampton at 100–9, ridden by Jack Watts, owned by Mr George Baird.

The young owner had inherited two fortunes and died at the age of 32, having squandered most of them 'in horse-racing, prize-fighting and harlotry', according to the press. He was a good rider himself, but a boor, and refused to lead Merry Hampton into the winner's enclosure.

1888: won by Ayrshire at 6–5 on, ridden by Fred Barrett, owned by the Duke of Portland.

The Duke won fourteen classics between 1884 and 1902, including the Oaks four times, but his real fame rested on his ownership of St Simon, which he bought after Prince Batthyany's death: it sired the winners of 571 races.

1889: won by Donovan at 11–8 on, ridden by Tommy Loates, owned by the Duke of Portland.

By now the EGSA, through H. M. Dorling, had bought from the Lord of the Manor of Walton not only that part of his land which the racecourse crossed, but also the great gallops on Six Mile Hill – 205 acres in all, at a price of £20,000.

1890: won by Sainfoin at 100–15, ridden by Jack Watts, owned by Sir James Miller.

Coincidentally with Louis Curzon's attack on 'the most niggardly racing corporation in the kingdom', Epsom at last decided – under pressure from the Jockey Club – to contribute to the stakes. The race was given a guaranteed value of £5,000. Two years earlier, with only 169 entries, it had fallen well below £4,000. Also, for the first time, the EGSA now controlled, on a long lease, the whole of the Downs and not just the racecourse.

1891: won by Common at 11–10 on, ridden by George Barrett, owned by Sir Frederick Johnstone.

Common won the 2,000 Guineas, the Derby and the Leger, immediately after which it was sold to Sir Blundell Maple, the furniture man, for 15,000 guineas. The Austrian government offered him 20,000, but he refused, and was then devastated to find that the horse was a failure at stud.

1892: won by Sir Hugo at 40–1, ridden by F. Allsop, owned by the Earl of Bradford.

The failure to win of La Flêche, the favourite, would have been inexplicable but for the extraordinary behaviour of its jockey, Barrett, who spent the early stages of the race shouting at the other riders.

1893: won by Isinglass at 9–4, ridden by Tommy Loates, owned by Mr Harry McCalmont.

Only beaten once in its racing life, Isinglass won the Guineas, the Derby and the Leger, and, altogether, more than £57,000 in stake money – a British record that was not beaten until 1952.

1894: won by Ladas at 9–2 on, ridden by Jack Watts, owned by the Earl of Rosebery.

Locally, the most popular win ever seen at Epsom. Rosebery, the fifth Earl, had bought Durdans from the Heathcotes, was a steward of Epsom races, and prime minister to boot. The Downs danced with joy. Ladas, which had never been beaten, ran at desperately short odds, and strangely enough never won another race.

1895: won by Sir Visto at 9–1, ridden by Sam Loates, owned by the Earl of Rosebery.

In a poor quality field, Rosebery's second win did not arouse such excitement as his first. Though Sir Visto won the Leger, it was beaten in all the five races it was entered for the next season.

1896: won by Persimmon at 5–1, ridden by Jack Watts, owned by the Prince of Wales.

Epsom had never seen scenes like those that greeted this royal win against Leopold de Rothschild's hot favourite, St Frusquin, which was beaten by a neck after a thrilling gallop over the last quarter-mile. Persimmon had had to be scratched from the Guineas, which accounted for its comparatively long odds: it was sired by St Simon.

1897: won by Galtee More at 4–1 on, ridden by Charles Wood, owned by Mr John Gubbins.

An Irish-bred winner of the Triple Crown, Galtee More was sold at the end of the year to the Russian government for £21,000 and subsequently to Germany for £14,000. It had already won more than £26,000 in British prize money.

1898: won by Jeddah at 100–1, ridden by Otton Madden, owned by Mr J. W. Larnach.

No less fancied an outsider had ever won the Derby, and the bookmakers went home exceedingly happy. The owner, unfortunately for him, was not a betting man.

1899: won by Flying Fox at 5–2 on, ridden by Mornington Cannon, owned by the Duke of Westminster.

The last Derby to be started by the flag, this soon developed into a duel between Flying Fox and Holocauste. With two furlongs to go, Holocauste broke a fetlock and had to be shot on the course.

1900: won by Diamond Jubilee at 6–4, ridden by Herbert Jones, owned by the Prince of Wales.

Another of the Prince's St Simon colts, Diamond Jubilee was born in the sixtieth glorious year of the Queen's reign and was, from the start, excessively excitable. Roger Mortimer records that at Ascot it kicked a bystander in the paddock, and at Newmarket unseated Jack Watts and bolted. Cannon was to have ridden it in the Guineas, but was viciously attacked by the horse. At Epsom, astonishingly, it did not even object to the starting gate.

1901: won by Volodyovski at 5–2, ridden by Lester Reiff, owned by Mr W. C. Whitney.

Owned, trained and ridden by Americans (though born and bred in England), Volodyovski set a new record time for the race and confirmed, if confirmation was needed, that the old style English methods of riding, upright and elegant, had to change.

1902: won by Ard Patrick at 100–14, ridden by Skeets Martin, owned by Mr John Gubbins.

A fine horse, but the outstanding favourite was the superb filly Sceptre, which had already won both the 1,000 and 2,000 Guineas and was to win the Oaks and the Leger. In the Derby it could only finish fourth, and Ard Patrick came in with plenty in hand.

1903: won by Rock Sand at 6–4 on, ridden by Danny Maher, owned by Sir James Miller.

For the third successive year, the Derby was won by an American jockey. Otherwise, all was well with the EGSA; there was electric light in the grandstand, and it had taken out a 106-year lease on the whole of Epsom Downs.

1904: won by St Amant at 5–1, ridden by Kempton Cannon, owned by Mr Leopold de Rothschild.

The Derby does not carry a happy record of sunshine; this time the heavens opened to dispose of a tremendous thunderstorm just before the race. Just the same, Leopold de Rothschild was happy enough; he had waited a quarter of a century to see one of his Derby runners win.

1905: won by Cicero at 11–4, ridden by Danny Maher, owned by the Earl of Rosebery.

Epsom's fortunes were at the bottom of a disastrous slump at this time, the annual profits having fallen from £24,000 in 1899 to £10,000 in 1904. Guaranteed prize money was, perforce, rising fast and the Derby now topped £7,000.

1906: won by Spearmint at 6–1, ridden by Danny Maher, owned by Major Eustace Loder.

No amateur rider has ever won the Derby, but George Thursby (later Sir George) was placed twice. This time he was second on Picton, and Danny Maher won his third Derby in four years.

1907: won by Orby at 100–9, ridden by John Reiff, owned by Mr Richard Croker.

The first Irish-trained horse to win the Derby, Orby was owned by an Irish-American and ridden by an American (brother of the 1901 winning jockey).

1908: won by Signorinetta at 100–1, ridden by William Bullock, owned by Chevalier Ginistrelli.

An exuberant little Italian who had lived in Newmarket for

fifteen years, Ginistrelli's totally unexpected win with Signorinetta was received with stunned surprise on the course, and disbelief in Newmarket. The pair of them rubbed it in two days later, when the filly won the Oaks as well.

1909: won by Minoru at 7–2, ridden by Herbert Jones, owned by King Edward VII.

Another close decision (officially 'half a head') brought much needed success to the royal stud and jubilation to the Derby crowd. In less than a year the King was dead: 'The Herculean pillar lost to our manly pastime,' wrote one racing journalist.

1910: won by Lemberg at 7–4, ridden by Bernard Dillon, owned by Mr A. W. Cox.

The Dillon family were still active on the Downs 60 years later. This particular member of it had a short riding career, after which he married Marie Lloyd. Cox, who had been fancied to win the previous year with Bayardo, was an Australian who chose to race under the name of Mr Fairie.

1911: won by Sunstar at 13–8, ridden by George Stern, owned by Mr Jack Joel.

Sunstar ran with a strained ligament, could hardly get to the paddock after the race, and never ran again, as its trainer predicted. The owner insisted that, because of the huge amount of public money on the horse, it must be got to the post.

1912: won by Tagalie at 100–8, ridden by John Rieff, owned by Mr Walter Raphael.

Raphael's horse Louviers had been doubtfully beaten by Minoru in 1909; this time he won with a filly, only the fifth of that sex to take the Derby since 1780. It was unplaced in the only two races it subsequently ran.

1913: won by Aboyeur at 100–1, ridden by E. Piper, owned by Mr A. P. Cunliffe.

As King George V noted in his diary, this was a disastrous Derby, the details of which have been fully chronicled in an earlier chapter. The favourite, Craganour, won by a head and was then disqualified by the stewards, on their own objection, for bumping and boring. The King's horse, Anmer, was brought down by a suffragette who ran onto the course at Tattenham Corner. Her skull was fractured and she died a few days later.

1914: won by Durbar II at 20–1, ridden by Matt MacGee, owned by Mr H. B. Duryea.

Owned, trained, and ridden by Americans, Durbar II was bred and did most of its racing in France, from which country it arrived a few days before the Derby. Within three months war was declared, and racing at Epsom was suspended.

1915–1918: 'The New Derby Stakes' were run at Newmarket, where Steve Donoghue had two of his six Derby wins.

1919: won by Grand Parade at 33–1, ridden by Fred Templeman, owned by Lord Glanely.

A tremendous crowd came for the 'Peace Derby', including an impressive royal contingent. The favourite, The Panther, failed sadly and was found, after its death several years later, to be suffering from heart disease.

1920: won by Spion Kop at 100–6, ridden by Frank O'Neill, owned by Major Giles Loder.

The time went down to less than 2 minutes 35 seconds, but the race was mostly remembered as the Derby in which Steve Donoghue fell. His mount, Abbots Trace, lost its footing after a collision, and Donoghue, then among the leaders, fell in the path of the field. He was not injured.

1921: won by Humorist at 6–1, ridden by Steve Donoghue, owned by Mr Jack Joel.

Within a fortnight of its win, Humorist dropped dead in its box at Wantage, almost without warning, and was found to have a tubercular lung. In the circumstances, it was an incredible performance in an extremely testing race, and a highly popular result.

1922: won by Captain Cuttle at 10–1, ridden by Steve Donoghue, owned by Lord Woolavington.

Criticism of the overcrowded conditions of the stands was now rife, and in seeking more building land from the Lord of the Manor of Epsom, the EGSA admitted that both the Jockey Club and the Urban District Council had made it clear that the licence to race was in jeopardy unless improvements could be made.

1923: won by Papyrus at 100–15, ridden by Steve Donoghue, owned by Mr Ben Jarvis.

Donoghue's third successive win was for a Suffolk farmer, whose horse was only the second he had ever possessed. Donoghue had insisted on the mount, though he was retained by Lord Woolavington, who had two runners in the race.

1924: won by Sansovina at 9–2, ridden by Tommy Weston, owned by the Earl of Derby.

The Derby family had to look back to Sir Peter Teazle in 1787 to find its last winner of the race that the twelfth Earl had originated. The seventeenth Earl's big, strong horse was helped by the wettest Derby meeting ever known, at which the track for the big race was a river of mud. Nearby, buses sank up to their axles and were unable to leave the Downs that day.

1925: won by Manna at 9–1, ridden by Steve Donoghue, owned by Mr H. E. Morriss.

This was a runaway win by a high-spirited colt that was twice beaten later in the year by Solario (fourth in the Derby) and never ran again. It was Donoghue's last Derby win.

1926: won by Coronach at 11–2, ridden by J. Childs, owned by Lord Woolavington.

By now the EGSA had bought the freehold of Epsom Downs for £58,000 (and sold Six Mile Hill to Stanley Wootton for £35,000), and as soon as the meeting was over, work commenced on the demolition of the stands and their rebuilding, it was hoped, in time for the spring meeting. But the General Strike prevented this.

1927: won by Call Boy at 4–1, ridden by Charles Elliott, owned by Mr Frank Curzon.

The evening before the Derby meeting began, the painters were still at work on the new stands, but they were ready for the day. It was also the year of the BBC's first radio commentary. The winning owner, a theatrical impresario and former actor, died within a month of the race.

1928: won by Felstead at 33–1, ridden by Harry Wragg, owned by Sir Hugo Cunliffe-Owen.

Lord Derby's Fairway was expected to win this one, but while being walked from the paddock to the course for the parade, admirers surrounded the animal and began plucking hairs from its tail as souvenirs. Understandably, it had a poor race.

1929: won by Trigo at 33–1, ridden by Joe Marshall, owned by Mr William Barnett.

Only Belfast bookmakers suffered from this race, and were said to have paid out £100,000. Trigo came to England after its two-year-old season, and was then rated by its trainer as the best colt ever to have left Ireland.

1930: won by Blenheim at 18–1, ridden by Harry Wragg, owned by the Aga Khan.

Without much question the most successful owner British racing has ever seen, the Aga Khan won the Derby and the Leger five times each, and altogether took more than £1 million in prize money.

1931: won by Cameronian at 7–2, ridden by Fred Fox, owned by Mr J. A. Dewar.

Thanks to some determined action by Edgar Wallace, the Jockey Club rule about classic nominations becoming void on the death of the nominator was changed in time for Lord Dewar's Cameronian to stay in the Derby field when it passed, with the rest of his string of racehorses, a stud and £1 million, to his nephew.

1932: won by April the Fifth at 100–6, ridden by Fred Lane, owned by Mr Tom Walls.

Tom Walls was only slightly less successful on the race track than he was on the stage of the Aldwych Theatre, and this horse he not only owned, but trained himself, at Epsom. The two of them only just made it by curtain up, as the horse box was stuck in a traffic jam and they had to get out and walk.

1933: won by Hyperion at 6–1, ridden by Tommy Weston, owned by the Earl of Derby.

A comparatively small colt, and weak as a foal, Hyperion was one of the dozen this century that, mysteriously, caught the imagination of the public. Its victory, at long odds for a favourite, made it a happy day on the Downs for the crowd, but an extremely uneasy one for the bookies.

1934: won by Windsor Lad at 15–2, ridden by Charlie Smirke, owned by the Maharaja of Rajpipla.

It was the exotic Maharaja's first Derby runner, and the first of four Derby wins for Smirke, who had been in the race since 1924 and was to continue till 1958.

1935: won by Bahram at 5–4, ridden by Fred Fox, owned by the Aga Khan.

This brilliant, unbeaten horse was so lazy that even its trainer never found out just how good it was. Roger Mortimer tells us that Bahram 'seemed to enjoy being admired and would lean nonchalantly against a wall with its front legs crossed, looking extremely pleased with himself'.

1936: won by Mahmoud at 100–8, ridden by Charlie Smirke, owned by the Aga Khan.

The Aga Khan's third Derby winner set a time for the race, 2 minutes 33.8 seconds, that was still the record nearly forty years later. He also owned the second horse, ridden by Gordon Richards – the second of the three times he was runner-up before the win in 1953 that he had waited twenty years for.

1937: won by Mid-day Sun at 100–7, ridden by Michael Beary, owned by Mrs G. B. Miller.

Another coronation year Derby. King George VI was present for the big occasion, though – despite his many racecourse wins – he never seemed much more personally interested in the turf than was his father.

1938: won by Bois Roussel at 20–1, ridden by Charles Elliott, owned by Mr Peter Beatty.

The first Derby to be televised and the last for more than twenty years. Also the first with a Tote on the Hill.

1939: won by Blue Peter at 7–2, ridden by Eph Smith, owned by the Earl of Rosebery.

How many of the thousands on the Downs that day never saw another Derby, never saw another racecourse? How many never saw another summer?

1940–1945: a substitute Derby was run each year at New-market. In three of the six races the winner was ridden by William Nevett.

1946: won by Airborne at 50–1, ridden by Tommy Lowrey, owned by Mr John Ferguson.

War-weary Epsom, still showing signs of bomb damage and army occupation, was glad to see the crowds again. Though it had little to offer by way of entertainment, the sun came out just in time for the big race in what had been a wet and blustery day.

1947: won by Pearl Diver at 40–1, ridden by G. Bridgland, owned by Baron de Waldner.

Photo-finish equipment was in use, but not needed: the French-bred and French-trained horse won by four lengths, with Gordon Richards fourth on the 7–4 on favourite, Tudor Minstrel. By government request, the Derby was run on a Saturday, so as to interfere as little as possible with industrial production.

1948: won by My Love at 100–9, ridden by Rae Johnstone, owned by the Aga Khan.

Now the French rubbed British noses in the dust of the track, coming home with the first two and the fourth, which happened to be the favourite. An hour before the race it was rumoured that My Love had dropped dead in its box.

1949: won by Nimbus, at 7–1, ridden by Charles Elliott, owned by Mrs H. A. Glenister.

Only a photograph separated the first two, denying the French another win with Amour Drake. M. Leon Volterra, who owned the runner-up both this and the previous year, died in Paris the next day.

1950: won by Galcador at 100–9, ridden by Rae Johnstone, owned by Monsieur M. Boussac.

Another French win, and that year they also won the Oaks, the Leger, and 1,000 Guineas, the Eclipse Stakes, the Coronation Cup and the Goodwood Cup.

1951: won by Arctic Prince at 28–1, ridden by Charlie Spares, owned by Mr Joseph McGrath.

Arctic Prince was owned by a leading Irish Republican, and bred in that country. It won by a street from a moderate field, in which the Gordon Richards mount was again well back.

1952: won by Tulyar at 11–2, ridden by Charlie Smirke, owned by the Aga Khan.

At 16, Lester Piggott on Gay Time was less than a length off a Derby win. The horse unseated him after the post and galloped off towards Epsom. It was caught just in time for Piggott, by then dressed for the next race, to be weighed in with the saddle.

1953: won by Pinza at 5–1, ridden by Sir Gordon Richards, owned by Sir Victor Sassoon.

Nobody will ever forget this one: the dilemma of which to back – the newly-knighted Richards in his 28th attempt to win, or Aureole, owned by the Queen who had been crowned only four days previously? (After having reverted to Wednesday in 1951, the Derby was, for this year only, run again on a Saturday). In the event, Sir Gordon did it cleanly, the Queen came second, and the bookies last.

1954: won by Never Say Die at 33–1, ridden by Lester Piggott, owned by Mr Robert Clark.

A totally unexpected win for the new young master of the

Epsom course, at an age (18) which seems ridiculous today but which would have been quite unremarkable a century earlier. After an incident at Ascot a fortnight later, on the same horse, Piggott was suspended by the Jockey Club for dangerous riding.

1955: won by Phil Drake at 100–8, ridden by Fred Palmer, owned by Madame Leon Volterra.

A totally French win (even the jockey, despite that name) and a thrilling one, with Phil Drake weaving its way through fifteen runners in the straight to win with a magnificent final burst.

1956: won by Lavandin at 7–1, ridden by Rae Johnstone, owned by Monsieur P. Wertheimer.

That week the French took the first two places in the Derby and the first three in the Oaks, and the weather for the Derby could hardly have been wetter.

1957: won by Crepello at 7–4, ridden by Lester Piggott, owned by Sir Victor Sassoon.

One of those hard luck years: hard luck on the runner-up, Ballymoss, that there was a three-year-old even better than that fine colt, which started at 33–1 but proved the next year to be the outstanding horse on any track.

1958: won by Hard Ridden at 18–1, ridden by Charlie Smirke, owned by Sir Victor Sassoon.

An Irish win, and one that astonished the experts: for Hard Ridden was sired by a sprinter, and not by the classic distance horse that is always thought to be an essential ingredient of any Derby winner. Luckily for Smirke, the race began at a gentle gallop and was won in the slowest time for nine years.

1959: won by Parthia at 10–1, ridden by Harry Carr, owned by Sir Humphrey de Trafford.

There was a huge increase in prize money this year, with the entry fees rising and the promoters adding £10,000. Sir Humphrey, who had expected to win the previous year with Alcide, thus took home £36,000 instead of £20,000.

1960: won by St Paddy at 7–1, ridden by Lester Piggott, owned by Sir Victor Sassoon.

Piggott's third win in seven years was Sir Victor's fourth in eight years, an even less likely achievement. Both might have been frustrated but for the favourite, the French Angers, breaking a fetlock on the way round and having to be destroyed.

1961: won by Psidium at 66–1, ridden by Roger Poincelet, owned by Mrs A. Plesch.

After this meeting the most knowledgeable of racing journalists suggested that, unless the course was watered, the Epsom Derby could no longer hold its international status. Many thought, he said, that it was 'a pointless, dangerous, free-for-all'. That aside, this was a deeply surprising win. For the first time, incidentally, the owners of the first three horses were women.

1962: won by Larkspur at 22–1, ridden by N. Sellwood, owned by Mr R. R. Guest.

A dreadful Derby, in which seven horses fell at Tattenham Corner, including the favourite, one was destroyed and four jockeys were detained in hospital. The stewards regretted 'that so many horses which had no right to be in the field were allowed by owners and trainers to start'.

1963: won by Relko at 5–1, ridden by Yves Saint-Martin, owned by Monsieur M. F. Dupré.

Four tons of powdered seaweed had been put on the course to keep it moist, and foundry sand was used instead of peat to cover the public crossings. The start was long delayed while Hullabuloo came into line, then it was left standing and took no part in the race.

1964: won by Santa Claus at 15–8, ridden by Scobie Breasley, owned by Mr J. Ismay.

Breasley's first Derby win, at the age of fifty. Public crossings were now covered with coconut matting, and the most used had been replaced by a pedestrian tunnel. Heavy spring rain prevented the new turf from knitting, and for a while it looked as though the Derby, with £80,000 at stake, might be in jeopardy.

1965: won by Sea Bird II at 17–4, ridden by Tommy Glennon, owned by Mr M. J. Ternynck.

A watering system had been installed, patrons of the face-lifted Rosebery Stand could buy hot meals for the first time, and the favourite won comfortably from Lester Piggott on an Irish colt.

1966: won by Charlottown at 5–1, ridden by Scobie Breasley, owned by Lady Zia Wernher.

There was a fifteen-minute delay before the start while a blacksmith was found to re-shoe the eventual winner. The race, which was run in steady rain, was a triumph for G. Smyth, in his first season as a public trainer.

1967: won by Royal Palace at 7–2, ridden by George Moore, owned by Mr Herbert Joel.

Money poured onto an outsider, El Mighty, after a much publicised dream: its odds dropped from 200–1 to 22–1, but it finished 17th. Mr Joel gave part of his winnings to the Israeli fighting fund, and George Moore's daughter nearly ruined it all by trying to kiss her father before the weigh-in – against Jockey Club rules.

1968: won by Sir Ivor at 5–4 on, ridden by Lester Piggott, owned by Mr Raymond Guest.

After this win, Sir Ivor was worth £1 million and the bookies paid out £1 million. Mr Guest, the United States ambassador in Dublin, did not see his second Derby win as he was unveiling the Kennedy Memorial in Ireland at the time.

1969: won by Blakeney at 15–2, ridden by Ernie Johnson, owned by Mr Arthur Budgett.

The gipsies' threat, though not their curse, hung over this Derby; 160 summonses for trespass or illegal parking were issued in an attempt to stop their age-old custom of camping on the Downs during the meeting. It failed. Johnson succeeded, he said, by watching, the previous evening, films of Piggott's four wins.

1970: won by Nijinsky at 11–8, ridden by Lester Piggott, owned by Mr Charles Englehard.

Undefeated Nijinsky, one of the century's great horses, returned the second fastest time in history. His owner valued him after the race at £1.2 million.

1971: won by Mill Reef at 100–30, ridden by Geoff Lewis, owned by Mr Paul Mellon.

Trainer Ian Balding was stuck in a traffic jam, as Tom Walls had been 40 years earlier, and had to leap out and run two miles in top hat and tails to saddle his runner for an earlier race. Five furlongs from home Mill Reef's jockey called out to Joe Mercer, ahead, to make room for him to come through, and he did.

1972: won by Roberto at 3–1, ridden by Lester Piggott, owned by Mr John Galbraith.

Piggott's historic sixth Epsom Derby win, equalling Jem Robinson's record, was accomplished under a cloud: at the eleventh hour he replaced the intended jockey, Australian Bill Williamson, supposedly not fit. When Williamson won a race later that day, his reception was much warmer than Piggott's had been.

1973: won by Morston at 25–1, ridden by Edward Hide, owned by Mr Arthur Budgett.

The most open Derby for years, won by a horse that had run before only once, had never before been ridden by its jockey, and started at the longest odds since Piggott's first win, in 1954. This time he was half a length behind.

Index